SPIRO AGNEW'S
America

BY THEO LIPPMAN, JR.
SPIRO AGNEW'S AMERICA

BY THEO LIPPMAN, JR.,
    AND DONALD C. HANSEN
MUSKIE

SPIRO AGNEW'S
America

BY THEO LIPPMAN, JR.

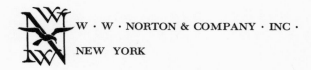W · W · NORTON & COMPANY · INC ·
NEW YORK

973.924
L76a

FIRST EDITION

m. R.

Library of Congress Cataloging in Publication Data
Lippman, Theo.
    Spiro Agnew's America.
    1. Agnew, Spiro T., 1918–   I. Title.
E840.8.A34L5   973.924'0924 [B]   71-38950
ISBN 0-393-07470-6

1 2 3 4 5 6 7 8 9 0

FOR MY MOTHER AND FATHER

Contents

Acknowledgments

MY FIRST AND GREATEST DEBT is to my wife, Madeline, who managed a home and a career, and still found time to give me advice on this project and do the typing. Vice-president Agnew was kind enough to lower the barricades raised against me by many of his friends and associates who, either because of my own reputation or that of the Baltimore *Sun*, did not choose to be interviewed. Mr. Agnew did this even though he had reason to believe my book would be an unfriendly one. Many members of his staff also assisted me, particularly Mrs. Alice Fringer, who graciously shared her own research into the Agnew family, and Mr. and Mrs. Herbert Thompson. The library staff at the *Sunpapers* was also very helpful.

Two previous biographies of Vice-president Agnew were of assistance. They are *Agnew: Profile in Conflict*, by Jim G. Lucas, Award House, New York, 1970; and *Agnew: the Unexamined Man*, by Robert Marsh, M. Evans and Company, New York, 1971. There is a chapter devoted to Agnew in *Nixon Agonistes*, by Garry Wills, Houghton Mifflin Company, Boston, 1970. The following books were also quoted from directly or indirectly in *Spiro Agnew's America: Firsthand Report*, by Sherman Adams, Harper & Brothers, New York, 1961; *Witness*, by Whittaker Chambers, Random House, New York, 1952; *An American Melodrama*, by Lewis Chester, Godfrey Hodgson, and Bruce Page, the Viking Press, New York, 1969; *The National Election of 1964*, edited by Milton C. Cummins, The Brookings Institution, Washington, 1966; *Mandate for Change*, by Dwight D. Eisenhower, Doubleday & Company, Garden City, 1963; *Waging Peace*, by Dwight D. Eisenhower, Doubleday & Company, Garden City, 1965; *The Levittowners*, by Herbert J. Gans, Pantheon Books, New York, 1967; *The Republican Establishment*, by Stephen Hess and David S. Broder, Harper & Row, New York, 1967; *The Crack in the Picture Window*, by John Keats, Houghton Mifflin Company, Boston, 1956; *Revolt of the Moderates*, by Samuel Lubell, Harper & Brothers, New York, 1956; *Richard Nixon*, by Earl Mazo, Harper & Brothers, New York, 1959; *Happy Days*, by H. L. Mencken, Alfred A. Knopf, New York, 1940; *The Republicans*, by Malcolm Moos, Random House, New York, 1956; *The*

Southern *Strategy* by Reg Murphy and Hal Gulliver, Charles Scribner's Sons, New York, 1971; *Six Crises,* by Richard M. Nixon, Doubleday & Company, Garden City, 1962; *The Agony of the G.O.P. 1964,* by Robert D. Novak, The Macmillan Company, New York, 1965; *The Nixon Watch,* by John Osborne, Liveright, New York, 1970; *The Second Year of the Nixon Watch,* by John Osborne, Liveright, New York, 1971; *Bring Us Together,* by Leon E. Panetta and Peter Gall, J. B. Lippincott Company, Philadelphia and New York, 1971; *The Emerging Republican Majority,* by Kevin Phillips, Arlington House, New Rochelle, 1969; *The Lessons of Victory,* by the Ripon Society, The Dial Press, New York, 1969; *The Real Majority,* by Richard M. Scammon and Ben J. Wattenberg, Coward-McCann, New York, 1970; *Negroes in Cities,* by Karl E. Taeuber and Alma F. Taeuber, Aldine Publishing Company, Chicago, 1965; *Zoned American,* by Seymour I. Toll, Grossman, New York, 1969; *The Making of the President—1968,* by Theodore H. White, Atheneum, New York, 1969; *The Organization Man,* by William H. Whyte, Jr., Simon and Schuster, New York, 1956; *The Resurrection of Richard Nixon,* by Jules Witcover, G. P. Putnam's Sons, New York, 1970; *We Who Built America,* by Carl Wittke, The Press of Western Reserve University, Cleveland, 1964; *Suburbia: Its People and Their Politics,* by Robert C. Wood, Houghton Mifflin Company, Boston, 1958.

I have quoted directly or indirectly from the following magazine articles: "Continuity and Change in American Politics: Parties and Issues in the 1968 Election," by Philip E. Converse and others, *American Political Science Review,* December, 1969; "History of a Changing Neighborhood," by Robert E. Curran, *America,* June 15, 1968; "The New Suburbia," by G. Edward Janosik, *Current History,* August, 1956; "Baltimore Boy," by Robert Kotlowitz, *Harper's,* December, 1965; "Suburban Residence and Political Behavior," by Jerome G. Manis and Leo C. Stine, *Public Opinion Quarterly,* Winter, 1958–1959; "Cage of Fear," by Jack Rosenthal, *Life,* July 11, 1969; "Life-Style Differences Among Urban and Suburban Blue-Collar Families," by Irving Tallman and Ramona Morgner, *Social Forces,* March, 1970; "Political Sociology of American Suburbia: A Reinterpretation," by Frederick M. Wirt, *Journal of Politics,* August, 1965; "The Suburbs and Shifting Party Loyalties," by Raymond E. Wolfinger and Fred I. Greenstein, *Public Opinion Quarterly,* Winter, 1958–1959; "A Comparison of Political Attitude and Activity Patterns in Central Cities and Suburbs," by Joseph Zikmund, *Public Opinion Quarterly,* Spring, 1967.

Finally, I must express my thanks to Evan Thomas and Mrs. Louis Jacobson for their creative editing. Whatever errors and flaws remain in this book are, of course, solely the responsibility of the author.

THEO LIPPMAN, JR.

Baltimore, October, 1971

SPIRO AGNEW'S
America

Chapter One

Forward Together

BAND AFTER COLORFUL BAND, float after float, military marching units, state and Federal dignitaries, filled the middle of the long and famous avenue, striding or riding toward the specially constructed reviewing stand in front of the White House. For over a mile, from Capitol Hill, in a straight line descending to the Treasury Building, then around it by the White House, the richness, power, and diversity of America were massed in a moving line of tribute to the new president and vice-president. The scene was an imperial one. Before they took their places behind the bulletproof glass in front of the White House, the new president and vice-president had driven down the inaugural-parade route themselves. They came slowly in limousines, to the cheers of thousands, behind the service bands and ceremonial platoons. It was a gray Washington winter day, the temperature in the 30's, a damp cold, with low-hanging clouds and a wind from the northeast. For President Nixon, it was a day he must several times have doubted would ever come. In 1960 he had been defeated for the presidency. In 1962 he had been defeated for the governorship of California. In 1964 he had failed in a bid for the Republican presidential nomination. In 1968 he had seen a big lead in the polls at the beginning of the campaign dwindle to nothing by election eve. But he had won, and now, on January 20, 1969, he sat in a protected stand and watched America go by—its history and its future. Down past the stand a fife-and-drum corps in black tricorn hats, white wigs, red greatcoats over breeches and stockings, marched to the slow, ninety-step-a-minute pace of the eighteenth century. Next came motorcycle policemen from the Park Police and the District of Columbia police force. Then a Marine band and modern warriors of every service.

For the new vice-president sitting at Nixon's side, it was a moment he surely could not have anticipated in 1960, when he ran for county judge in Maryland and finished fifth in a field of five. In 1962 he was elected to his first public office, county executive of suburban Baltimore County, fifty miles from the White House by car, but light years away politically. Even in 1966, when Agnew became governor of his state in a fluke election, he probably did not dare to hope that some day he would be where he now was. If he had ever had dreams of such exalted glory, it may have been in early 1968 when he formed a committee to help an eminent Republican toward the presidency—not Richard Nixon, but Nixon's then chief rival, Governor Nelson Rockefeller of New York. But here he was, in the front row of the presidential reviewing stand, tanned, immaculately groomed, smiling a tight, forced smile, in the seat next to the seat of honor, watching the theme float roll below him. It was a large float, carrying youths from every state and territory, among them the young lady whose homemade campaign sign had suggested the theme. Nixon had seen her in Deshler, Ohio, waving a placard that said, "Bring Us Together"; the theme of the inaugural parade, at a time when the nation was more divided than it had been in a hundred years, was "Forward Together."

Moving along Pennsylvania Avenue now were cadets from the Military Academy in their long gray coats, middies from Annapolis in blue and white, a fake lunar module resting on a fake lunar landscape. There were reminders of the old and the new. A pretty fire-baton twirler strutted in front of the Pilgrim High School band from Rhode Island. The New York float was decorated with red, white, and blue lines converging to symbolize "Forward Together." Below a small Statue of Liberty were the words "Liberty and Justice for All." Louisiana's float bore a Dixieland band. The Ohio State University Marching Band, hearty and vigorous, from Big Ten football country, had trombonists as large as tackles. Down between the massed spectators and the ten thousand soldiers lining the route the parade came.

The soldiers were only part of the security apparatus on that cold day; the precautions taken along the route were the most thorough ever. Over five thousand policemen and Secret Service agents were on duty. Police experts in crowd work had come from many cities to help guard the President, the other dignitaries, and the onlookers. Lawmen, spectators, and paraders were not the only Americans who had converged on Washington. Several thousand enemies of the government had come too, invited by the National Mobilization Committee to End the War in Vietnam. The day before the inaugural they had staged a counter-inaugural. They had paraded up Pennsylvania Avenue in the opposite direction, then started a rock-throwing melee outside the Smithsonian Institution, where a reception for Spiro Agnew was being held. Many were arrested. On the day of the inaugural parade, a number threw debris at the President's armored Lincoln as he rode slowly from his swearing in to the reviewing stand. They chanted obscenely at the vice-presidential car. As a result, the national capital was more tense on this Inauguration Day than on any previous one, at least since the Civil War. There was an ugliness abroad throughout the nation. The swearing-in ceremonies at the Capitol's east front were conducted behind the same sort of bulletproof glass that guarded the President and the others in the reviewing stand. When the President rode from one protective stand to the other, two helicopters buzzed back and forth over his head. Every manhole cover along that route had previously been locked shut. No one was allowed in any building along either side of the ceremonial avenue without previous clearance. Additional clearance was required for those who wished to look out the windows. And the windows were kept shut; there could be no ticker tape or confetti. The roofs of the buildings were off limits to all but uniformed guards.

Much of the despair and turmoil in the nation were the legacy of the outgoing president to his successor. *His* predecessor had been assassinated. So had that victim's brother, also a political leader. So had the two most acclaimed Negro civil-rights leaders of the day. The war in Vietnam, the racial divisions at home—these were long-festering problems. But Richard Nixon was not exactly an innocent heir to all the troubles that divided the nation. Using as his instrument the running mate who now sat by his side, he had helped turn a number of Americans against each other. Spiro Agnew was a newcomer to his party's and his nation's high councils. Among the Republicans he overshadowed there on the platform that day were some who had long been honored nationally: Everett Dirksen, the Senate minority leader; Earl Warren, the chief justice of the United States; Gerald Ford, the House minority leader; George Romney; Melvin Laird. . . . Today, Spiro Agnew was better known than any of them. He had achieved this fame in the ten weeks of campaign for the 1968 election, an election which he was accused of almost losing for Nixon and praised for saving for him. Agnew's reputation was for part bumble, part coarseness, part vituperativeness, part vindictiveness. He was ridiculed for foot-in-mouth statements. He was thoroughly disliked and distrusted by most liberals, most college youths, and particularly, by most Negroes. Among the themes he had emphasized in his campaign were attacks on these groups. He had assailed "scroungy dissenters" in Missouri, called antipoverty programs "pay-offs to militants" in Texas, derided "phony intellectuals" in New Jersey. The last epithet was an echo of racist presidential candidate George Wallace. Agnew echoed Wallace a great deal; indeed, many commentators saw in the Republican campaign a "Southern Strategy." Agnew seemed to have been assigned to win over the voters who were attracted to Wallace—in the South and elsewhere. So while Wallace said repeatedly, "Stand up for America," Agnew said, in Charleston, South Carolina, "Let's stand up and say America is a great country." He declared on national television that he opposed civil-rights demonstrations, even such historic and peaceful ones as the 1955 Montgomery bus boycott. He used the phrase "law and order" as often as Wallace did. Republican congressional leaders suggested gently that the emotionally charged phrase was inappropriate, but Agnew refused to drop it. He had shown this readiness to make a bitter enemy of the black man in earlier campaigns as well, and that may have been why he was chosen for the ticket.

The Whittier High School Cardinal Band marched exuberantly past the reviewing stand, 113 strong—sunny, young Californians from the high school Richard Nixon had attended. The California float flowed by, emphasizing the state's two hundred-year history of going "forward together." America's even older history was dramatized by a contingent of Indians. Miss American Indian XV rode on a gray horse, with Indian escorts, followed by dancers in the costumes of twenty different tribes. Also in the parade were cowboys from Arizona. The most sobering floats were those of two states associated with another Republican president who had been concerned about America's being held together. Kentucky, where Abraham Lincoln was born, displayed a giant reproduction of its state seal; "United We Stand, Divided We Fall," read the motto. Illinois, where Lincoln lived and is buried, offered the sadly familiar black stovepipe hat and a scroll with Lincoln's words "A house divided against itself cannot stand." Hawaiian leis, Colorado's ski slopes, cowboys and Indians, Grand Old Opry, farmers, laborers, militiamen—all the majesty of a continental nation rolled forward for the approval of its new magistrates. The Forest Park High School band, of Baltimore, turned the corner by the Treasury Building and moved arrow straight down the street to the White House. Spiro Agnew and his wife, Judy, had gone to that school. It meant a lot to them. Agnew did not complete college, and finally won his law degree at a night school in Baltimore. Now he smiled his precision grin through the bulletproof glass and waved as the fifty-member band drew abreast, proud students performing in the most glamorous event in their lives and in the school's history. "Maryland, My Maryland" they played martially. Left-right-left-right they marched in rhythmic lockstep, their fifty forest-green and gray uniforms splendidly clean, their silver and gold instruments gleaming under the low January clouds, their scrubbed black faces dully glowing.

Chapter Two

The Young Manhood of Spiro Agnew

The First Suburb

WHEN SPIRO THEODORE AGNEW moved to Forest Park in the first year of his life, in 1919, it had neither black residents nor its own high school. Agnew was born in November 9, 1918, in an apartment over a florist's shop in downtown Baltimore, at 226 West Madison Street. Within months, the Agnew family moved to the brand-new house on a street of new houses in the neighborhood that was Baltimore's latest addition. Like most cities of size at that time, Baltimore had steadily been expanding out from its center as population and mobility increased. H. L. Mencken, a city boy, had noticed the drift to suburbia as early as the 1880's. "Baltimore was creeping out block by block, year by year," he wrote of that preautomobile decade. Forest Park was then just cornfields, meadows and woods, for the most part. By the turn of the century, however, it boasted many summer houses and a rambling hotel, where Baltimoreans of some means would go to escape the humid, mosquito-dominated summers of the low-lying port city. Part of Forest Park was annexed to the city in 1888, the rest in 1918. It was almost exclusively a community of detached houses, separated one from the other by ten to twenty feet of grass and shrubs. This arrangement distinguished suburb from city in Baltimore, that collection of street after street of narrow brick row houses. Row housing was banned in Forest Park.

The Agnews' new house at 3707 Ashburton Street (later renamed Sequoia Avenue), was a two-story, brown, shingled structure with a porch, large enough for a family that included the future vice-president, his father and mother, a half brother, and a maiden aunt. His father—Theodore Spiro Agnew—owned a restaurant on Baltimore's busy Howard Street, about seven miles away, and each day he commuted to his place of business, along with most of the residents of Forest Park. Through the early 1920's, job opportunities in the neighborhood were scant. There were a couple of stores, a branch library, and two churches when the Agnews arrived. During Spiro Agnew's youth these were joined by a fire station, more stores, several new schools and churches and synagogues, even a theater.

In the 1920's and 1930's, when Spiro Agnew was growing up there, Forest Park was almost the ideal American suburb, ideal even to the point of being open to Greek-Americans, like Theodore S. Agnew, and to Jews. "[It] looked precisely like every other self-contained suburb on the American continent, give or take a few odd features. Old oaks and sycamores overgrew the street. Flowers grew in everyone's backyard. . . . Hills garlanded the western edge of Forest Park, gradually leading into Gwynns Falls Valley and making, along the way, perfect slopes for sledding, which we used each winter. Nothing ever really happened on those hills and streets except a certain amount of necessary movement to and fro and the steady, subversive activity, mostly invisible to adults, of children picking up misinformation about life." So a Forest Park boy, Robert Kotlowitz, wrote later in *Harper's*. It sounds idyllic because it was. Later Forest Park would be an "urban" neighborhood, but by then the Agnews would all be gone. Forest Park was Spiro Agnew's first suburb, but not his last.

The Greek

A liberal Maryland Democrat of Greek extraction once said that the only thing Agnew did for the Greek community was to leave it. That is not true. Baltimore's Greeks took pride in his rise through the levels of political power and eminence. During that rise, newspapers dutifully interviewed members of the community —"leaders" and "rank and file"—and dutifully reported that they rejoiced in the reflected glory. Providing this glory was doing something for a community. But the Maryland Democrat was wrong for a more basic reason: Agnew never left the Greek community; he was never a part of it. His father was very much involved in its affairs, but the son never was.

Theofrastos Anagnostopoulos was born in Gargalianoi, Greece, in 1878. He grew up in that village, apparently a member of a family of landowners, though the record now is not clear. At any rate, at twenty-four he emigrated to America, part of one of the most remarkable surges across the Atlantic. There were fewer than a thousand Greeks living in the United States when he was born. By 1920, there were over 176,000 Greek-born residents here. They had few qualifications for succeeding in an industrial and commercial society: they were almost all poor, almost all uneducated and untrained, almost all from peasant homes; they almost all settled in cities, however, and by and large they enjoyed prompt success. Typically, they began in some sort of menial job, quickly moved to a better one, then to a still better one—none highly prestigious— and then to entrepreneurship. Almost all the Greek immigrants of this period were young men, and once successful they generally returned to Greece to marry their childhood sweethearts. Except in this last particular, Anagnostopoulos followed this pattern exactly.

The future vice-president's father arrived in New York City on a Red Star Line steamer on September 19, 1902. He listed his occupation as "laborer." He was twenty-five, short, slight, and dark. He was en route to Schenectady, to live with a cousin. Four years later his declaration of intent to become a citizen listed his family name as "Anagnost" and included the middle name "Spiro." He now said he was a barber. In 1907, when he petitioned for naturalization, he described himself as a merchant, having graduated to the calling of restaurateur. His first cafe, opened in Schenectady in 1907 was a failure. So was a second, opened in 1908 in Troy, New York. In 1910 or thereabouts he moved to Baltimore, for reasons unknown, and opened a third restaurant, the Brighton, on a busy downtown street. This one prospered. As he approached forty, the now thoroughly Americanized Theodore Spiro Agnew decided he needed a family. Instead of returning to Greece or choosing from the local, small Greek community, he proposed to a Virginian, Mrs. William R. Pollard, who was the widow of a late friend. Her husband had had a well-paying job as a government meat inspector, and they and their one child, W. Roy, had lived a pleasant life of comfort and some prestige in a row house in west Baltimore. They had often dined at the Brighton, and Agnew had often dined in their home. Agnew and Mrs. Pollard were married in late 1917 or early 1918, and moved to the apartment over the florist's shop, where their son Spiro was born.

The life-style of the new Mrs. Agnew and her older son, ten-year-old Roy, changed with her remarriage. The standard of living was the same, but because Mr. Agnew's restaurant was more demanding of his time than Mr. Pollard's profession had been, their home life became much less conventional. Mrs. Agnew took an increasing interest in outside activities, even helping with the staff at the restaurant. The family ate out almost all the time. Mrs. Agnew also became much more sociable. She liked the races, as did her new husband. She liked long shopping expeditions. "She was a real gad-about," says Roy Pollard. When Spiro was born and the family moved to the suburbs, Mrs. Agnew's unmarried sister, Lillie Akers, took over much of the responsibility for rearing both children. She fixed their meals at home, she herded them to Sunday school. (Mrs. Agnew and her sister were lifelong Episcopalians.)

Spiro Agnew's father would have liked to see his only son take more of an interest in his Greek heritage. The situation was delicate. Though he was a stern parent, a strict disciplinarian, he shied away from forcing the boy. Agnew senior was a leading figure in the small Greek community of perhaps two thousand people, active in the American Hellenic Educational and Progressive Association and looked up to particularly by the many Greeks in businesses related to food and dining. He never went beyond offering Spiro bribes to attend Greek school. When these were refused, the matter was closed. He offered to teach the son a little of the language at home, but Spiro again refused. The very fact that his father spoke English with an accent was embarrassing to him. And for his father to speak Greek in the presence of one of young Agnew's WASP friends was agony. "It made me vaguely uneasy and embarrassed to have to be there when another child was. You resent differences at that age [pre-teens and early teens]. . . . I was very sensitive to the fact that my father was Greek and spoke with an accent, and this was sometimes a source of ridicule in my peer group," Spiro Agnew said later.

The elder Agnew, in *his* peer group, had embarrassments, too. "Mr. Agnew would have been a more contented married man had he gone among the Greek community to find himself a wife," his stepson said later. "My mother was always strictly American. And if she was at a Greek gathering, she so conducted herself that it showed she was obviously an American." So the son, with help from his Virginia mother and aunt, the Episcopal church, and a comfortable middle-class group of playmates, went beyond the father's Anglicization to Anglo-Saxonism.

A Good Depression

The depression redeemed Agnew senior in the eyes of his son. After he became vice-president, Agnew was described by a British writer as one who had "a good war." He also had a "good" depression. That is, in both of the great watershed events of his generation he was touched by their central meaning, shared some of their informing experience, without being subjected to the full rigors or horrors they were capable of inflicting. By the time of the 1929 crash, Agnew senior had given up the Brighton and was running an even more successful restaurant, the Picadilly, also in downtown Baltimore, on Howard Street. The money was rolling in, so much so that Spiro Agnew could later accurately claim, "We were upper middle class, well to do." The depression first wiped out the downtown corporation whose many employees were the Picadilly's regular customers; the restaurant suffered, finally closed. Then came the failure of the savings and loan association where the Agnew savings were deposited. "We were wiped out," the vice-president says, but that may be putting it strongly. Several more years passed before the depression's weight was so heavy that the Agnews had to sell their home and move to a smaller, cheaper, rented house. The family kept going because Theodore S. Agnew went to work as a commission agent, buying produce wholesale and selling it to retail establishments. Agnew sold mostly to his fellow Greek restaurant owners. Though he did well, the change represented a drop on the social ladder. Their income went down. The work was much more physically demanding than running a downtown restaurant had been. But Theodore Agnew was never the fruit peddler that some publicists tried to make him in later years.

Spiro Agnew was just approaching the age at which many first-generation sons get over their unease regarding their parents. The manner in which his father rebounded from his loss of the restaurant and the savings account seemed especially heroic to him, and he even accompanied his father to a few Greek meetings. He also began to give expression to a new-found love of big words and fancy rhetoric, by writing speeches for his father. Theodore Agnew was a frequent speaker at both Greek and Democratic-party meetings.

The depression's blow was so blunted by the father's enterprise and resourcefulness that, after graduation from high school in 1937, Spiro could take a step not possible for the overwhelming majority of the members of his generation. He enrolled as a full-time, nonworking student at an expensive private university.

School Days

Forest Park High School was a yeasty, innovative, highly competitive place in the middle 1930's Spiro Agnew was out of his element there, in a sense. He took part in no activities, won no honors, played no sports, made no enduring friendships. Like the community it served, the school was a one-class social organization. Because of the depression, some of the students were from families with little money, but none were from what could be called the culture of poverty—of those who had been, were, and would continue to be poor. Despite the social uniformity, there were distinctions, and young Agnew was ultrasensitive to them. They repelled him in some way, and after school, while others stayed there for fun and games or serious work, he fled home to the familiar, comfortable, and homogeneous block. He noticed this in himself early. Talking of his grammar-school days, he said, "I lived in the 3700 block. Kids in the 3800 block were an entirely different bunch of kids. Just to give you an idea of how insulated we were during those years, I went to [Public School] 69, which didn't have shop or vocational training facilities. That was required. So our sixth grade class had to walk down to 64. It was like going into another world. This was an older school. The neighborhood was almost imperceptibly less affluent, but [that was] very apparent to us in the way the kids were dressed, in their mannerisms, in the way they acted." The two schools were a half mile apart.

Agnew felt the same way in high school. For most of his class-mates, the school was the neighborhood social center. Even students who had jobs made it a point to spend some time there, taking part in extracurricular activities. Forest Park was the city's first coeducational school. Its faculty and staff were eager to outperform the older, stuffier boys' schools and girls' schools. Also, the student body included a large number of Jews. They were mostly second-generation sons and daughters of Eastern European Jews, and saw a good education as their best hope of overcoming the obstacles non-Jews and even some of the German Jews of the city raised in their paths. All these circumstances, along with the depression, made Forest Park an arena of social and educational over-achievers. Though Agnew scored well on intelligence tests, his shyness, sensitivity, and lack of ease held him back. His grades were above average, but he was lost to sight in a sea of ambition. Many of his classmates and teachers never knew him, or forgot him soon afterward. His one claim to visibility was his piano playing. His mother played, and he had shown an early interest in the piano. By high school he was good enough to be chosen to play at assemblies. Those who remember him at all remember him best as sitting ramrod straight (and ramrod thin, another cause of his shyness), banging out "The Star-Spangled Banner" at the weekly morning assembly. The 1937 class yearbook lists no achievement or interest under his picture; he is one of only 4 in a class of 163 who were so undistinguished. One reason Agnew avoided activities and rushed home right after school was that he thought his classmates talked about him, about his Greekness. Ironically, his rushing home was interpreted erroneously. "I didn't know he was Greek. I thought, I think we all thought, he was never around because he was poor and had to work after school," said one friend who had believed he knew him fairly well.

The 3700 block of Sequoia was a comfortable and homogeneous retreat, a snug harbor for an uncertain adolescent. A contemporary who grew up there when Agnew did, who played sandlot games with him and engaged in acorn fights among the big oaks, who later doubled-dated with him, going to movies, to the neighborhood drugstore, to girls' houses to dance, thought the most significant fact about the block was that "everybody's standards were the same. Everybody had about the same income." Another contempo-

rary on the block said that even during the depression, children
there were aware that they had "more than an average amount of
money." The only Negroes the people there ever saw came to be
shared by two or three families as yardmen or domestics. "Some of
us even had maids with starched blouses," a former resident recalls. Except in part for the Agnews, and for one other family of
Greek extraction, all the people on the block were Protestant or
Roman Catholic. The many Jews of Forest Park lived on other
streets. (Most other middle-class suburban neighborhoods in Baltimore still enforced restrictive covenants in the 1930's.) So the street
was a community within a community, with its own standards, if
one were perceptive enough to notice. Agnew always explained his
determination not to go to Greek school in this way: "I resented
the suggestion fiercely, because I didn't want anything that connected me with something different from my neighborhood."

Most Americans who graduated from high school in the period
did not go to college. In Maryland about 30 percent of the white
graduates continued their education. But more than 50 percent of
the Forest Park graduates of 1937 went promptly to college, and
others attended later. Agnew chose Baltimore's Johns Hopkins University, a private school which then had already earned such distinction for its graduate programs that they attracted good students from all over the nation. Its undergraduate programs were
less magnetic. Most of the undergraduates of the day were from
Baltimore or the surrounding Maryland counties. Tuition was $450
a year. Anyone who could pay the tuition and had an 80 average
in high school could get in. Hopkins was pretty much a no-non-
sense school, not known for either sports or goldfish-swallowing. It
did have a social life, however, organized around the fraternities.
The principal events of the year were dances at the downtown hotels, to the music of touring big-name bands, the winter cotillion,
and June Week. Hopkins was an urban university, during the last
decades of urban splendor, in a city that may have actually deserved to be called splendid. An eloquent and unprejudiced so-
journer said this of the Baltimore of 1938: "My wife and I had come
to love Baltimore above all cities. We were at home in it. . . . We
loved the physical city, its old brick houses . . . its gaslit streets at
night. We loved the touch of the continuing past." That was Whittaker Chambers, who soon after 1938 took flight to what he consid-

ered a remote hiding place, Baltimore County, a flight Spiro Agnew would duplicate later, for different reasons. And with different results.

In February, 1937, Agnew began the study of chemistry at Hopkins. Chemistry and English had been his best subjects in high school. He joined a small, new fraternity on the edge of social acceptability, Alpha Chi Rho. Several of the members of the day do not recall knowing him. One who does says he often came to the fraternity house to eat lunch, and stayed for endless games of Ping-Pong. Once in a while he played the piano there. He was eighteen years old now, and beginning to break out of his shell. He dated some. He had become a good dancer. But something was distracting him from studies, and he failed several subjects. He says he was worried about the situation in Europe and lost interest in education. A professor who was there at the time says that seems unlikely, since he saw little evidence among the undergraduates of concern with the approaching war. A fellow student says Agnew told him he flunked out. According to the records, he "withdrew" in February, 1939.

Judy Agnew

"The most likeable thing about him," wrote Baltimore journalist Gary Wills. He was talking about Agnew's wife, Judy. Having praiseworthy wives seems to be a modern Republican trait. Richard Nixon described his own marriage by quoting Eisenhower on his: "Like all successful politicians, I married above myself." Judy was Elinor Isabel Judefind when Agnew met her in November, 1940. Both were working at the Maryland Casualty Company in Baltimore. Agnew had gone there after dropping out of Hopkins. He was an "assistant underwriter in the sprinkler leakage and water damage division." She was a file clerk. The gulf between them was not as great as the two titles might suggest. He never made more than eighteen dollars a week there, and she reached seventeen. Judy was from a good middle-class French-German family that lived in a good middle-class neighborhood—Forest Park. She grew up only a few blocks from where Agnew did, and attended Forest Park High School just two years behind him, but she had not known him there. Agnew was, in her view, still a little shy when they met, but he had come a long way. They met in a car pool going home from work one afternoon, and he asked her for a date that night. Within a few weeks they were dating regularly, and began to talk of marriage. He gave her an engagement ring in April, 1941. They planned to wed in December, but he was drafted in September, and his service duties forced postponement of the marriage. It took place instead in May, 1942, in the living room of the Judefind home on Chatham Road in Forest Park.

World War II

Many of the men in their circle were being drafted in 1941 and 1942. The women retired to "hen parties." Agnew's career in the military was unexceptional, but he did earn two medals, and he did come out of the Army with a lot more confidence in himself than he had when he went in. He told his wife this experience made him realize he could be a leader of men. Certainly the record shows he was more assertive after the war than before it. So his experience is worth noting in detail.

He entered the Army as an enlisted man on September 24, 1941. He trained for three months at Camp Lee, Virginia, and for three months at Camp Croft, South Carolina. Then he went to the officer candidate school attached to the armored force school at Fort Knox, Kentucky, receiving a second lieutenant's commission on May 23, 1942. He served in various low-level jobs at Knox and at Camp Campbell, Kentucky, until July, 1943, when he was sent to a replacement depot at Fort Meade, Maryland, just a few miles from Baltimore. This was a fortuitous assignment, for Judy, who had been living near the Kentucky camps, had returned to Baltimore in April, 1943, to prepare for the birth of their first child. A daughter—Pam—was born in July. In March, 1944, Agnew was himself placed in a replacement battalion. He was sent to England, then to France, where he was assigned there to the 54th Armored Infantry Battalion of the 10th Armored Division, just in time to participate in the Battle of the Bulge. In this brief encounter with responsibility and danger, he acquitted himself well.

Until that time, Agnew had served as assistant special-service officer of one outfit, special-service officer of another, pool officer in one place, replacement officer in another, always far from the sounds of battle. In December, 1944, he was both rifle-platoon leader and motor officer. His job was to bring rations, supplies of all sorts, and green recruits to the units around the Bastogne area, which were under attack in the last-gasp German winter offensive. Agnew was as green as the recruits in his charge. The first day they came under fire, he perhaps surprised even himself. Here is how his first sergeant, John F. Bevilaqua, recalls the episode: "All of us were dog tired. Suddenly there were short swishes and loud roars as German 88-millimeter cannons began to bracket the convoy. Within seconds Lt. Agnew had stopped the convoy and had everyone in ditches. As round after round fell on us and around us, many of the recruits began to panic and wanted to run, but the lieutenant kept hollering at them that everything would be all right. He used a firm confident voice and the soldiers believed him. . . . The company suffered only eight casualties and I believe the leadership of the man who was later to become Vice President of the United States had a lot to do with this low casualty rate."

Agnew's unit supplied troops in the area for thirty-nine days, usually under fire, according to Bevilaqua, and he himself determined the apportionments when there were shortages or conflicting claims, Bevilaqua said. The following month Agnew was awarded the Combat Infantryman's Badge and the Bronze Star. There is no citation accompanying the latter, which apparently was awarded under a procedure that allowed any man with the Combat Infantryman's Badge to request it. Agnew's tour of duty after the Battle of the Bulge was not exceptional. He returned to Fort Meade in November, 1945, still a lieutenant, to begin terminal leave. He and Judy and Pam, now two, first lived with Judy's mother in Baltimore, then—after the birth of another child—moved to their second suburb, joining one of the most significant migrations in American history.

Chapter Three

The Making of a Suburbanite

Country Club Park

FIFTEEN MILLION STRONG, American veterans began reentering the mainstream of national life in 1945, determined to create a better life than the one they remembered from the previous decade. They were armed with some impressive tools, particularly the famous "GI Bill," the Servicemen's Readjustment Act of 1944. Among other things this program made it easier for veterans to buy homes, and paid them to attend school, or to learn a trade or profession by training on the job. Two million veterans took immediate advantage of the school program, including Agnew. While he was on terminal leave, he enrolled in the night law school of the University of Baltimore. He had attended this night law school back in 1939, after his failure as a chemistry student at Johns Hopkins, but at that time he did poorly and cut many classes, and he dropped out eventually to enter the service. His postwar resolve was stronger. He stayed in attendance at the school until graduating in 1947; a school official later described him as a "slightly better than average student."

During this period he also worked as a law clerk in the downtown Baltimore firm of Smith and Barrett. The partners were old associates of Theodore Roosevelt McKeldin, Maryland's leading Republican up to that time, who was to be twice mayor and twice governor before his retirement in the 1960's. He got the job through the influence of the company then employing his father, Koontz Creamery, which was the law firm's largest client. The clerkship paid twenty-five dollars a week, about the same amount Agnew was receiving under the GI Bill. When he passed the bar in 1947, the GI benefits stopped. Michael Paul Smith, one of the firm's partners, brusquely vetoed any raise for Agnew, and not long thereafter Agnew left to try it on his own. He did poorly. In 1949 he obtained a job with Lumbermen's Mutual Insurance Company as an investigator and adjuster. In his application for this job he described his income while on his own as "erratic." His salary at the insurance company was about what it had been at the law firm. Agnew always bore Smith a grudge, according to some of his intimates, and eventually got revenge.

One of the biggest problems facing young veterans with families was the housing shortage, and the Agnews were no exception. With Spiro, Judy, Pam, and Judy's mother all living together, the Judefind home was crowded, and in September, 1946, when son J. Rand Agnew came along, there simply wasn't enough room. So in December, 1946, the young family moved out of Baltimore to the beckoning county, into a small but adequate detached house on Goucher Avenue, in a development that was booming thanks to veterans' loans and guarantees. They could have bought the house and lot without a down payment, but Mrs. Judefind had saved the money from the allotment checks Judy had given her as rent during the war, and she gave it back now, enabling the Agnews to purchase two small lots. This purchase served as their down payment on the house, and as a result, their monthly payments were low—about fifty dollars, all told.

In some ways Country Club Park was an atypical suburb. In many such new suburban developments there was outright fraud. Scandals abounded around the country as exploiters rushed to take advantage of the veterans' money and the housing shortage. Congress investigated several developments and uncovered chicanery, duplicity, and worse. The Country Club Park development held up well, and is a settled, trim neighborhood today. In fact, it is still growing. The development was different enough from the perhaps more typical suburb to leave the Agnews with pleasant memories of their first home, the kind of memories many members of their generation do not have. They had a happy introduction to the new suburbia of the county. The Agnews became good friends with the developer, himself a former Forest Parker, and years later he became one of Agnew's most generous backers.

By the hundreds of thousands, by the millions, all across the country, the lure of subsidized low-cost housing in just such suburban settings as this was drawing young middle-class whites out of the central cities of metropolitan areas. Already, in fact, the divisions that would come to plague America in the two decades ahead were noticeable. In Baltimore County, for example, shortly after the Agnews made their move, the median annual family income was $400 greater than in Baltimore city—$3,600 to $3,200. County residents were already slightly better educated. The county had been growing much faster than the city in the war decade, its population jumping 73 percent while that of the city rose only 10 percent from 1940 to 1950. The flood of migration was just beginning, however. The Agnews were almost pioneers. In the ten years after the end of the war, so many Americans would move from city to suburb, that Robert Wood could write in the mid-fifties that what had happened was the "greatest migration in the shortest time in the nation's history."

Most of this migration was to what William H. Whyte and others called "dormitories," because the breadwinners commuted back to work in the city they had left. Baltimore County was no exception to the continued emigration from the cities. Between 1950 and 1960, during the years in which Spiro Agnew carved out a place for himself and, significantly, moved his law practice from a city skyscraper to a county medium-rise office building, Baltimore County's population grew by 82.2 percent, while Baltimore city's *declined* by 1.1 percent. Migration was the principal cause for both changes. The most ominous statistics, as it turned out, were probably those concerning income differential (by 1960 the median income in the county was $1,400 higher than that of the city) and racial composition. When the Agnews moved from Baltimore city to Baltimore County, 23 percent of the city population was black, but only 6.7 percent of the county's. In the boom decade of the 1950's, the proportion of blacks grew in the city to 34.7 percent while in the county it declined to 3.5 percent, and there was an actual decrease in the number of blacks as well as percentage! By 1970, the city was 47 percent black and the county still only 3.5 percent. Towson High School, where Agnew's oldest children went to school in the 1960's, was almost all white. By then Forest Park High School was all black. In the 1930's, the law had made Forest Park all white. The causes were a little more complicated by the 1960's in such suburban areas as Baltimore County, but the effect was the same. In states where there had never been dual school systems, there was less racial mingling, more isolation, in the 1960's, than before the great suburban migration.

In the 1950's almost all the critics of suburbia dwelt on the rootlessness of the residents; they were all newcomers. And indeed in the Baltimore County the Agnews moved to, a much higher percentage of the residents were newcomers (people who lived in the county in 1950, but had lived elsewhere in 1949) than was true in Baltimore city. But still only 21,000 of the county's total population of 270,000 were such newcomers. And many of those were from the city, like the Agnews. They made some friends in their new neighborhood, but they had many friends who still lived in the city or had recently moved to some other county suburb. Later the Agnews would buy another house, then another, but they would always live in the county. They did have roots.

In late 1950 they sold their Country Club Park house, when Agnew was called back into the Army for the Korean War. He bitterly resented this recall, as did thousands of other veterans, who believed that one war was enough, for an individual if not a nation. He fought against it, and in 1951, after having been assigned to infantry school at Fort Benning, and after less than a year back in uniform, he was released. A third child, Susan, had been born in October, 1947. When Agnew left the Army in 1951, they bought a larger house in the Loch Raven Village section of the county. It was a unit of what was being called "group housing" in the suburbs, really just a newer version of the old Baltimore row house. Today the same thing is dignified as a "town house." Housing of this type is economical, still a principal consideration for the Agnews in 1951.

Practicing Law

A Baltimore University Law School degree was not the most helpful asset for a young lawyer, as Agnew had learned at Smith and Barrett. The school had once been considered nothing more than a degree factory. By the postwar era it was moving up, but not fast. It was not accredited when Agnew received his degree. Though some of the school's graduates earned respect in the Baltimore legal community, the fact was that when firms had a choice they almost always preferred a young man with a Maryland or Ivy League degree to one with a Baltimore University degree. In 1949 Agnew had gone to work for Lumbermen's Mutual in desperation. In little over a year, he had had enough of that, but still did not believe he could make a living as a lawyer. He took a job as an assistant in a downtown food store, a family-owned supermarket called Schreiber Brothers. He was one of two assistants to a family member who served as the personnel manager. The job involved some timekeeping, some hiring and firing and other work with the store's three hundred employees at two locations, some legal counseling in cases of accidents and shoplifting (though the store used a firm of attorneys for most legal work). Occasionally Agnew would pitch in and help customers, donning a long white butcher's gown with the legend "No Tipping" sewn on one breast. At times he would lecture employees on their responsibilities to the management, warning them on one occasion, for instance, that they would bankrupt the store if they kept putting more than five pounds of sugar in the five-pound bags. The job was not very challenging, but it paid about five thousand dollars a year, more than he could expect to make—more than *he* expected he could make —practicing law. He performed well enough so that when he returned from the Army in 1951, he was rehired and given a promotion of sorts, to co-personnel manager. He remained until 1953 despite increasing disagreements, apparently personal, with some members of the Schreiber family. Then he quit or was fired— stories differ—and took up for good, at the age of thirty-five, the practice of law on his own. It was now or never. He knew he was late starting and figured he would have a lot of catching up to do. He was right.

Aberdeen Road, in Loch Raven, was a very democratic community. Attached to one side of the house of Spiro Agnew, lawyer, was the house of a bus driver for the Baltimore Transit Company. On the other side lived a postman. Every day everyone commuted to town. Agnew was probably not earning any more than his less professional neighbors. As a young associate (not as young as the other associates) in the firm of Karl F. Steinmann, he was probably still making about five thousand dollars a year, as he had at Schreiber's. Maybe less.

The Steinmann firm holds a peculiar place in the history of

legal practice in Baltimore. Steinmann was a brilliant member of one of Baltimore's largest and most established ethnic groups, the Germans. He had risen from poverty to wealth and influence by the 1950's, owned his own part of the skyline, the Tower Building, represented the interests of the richest family in town, the Blausteins, founders of the American Oil Company, and had several other influential accounts, like the local Hearst interests, Emerson Drugs, and the Old Bay Line, a steamship company. The law firm was not "establishment" in the sense of having members or clients with old money, or membership in the Maryland Club, but it was powerful and influential in the business community. It was also declining and perilously close to disaster when Agnew went there. Steinmann was autocratic and eccentric, and his personal traits had begun to interfere with the firm's operations. Less than a year after Agnew arrived, the other partners walked out on Steinmann, and formed their own firm, now known as Cable, McDaniel, Bowie and Bond. They took with them 90 percent of the clients, including the best ones. They also took most of the young associates of the firm, but not Agnew. The others had more to offer, in education, experience, or demonstrated expertise. Agnew fell down on all three counts. Steinmann had assigned him to corporate tax work, but he could not develop much expertise in this. He hated the detail work involved, even after a stint at night school helped him understand accounting procedures better. Neither then nor later was he to display much competence in those fields of law that require scholarship or concentration. Surprisingly, in view of his reputation as a polarizer when vice-president, he was at his best professionally when conciliation and person-to-person negotiations were called for. In the later years of his practice he was an excellent mediator, able to bring people together.

The Steinmann firm floundered after the breakup. Agnew found Steinmann more and more difficult to take. Some of the others who stayed said later that Steinmann made no distinction between Agnew and the associates still in their twenties. He treated them all with abuse. The younger ones took it, but in February, 1955, with few or no prospects, Agnew decided he didn't have to take it and he quit. In February, 1955, he rented an office from another lawyer for twenty-five dollars a month, furnished. He couldn't afford even that amount, so he sublet half the space to another lawyer he had met, Sam Kimmel, for $12.50. Also, he obtained a salaried job as assistant reporter for the Committee on Rules of Practice and Procedure for the Maryland Court of Appeals. This was a research job, dry as dust. Agnew found it no more interesting than corporate tax work. And he was no better at it; one of the lawyers on the committee who oversaw the staff termed Agnew's performance "deficient." But it paid $2,500 a year and he needed the money badly. So he stuck it out. Fees picked up from the practice of a little labor law, for contacts he had made at Schreiber's, brought his income up to perhaps $5,000 or $6,000 a year.

Gradually, he built a small practice, with increasing emphasis on labor law. By the time the research job petered out, he was able to maintain his accustomed income through the practice alone. His principal client between 1955 and 1960 was Local 162 of the Amalgamated Meat Cutters and Butcher Workmen. The local paid him a retainer of a hundred dollars a month. In 1960, Local 162 and Local 149 merged, and Agnew was left without a client. The lawyer for the other local had a better reputation in labor law, and was retained after the merger. The international union, with headquarters in Washington, gave Agnew some consolation assignments as legal adviser to organizers working the hard and sometimes unproductive ground of packing plants in Virginia, where a right-to-work law added to their difficulties.

Meantime, Agnew had made another move. He and Sam Kimmel were still sharing that twenty-five-dollar-a-month office downtown, but in 1957, they opened a "branch" in Towson, in Baltimore County. The county courthouse was located here, and lawyers from the city often came to Towson to appear in court or search records. In many ways the legal profession there was a closed shop. Very few of the big Baltimore city firms even had permanent offices in Towson. Agnew and Kimmel barely had enough clients for one office, but both had friends in the county. Agnew lived there, and was moderately active in county civic affairs. Lester Barrett, of the first firm he worked for, had just come to Towson as a judge, and he liked Agnew. (Agnew said it was because of Barrett that he changed his registration from Democratic to Republican.) There would be some court-assigned work. So they rented space in Towson, sharing it with the firm of George White, another young lawyer who saw possibilities in a suburban practice.

He and several other lawyers had just left a big downtown firm to form their own firm, with offices downtown as well as in Towson. At first, most of White's time was spent in the city (where all of Kimmel's and some of Agnew's time was being spent). In a few years, White's firm had become one of the most successful in the area, and he found he was spending 80 percent of his time in the suburb. White and Agnew became close friends. White managed Agnew's campaign for vice-president in 1968 and is his attorney today. The one indication that Agnew became a respected lawyer that most friends cite today is that George White urged him to join his firm in the mid-1960's. One other bit of Agnew lore that surfaces from time to time in this regard is that he was offered $25,000 a year in 1961 to join a New York law firm. This isn't quite true. A member of the firm, Thomas Kerrigan, got to know Agnew in contract negotiations involving the captains and crews of the menhaden-fishing fleet in several of the Middle Atlantic States. Agnew represented the crewmen. Kerrigan was impressed enough with Agnew's negotiating skills and his devotion to his clients' interests to tell him that if he ever wanted to try his luck in the big city, he would introduce him to his partners. Agnew never wanted to try.

Within a year after moving to Towson, Agnew found he could practice full time there. He was developing a general practice, heavy with labor work. But there were also contracts, divorces, negligence cases (in which he sometimes represented union men against their employers, and sometimes defended his old employer, Lumbermen's Mutual, in actions that spilled over from the company's city law firm). He also received a number of criminal-defense assignments from the courts.* He would have preferred a more substantial practice. His income was only creeping up. The year Agnew turned forty, Kimmel closed up the downtown office and

---

* An embarrassing incident resulted from his court-appointed work. In 1962 Agnew was attorney for Lester L. Grogg, accused of murdering ninety-one-year-old Mrs. Katie Hoffheiser. Grogg allegedly ordered an accomplice, a teen-age boy named Robert A. Kelly, to shoot the woman during a robbery. Kelly was convicted of second-degree murder and served a year. Agnew argued that Grogg, who had a history of treatment for mental problems, was a paranoid schizophrenic. Agnew had state records and impressive legal arguments on his side. The prosecution cited the sanity rule then in effect—that if a man knew right from wrong and the consequences of his act, he was legally

moved full time to Towson himself. Agnew's income that year was probably in the neighborhood of ten thousand dollars, and that included a salary for serving on a county zoning-appeals board. Agnew approached at least one large downtown firm in this period, seeking an appointment, and was refused. He also approached his old colleagues from Steinmann's, now at Cable, McDaniel, suggesting that his Towson office and their Baltimore office be somehow united, formally or informally. He was politely turned down. So he decided to form his own firm. In 1960, when he was forty-two, he and two other Towson lawyers agreed to form a partnership. This was five years before the George White offer. In all the years he had been practicing, Agnew had operated as an individual. He and Kimmel were never partners. This was to be a new venture for him.

At the time the partnership was formed, Agnew was at last beginning to see some results in his legal career. In 1960 he won what was probably his most remunerative case up to that time. He was legal representative for a Teamsters local that had just organized Koontz Creamery. Koontz was a large firm, with four hundred employees to be covered by the contract. It was a Koontz executive who had gotten Agnew his first job with Smith and Barrett, at the request of Agnew's father. There were several other crosscurrents involved in the negotiations. The Koontz lawyer was Michael Paul Smith, Agnew's old boss, who had not approved a raise for him in 1947. Another Koontz lawyer involved in the negotiations was an old personal friend of Agnew's. Agnew had been brought in because the negotiations had become incandescent; personal feelings were running so high that one side or the other had to change lawyers. The Teamsters did, and Agnew displayed the talents that he had developed over the past five years—calming people down, working out compromises, lowering voices. People

---

sane. The jury agreed and Grogg was sentenced to life imprisonment. Grogg then asked for a rehearing on the grounds that he had not been adequately represented. In 1967, Agnew, then governor of the state, had to go on the stand in Federal court in Baltimore to answer, in effect, the charge that he was not a good lawyer. Judge Roszel C. Thomsen, who later gained some fame by presiding in the trial of the Catonsville Nine, refused to order a new trial for Grogg. He said Agnew had provided him with a defense "far more than adequate" and had kept him from being sentenced to death "for a shocking murder."

who remember him from those years find his political career mysti-
fying. He was never the divider and polarizer he later became.
(Similarly, his childhood friends always remark on how his personality changed, how he moved from shyness to outspokenness.)

Agnew's principal goal in the negotiations was, naturally, to
win a good settlement. He felt he might be at a watershed in his
career. The zoning-board job was now paying $8,000. He was earn-
ing about $1,000 as a teacher of torts in his old night law school.
Altogether in 1960 his income was about $15,000, or slightly more,
with about $3,000 coming from the Teamsters. He told a Teamster
official, Joseph Townsley, that if he did well in the Koontz negotiations, he might specialize in labor law. He hoped the case would
give him the publicity he needed in the ranks of labor. He did do
well. He calmed everybody down, and got the company to agree
to benefits higher than the union had told him it was willing to accept. Agnew considered the settlement a triumph, and was puzzled
that the unions did not reward him with more business.

Once he and the two other Towson lawyers—Owen Hennegan
and John Armiger—had agreed to form their own firm, they began
interviewing younger men to come in as associates. They planned
to open an office in a new building by the summer of 1961, but
construction delays forced them to wait till fall. As it turned out,
the firm had a short life. Agnew was sidetracked. As 1961 ended,
Agnew, at forty-three, was moving into a new thirty-five-thousand-
dollar house in a suburb a mile farther from town, and practicing law as a member of a suburban firm ambitious enough to
have three partners and three associates—and then suddenly he
was lured from the practice of law deep into the trackless Baltimore County political thicket. It was not a plunge he could afford,
really. He lost the zoning-board salary. The authoritative lawyers'
guide, Martindale and Hubbell, estimated his net worth that year
at only between ten and twenty thousand dollars, new house and
all, and he couldn't run for office and still draw income from the
firm. However, the venture turned out well.

Chapter Four

County Politics

Political Baptism

WILLIAM H. WHYTE has called the young newcomers to suburban counties "the new elders," an instant establishment. In Agnew's case, there was to be a slow climb before he could identify himself in any way with such status. In 1950 he joined the Kiwanis Club of Loch Raven. Also, in the early 1950's, he was active in the Parent-Teacher Association at the Loch Raven Elementary School, and in 1959 was elected president of the P-T A of the Dumbarton Junior High School. By this time he was practicing law in the county, so the election had beneficial side effects. By this time, too, he had begun actively participating in politics of a sort.

In 1956, Baltimore County voters approved a change in their form of government from the traditional county commission to a council-executive form, with more home rule and a modern charter. Local control of local affairs had been an article of faith in the earliest days of the Republic, but the nineteenth century had seen increasing interference by state governments, especially in urban localities. Late in the century, the cities began to fight back, and many were able to wrest home rule from rurally dominated legislatures. After World War I, counties with urban characteristics—suburban counties, actually—also joined in the fight for home-rule charters. For these counties the horrors of commission government and state control were often even worse than they had been for the cities. In Baltimore County, for example, the voters in the rural sections were still strong enough to prevent the three-man county commission from doing those few things the residents of the built-up part of the county wanted and had a right to. It is a truism in American politics that the rural voters always seem to have their way, long after their numbers no longer entitle them to supremacy. In Baltimore County attempts to modernize government had always failed. The "progressive" elements in the county had tried as early as 1920 to get a home-rule charter. But that November the county voted for Harding, normalcy, and no charter. The majority of those Harding voters were probably Democrats.

After World War II, as the Agnews and the hundreds of other city types moved to the county, a new fight for a charter was launched. It was the League of Women Voters against the Farm Bureau again, and the farmers won. Ten thousand signatures were required to get a home-rule referendum, and the charterites could amass only six thousand. This humiliation came in 1950, and instead of discouraging the reformers, it spurred them to begin again immediately.

By 1954, county voters (their numbers growing by leaps and bounds as the great migration gathered momentum) had approved the writing of a draft charter. At that time all of Maryland's counties but one, Montgomery, had a commission form of government. But the county charter was an idea whose time had come; it was publicly supported even by the politicians with the most to lose in the county. The two most notable were Christian H. Kahl and Michael J. Birmingham, both former Democratic county commissioners (and commission chairmen). Kahl seemed to have been actually converted. Birmingham spoke for the charter, but all his lieutenants worked against it.

Basically what the charter did was to give the county direct control over much of its own governmental activity. It established a seven-member legislative council to replace the three-member commission; it created the office of an elected county executive, who would be in a position comparable to that of the strong mayor of the most progressive cities, with veto and budget-making powers; it set up several executive departments and offices out of the welter of boards and agencies that had multiplied and overlapped through the years; it provided for a hired administrator. In a county like Baltimore, where none of the towns or cities is incorporated and there are *no* municipal governments, such an instrument of government would be more meaningful than in most suburban counties. It is not unusual for metropolitan-area counties to be so fractionalized into governmental units that even the largest unit is reduced to impotent overseership.

In November, 1956, the suburbanites overwhelmed the old settlers and the charter was approved by about 60,000 to 40,000 votes. Under a special agreement, there would now be a council election in January, 1957, followed by a council and an executive election in November, 1958, with an appointed executive during the interim. The two parties immediately began heavy campaigning for the seven council seats.

Spiro Agnew, who was very shortly to move his practice to Towson full time, and who had only recently changed his registration from Democratic, walked into Republican headquarters and volunteered his services as a foot soldier in the short campaign. (If he had done any work in the charter drive, itself, it escaped the notice of the leaders of the drive.) He went door-to-door campaigning for the Republican slate. He licked stamps and addressed envelopes. He solicited contributions.

The county was a Democratic bastion. It had not then been run by a Republican in the twentieth century. In 1956, when the charter was approved, Dwight Eisenhower swamped Adlai Stevenson in the presidential voting in the county, but this was not really indicative of a suburban swing to Republicanism. Baltimore County's delegation to the state legislature was solidly Democratic, and the registration for the county, in May, 1956, was about 135,000 Democrats and 36,000 Republicans. The Republican party was definitely the party of opportunity, and of relatively little competition. Agnew had come to the right place. In January, 1957, county voters chose their first seven-man council. In a surprise upset, Republicans won a majority of the seven seats. They would lose control at the next election, but 1957 and 1958 were good years for the party and for Agnew.

Several things happened in 1957 that make it a turning point in Spiro Agnew's life. None of them was important in itself. But coming as they did in so short a span, the events set him finally on a course that he would stick to through smooth and rough waters until he reached the vice-presidency of the United States. They came at a time when he was thirty-eight years old, not successful by his own standards in his professional career, and a convert to a party that seldom enjoyed power in the state. In January or February, about the time he opened his Towson office, Agnew was chosen president of the Loch Raven Inter-Community Council, a group that was active in local affairs. This election was the first public recognition of those qualities of leadership which Agnew had seen in himself in wartime Europe twelve years before— coolness under stress, command presence. Also about this time, the United States attorney for Maryland, Leon H. A. Pierson, mentioned to Agnew that he would like him to join his staff of seven assistants. It was the sort of job that was usually offered to somewhat younger men, but almost always to those recognized as future successes, so Agnew, though unwilling to take it, was flattered, and his rebounding opinion of himself was augmented. Maybe recognition was coming at last. He didn't accept Pierson's offer because he had persuaded the Republicans who controlled the county council to reward his campaign work with a part-time job on the county board of zoning appeals. It paid three thousand dollars a year for one day's work. The job as assistant district attorney was an investment in the future that paid less than six thousand dollars a year for full-time work. Agnew couldn't afford that. And he knew that the zoning-board job too was an investment in the future.

Up from Planning

City officials in the United States began pressing for zoning ordinances around the turn of the century. The prime argument in favor of such laws was that, in a crowded setting, some uses of private property were nuisances to neighbors and should not be allowed. When the courts upheld this concept, the philosophy of zoning was carried forward to include the idea that certain land uses other than nuisances were undesirable enough for a community's development to be ruled illegal. In 1916 New York City passed the first zoning ordinance that embodied the theory that zoning was a useful and proper tool for community planning. City after city followed suit, particularly the smaller municipalities in suburban areas close to the large cities. Counties, too, began to enact zoning laws.

Baltimore County, which had no municipalities to pass such laws for their own small areas, passed a zoning law in 1939. Shortly after World War II, when the county also established a planning commission, it became the largest area in the nation under a single zoning-planning jurisdiction. The unprecedented growth of the county around the edges of Baltimore city made truly centralized planning impossible. The story of the 1950's was one of piecemeal redrawing of the county's zoning maps, of conflicts between citizens over land use, of conflicts between zoning officials and planners, and of growth, growth, growth. The original charter proposal in the 1950's called for a truly combined zoning-planning office, one that would avoid some of the problems of conflict that had plagued planners in the years before. But in the charter actually adopted, the zoning commissioner, though nominally under the planning commissioner, was in fact not required to follow his philosophy with respect to land use. The zoning commissioner was a full-time county officer who could make spot changes in zoning. His decisions were appealable to the three-man board of zoning appeals. This was a quasi-judicial body, though no legal training was necessary for appointment. It was the kind of body that was often involved in controversy, often of the sort that suggested unethical conduct. There was a lot of money to be made in real estate in Baltimore County in those years.

Agnew asked for appointment to the board apparently because he saw it as a stepping stone to what he then told friends was his only goal—a judgeship. In 1957 he saw the zoning appeals board as a setting in which he could display his judicial potential. In fact he did serve as a highly respected member of the board, at times being the only lawyer on it. He was chairman for one period.

Everyone who is willing to talk about the period today gives him high marks, even his enemies. "He tended to take things on a case-by-case basis, approach things on the basis of law and need rather than good planning principles," said one professional planner who followed his career in this period. "But they all did that. He understood planning better than many." "He was fair, firm, always in command," said one man who served with him on the board. "His only trouble was he couldn't take criticism. He was thin-skinned."

Agnew was appointed to the board in March, 1957, to a one-year term. Nathan Kaufman, a Democrat, was appointed to a two-year term. Charles G. Irish, a Republican, was appointed to a three-year term and was named chairman. Irish had learned about planning and zoning by selling cars. Agnew wanted to be chairman, and a year later, when he was reappointed to a three-year term, he got that job. Irish quit and was replaced by a Republican certified public accountant, Charles Steinbock, Jr., who had been Agnew's instructor a few years before when he briefly studied accounting in night school. Later they would have their political disputes, but Steinbock respected him.

Like everyone else asked to comment on rumors that Agnew might have profited from his position on the board, Steinbock maintains he was absolutely honest. It is difficult to understand the origin of these stories. While it is true that the suburban zoning decisions involved tens of thousands of dollars in profits for developers and landowners, and that some developers were not above offering bribes, the fact is that Agnew had very little wealth to show for his four years on the board. His decisions may have made him some influential friends who would help him financially in later years, but even that is not certain. Agnew has been quoted by friends as saying there were offers of money if he would rule in behalf of some interests. Steinbock says he was offered "bribes"—for instance the accounting business of a large building concern interested in developing a plot of land.° During this period there was always scandal swirling around the zoning board and the zoning commissioner. In 1959 a new member of the board, Daniel W. Hubers, was indicted for malfeasance in connection with a land deal. In 1960 the zoning commissioner, Wilsie H. Adams, was fired after conflict-of-interest charges were made against him. In 1961 and 1962 zoning-commission files were lost or stolen. Agnew was not implicated in any of this hanky-panky, but indirectly he benefited from it; for the aroma was rising from a Democratic administration, elected in 1958, and Republican Agnew was making a name for himself by criticizing its actions.

° The only specific charge of impropriety made against Agnew involved his actions as a lawyer, after he had left the board. Steinbock made the accusation in 1965. He said that in 1962 Agnew had asked him to overrule the zoning commissioner and grant apartment classification to some land on Slade Avenue owned by a client (and later contributor to Agnew's campaign chests). Steinbock said he refused and then Agnew got another Republican official to pressure him. Agnew denied the charge, giving conflicting stories, one to the effect that he had only asked Steinbock for information, another that he had only asked him to "accelerate" the decision. The rezoning petition was denied and this denial was upheld by the courts. Things being the way they are in suburbia, the property was later rezoned anyway and now has apartments on it.

"With the exception of taxation, no other aspect of suburban local government during the post-World War II era generated steadier bursts of intense public interest," Seymour Toll has written. Not only the scandals but the routine business of the board brought Agnew increasingly before the public eye. By the end of the 1950's, the board of zoning appeals was meeting twice a week. Agnew's name was often in the papers—the big Baltimore dailies and the suburban weeklies. In 1960 he decided to test the waters. He ran for judge. As it turned out, the attempt was made too soon, but, at the very least, he got his name a little more widely known.

It was quixotic to believe he had a real chance for a judgeship. The seat he sought was on the Third Judicial Circuit—Baltimore County—of the state court. Maryland, like many other states, followed the "sitting-judge principle." Judges were appointed by the governor, when vacancies occurred, then almost automatically re-elected. There were three judges up for election. The challengers did not run against particular individuals; the judgeships would go to the three candidates who received the most votes. Agnew and the Republican county chairman, Gordon G. Power, survived the primaries to challenge the three sitting judges: one Republican, on the bench since 1953, and two Democrats, appointed in 1959. Agnew attacked the sitting-judge principle, the county bar association, "the politicians," who, he correctly noted, were the real beneficiaries of a system that made the judgeships so secure, and the Democrats. He ran as a Republican, even emphasized his party affiliation, a very unjudicial thing to do. Power came in fourth and Agnew fifth. Agnew's fifty thousand votes were less than half the number received by the least successful incumbent. So, it was back to the practice of law for Spiro Agnew and Richard Nixon, who, unlike Agnew, had won the approval of Baltimore County voters on November 8, 1960. Agnew's law practice still only occupied three days a week; he devoted two days to his zoning-appeals board duties. But the Democrats in the county had some plans about that, too.

The Democrats, who had won control of the county in 1958, had been grumbling about Agnew for months. He got too many headlines to suit them, for one thing. He was harsh in his criticisms of some party officials, for another. He had made remarks in public about the slums owned by one party stalwart. His challenges to politicians in the judgeship race had often been insulting, particularly to those county old-timers who expected more gentility in public, conformity with the old ways. Knocking Agnew off again so soon after his humiliation in the judgeship race would also serve a partisan purpose. With the elimination in the 1958 election of Republican county councilmen and of a Republican congressman from the county, Agnew, incredibly, had become the highest ranking Republican in Baltimore County, as a member of the board of zoning appeals. His term was up in April, 1961. In January rumors to the effect that he would not be reappointed began to circulate freely. A maverick Democrat on the county council, W. Brooks Bradley, said "the hierarchy" was after Agnew—and after him for backing Agnew. The Republican central committee had endorsed Agnew for reappointment by the council, and Bradley said the party should have the right to select its own representative on the board.

Now the county Republicans were not the only ones to come to Agnew's defense. Civic organizations, led by the prestigious and quite liberal Citizens' Planning and Housing Association, also urged his reappointment. But in February the council voted him out, 5 to 2, with only Bradley and one other Democrat defending him. The session was stormy, with a crowded and angry roomful of citizens catcalling at the council. The defeat was the best thing that had happened to Agnew yet. He became a hero. Within a few days the papers were speculating that he would run for the House of Representatives or even the United States Senate. He hinted he might run for the House, to the consternation of the men who more or less controlled the party in the county and who had their own candidate. Promised finally that he could run unopposed for the county-executive nomination, Agnew agreed to shoot for that. It was a wise decision.

The Race for Executive

When family members fall out it is a shameful sight, the little rhyme goes. When Democrats fall out, it is a lovely sight for Republicans. Three times in the short span of six years, Democrats fell out and Spiro Agnew benefited. The first time was in 1962, and the Democrats involved were all in Baltimore County; the falling-

out led to his first election victory. That year there was also a fall-
ing-out of Republicans in Baltimore County—engineered by
Agnew. His party was so small there that a feud didn't make any
difference. But while not important in electoral terms, it was significant in that it revealed so starkly the new-type suburbanite con-
testing for party power with the old.

J. Fife Symington, a member of one of the county's older and
better-known families, a master of the hounds, husband of a Frick
of the Pittsburgh Fricks, had, like Agnew, switched his registration
from Democratic to Republican in the mid-fifties. He was the epit-
ome of the gentleman farmer, the kind that own so much of the
beautiful rolling countryside in the upper reaches of Baltimore
County. Politics was a lifeline to Spiro Agnew; it was a diversion
to Symington. He had run for Congress in 1958 and 1960 and lost
to a Democratic member of the horsey set, Daniel Brewster. Symington wanted to run again in 1962. He was able to align the
party behind Agnew for the executive race. But Agnew, after dropping out of the congressional race, endorsed a third Republican for
Congress, George H. C. Arrowsmith, against Symington. The result
was a struggle in the party, an "Agnew slate" versus a "Symington
slate" (though Agnew personally was unopposed by any Symington
candidate). In the May, 1962 primary, the Symington slate won,
but Agnew was to emerge as the new party power. It was his campaign that would draw the most attention between May and November, and he almost alone among Republican candidates would
win in November.

The race against the Democrat, too, would be somewhat symbolic of the new suburbanites taking power away from the old.

Agnew announced his candidacy for the county executive's job
in October, 1961. The incumbent executive was Christian H. Kahl,
a candidate for renomination against his predecessor, Michael J.
Birmingham. These two Democrats, natives of the county and lifelong politicians, had been alternating as party head since the
1930's. Both were long-time members of the old county commission
and both had served as chairman of the commission. Their long
tenure in office and in leadership roles in the Democratic party in
the county tainted them in the eyes of many county residents, especially the newcomers. The county had had many scandals, and
Kahl and Birmingham were "old pols." They were in the midst of a

bitter feud, a contest for power, but neither could blame the party's poor reputation just on the other. It was a party matter, in the headlines and in the minds of the voters.

Agnew had directly benefited from more than just the zoning scandals. A grand-jury report had criticized county purchasing practices during the periods when Kahl or Birmingham had been in power. There was a savings-and-loan scandal involving some county Democrats. Sleuths were employed to find out if county employees attended a fund-raising dinner. Building inspectors were reportedly being paid for work they did not do. Birmingham and other leading Democrats had met with county police officers in what appeared to be a political-strategy session. These and similar occurrences before and after the primaries were emphasized over and over again by Agnew. When he entered the race that October, Agnew pledged "honest government representing all the people of the county rather than government for the benefit of the profiteering special interest groups. . . . the leadership of Baltimore County must be pried from the tired but still greedy hands of the feuding majority party factions."

The following May, Birmingham pried the nomination from the hands of Kahl, with 37,000 votes to 35,000. Of the two, Kahl was less of an "old pol" (he was fifty-seven to Birmingham's seventy-one, for one thing, and in the primary he had attempted to picture himself as more up-to-date, like Agnew). Kahl lost the nomination only because of the candidacy of Independent-Democrat W. Brooks Bradley, the maverick who had supported Agnew most vociferously when the county council ousted him from the board of zoning appeals. Bradley won the votes of 17,000 liberal Democrats, most of which undoubtedly would have gone to Kahl. After his own defeat, Bradley supported Agnew. Kahl remained publicly neutral, which, since he was a Democrat, was a belligerent form of neutrality as far as Birmingham was concerned. Many Kahl allies worked for Agnew with Kahl's approval.

The summer and fall of 1962 were a new experience for Agnew. He found to his glee that he could compete with the most experienced of politicians in public speaking. And Birmingham was the ideal opponent for Agnew, who probably could have beaten even Kahl, but would have found the going tougher. "It's so easy," he boasted after a session before an audience shared with Birmingham. It was so easy and the contrast between the younger and more aggressive Agnew and the old and defensive Birmingham was so great that Birmingham refused to debate with Agnew, giving him a good issue. Throughout that summer Agnew dared Birmingham to debate him "on the issues." In a statement that his enemies might find ironic today, Agnew said that only such a debate would serve the people, that too often campaigns were based instead on "the vilification of personalities, or on catch phrases that divert public attention from the very real problems of the community." (But Agnew accused Birmingham of an "outrageous lie" for misrepresenting an Agnew position.) Agnew had the issues on his side. A newspaper political columnist called him "the self-styled 'Man with a Plan.'" Agnew told a meeting of architects that planning was the number-one issue—and obviously Birmingham, who had held so much power in years past and had *not* emphasized professional planning, could not reply. Agnew also preempted other issues dear to the hearts of the youthful family-oriented property-owning suburbanites. He was for new libraries, for more efforts to attract tax-base-broadening "high quality" industry. He was for cleaning up the county's tiny slum areas because their outhouses were a threat to everybody's health. He was for open space. He was even for talking about metropolitan cooperation, because "existing political subdivision lines are doomed eventually to destruction." He was for auto-exhaust control and stricter industrial-pollution control. Agnew was also for passage of a public-accommodations law banning racial discrimination in the county "promptly." Birmingham was for one, but not "hastily." All in all, Agnew offered a nice mix of liberalism, modernism, and pragmatism. In addition, Agnew had put together a competent campaign staff led by a suburbanite who typified the "organization man." He was Arthur Sohmer, young, a newcomer, the employee of a large corporation, and restless. Operating out of a storefront office in a shopping center, with a modest fifty-thousand-dollar budget, the candidate, his family, and the volunteers capitalized on all the assets they had going for them. Foremost, of course, was the apparent decay in the Democratic party. Time and again Agnew came back to this theme. "Bossism and government by crony must go," he kept saying.

His campaign won for him several important endorsements

from unions, civic groups, Democrats, and the local press. "Mr.
Agnew is not merely an acceptable head of ticket. He has a claim
on the job on the basis of his record and his campaign," said the
Sun. He won handily, with some 79,000 votes to Birmingham's
61,000. The victory was a personal one. Democrats swept almost
all of the other offices, with only one Republican winning a seat on
the county council and only one winning a seat in the state legislature. County voters demonstrated their interest in the office of
county executive by casting more votes in that race than in any
other except the one for the governorship. More voters indicated a
choice in the Agnew-Birmingham contest than in the contests for
seats in the United States Senate and the House of Representatives.

Chapter Five

Running a Modern County

Spiro Agnew's America

OVER FORTY YEARS AGO, Paul H. Douglas drew a distinction between the suburb of consumption and the suburb of production. It is the former, largely residential, almost totally middle class, white collar, and white, that hypnotized many of the critics of suburbs in the 1950's and early 1960's. But actually, even in the 1950's, many suburbs were beginning to add production to consumption. A few, like Delaware County, Pennsylvania, quickly became so heterogenous that G. Edward Janosik could say with truth, "Although many of the residents respond affirmatively when asked whether they consider themselves suburbanites, a goodly number possess little more than an address outside the geographic city limits. . . ." Baltimore County was in the forefront of those counties that combined consuming and producing. It was anchored at either end by giant organizations that employed thousands of people. On the east was Bethlehem Steel's rolling mill. On the west was Social Security's national headquarters. Many of the employees of both, particularly the black employees, lived in the city of Baltimore and commuted *out*. Though more county residents worked in the city than vice versa, the ratio was shifting.

Of the two largest employers, it was, symbolically, Social Security that gave the county its tone, which was white-collar, but just barely. When Agnew became county executive, the latest census figures showed that there were about one-third more white-collar than blue-collar workers living there. (The *male* work force, however, had slightly more blue-collar than white-collar members.) Glamorous Westchester County in New York and Montgomery County in Maryland had different characteristics. The former had two and a half times as many white-collar residents as blue-collar ones, and the latter had nearly four times as many. However, the distribution of jobholders in Baltimore County was not very different from that in some other big-city suburbs. St. Louis County, Missouri; Orange County, California; Bucks County, Pennsylvania; and Oakland County, Michigan—counties that do not include any part of their central cities—all resembled Baltimore County in having a very large percentage of blue-collar workers residing there.

It was not the white collars but the white skins of their residents that set the suburbs apart. None of the above-mentioned counties had a Negro population above 5 percent, as compared to a national proportion of 11 percent. Orange County was whiter than white, with only 0.5 percent of its 1960 population nonwhite. All of the big cities that had generated these suburbs had a percentage of Negro residents much higher than the national percentage. The trend was accelerating, and Baltimore County was ahead of the rest of the nation in this regard, too. Its neighboring city had a higher percentage of black residents in 1960 than any other large city except Washington, D.C. Agnew was a pioneer in many regards, and he was a pioneer in his willingness to come to grips with civil-rights problems even though his constituency was almost all white.

In almost every measurable way, the Baltimore County that Spiro Agnew took over in December, 1962, was another country from the Baltimore city he had so recently fled. It was more white, 96.5 percent to the city's 65.3 percent; and better off, with a median family income of $7,098 annually, compared to the city's $5,-659. Out of a ledger full of statistics contrasting the county and city, one need look at only a few more to recognize how great the difference was between urban and suburban life when Spiro Agnew became county executive. There were more than twenty times as many welfare recipients in the city. Measured as a percentage of population, there were half again as many homeowners in the county as in the city. The average education of the county resident was two full years above that of the city resident. The percentage of elderly in the county was less than two-thirds what it was in the city. The county was younger, richer, smarter, more stable, whiter. And becoming more so.

Employment was the key. Baltimore city was the first to be completely encircled by an interstate road system, alongside which sprang up those industries and commercial activities that could be as well served by fast trucks as the centrally located businesses could be served by trains. The ring was completed in 1962. By 1970 ten cities were so ringed, and seventy others will be in the next few years. By 1970, coincidentally, there were more automobiles registered in the county than in the city, though the county's population was about one-third less. Agnew had pledged in his campaign to increase spending for the department of government that worked to attract new industrial investment—more jobs. He could no more have stopped the growth of industrial activity in Baltimore County than King Canute could stop the sea. In 1963, Agnew's first year in office, there was almost as much capital expenditure for manufacturing in the county as in the city—$55,131,000, compared to $58,853,000, in the city. In the mid-sixties, it cost a resident of the city two dollars and several hours each day to get to a job in the fastest-growing sections of the county, using public transportation, and there were some jobs in the county which could not be reached by public transportation. But that was Baltimore city's problem, not the county's. So was the fact that there was no housing for blacks near those unreachable jobs. In December, 1962, there was no Federal open-housing legislation, only a pale, weak executive order President John Kennedy had just signed. It covered a very small part of the housing supply of the suburbs. Agnew, as governor, would be challenged to get an open-housing law passed in the state. He would do so, but to no avail, as we shall soon see.

Civil Rights

Though the county was lily-white, Agnew quickly found himself embroiled in problems concerning civil rights. The matter was in the air, for one thing. In early 1963, civil-rights demonstrations in behalf of ending segregation in such facilities as hotels and restaurants were cascading toward the climax of the August march on Washington, D. C. Maryland was not a Southern state in the sense that it had been in the Confederacy or had been aligned politically with the Southern states in Congress. But it was below the Mason-Dixon line. It had been a slave state. It was a member of the Southern Governors Conference. And much of its law and custom looked south rather than north. The state had required segregated schools until the Supreme Court ruled them unconstitutional in 1954. Baltimore hotels and restaurants were segregated (or excluded Negroes) until well into the 1950's. Not until 1962, the year Agnew became county executive, did the state's two most liberal subdivisions, Baltimore city and Montgomery County, pass public-accommodations laws. The same year, the state legislature refused to pass such a law.

The state was under double pressure, receiving it not only from the civil-rights movement, along with other states and private establishments, but from the Federal Government, which was especially concerned with the situation in Maryland because headlines had been created in 1961 and 1962 by incidents in which African diplomats had been refused service in hotels and restaurants along U. S. Route 40, part of the road system which links Washington and New York and runs through Baltimore city and Baltimore County. The Maryland governor at the time, J. Millard Tawes, was from the most Southern part of the state, the Eastern Shore. But duty and pressure led him to work for passage of a public-accommodations law.

In January, 1963, Executive Agnew reiterated that he favored a public-accommodations bill. He said he would like to see the state rather than the county pass the bill, but that if the state did not act, he would. Then he changed his position a little. He said the county did not have the authority to act, and asked the state to pass enabling legislation if it would not pass its own public-accommodations law. The state legislative delegation from Baltimore County knew a hot potato when it saw one and tossed it back to Agnew, asserting that he already had the authority. But this little feud turned out to be unnecessary. The state legislature did pass a public-accommodations law. It was limited to half the counties and Baltimore city, and it only covered hotels, motels, and restaurants, but it was still the first such law passed south of the Mason-Dixon line. But the idea of "freedom now" was gathering too much momentum for half measures. A large and very visible target of discrimination in Agnew's county was the Gwynn Oak Amusement Park, on the very edge of Baltimore city, and on the black, western edge at that. The brothers who owned it, Arthur, James, and David Price, had been fighting off attempts to integrate the park since 1952. Until now, Agnew had not been involved in the matter. But early in 1963, civil-rights leaders from several states announced their plans to demonstrate at the park in objection to its policies. The demonstrations were scheduled to be held after the state law on hotels, motels, and restaurants went into effect on June 1.

As the tension began to build, Agnew entered the dispute. On May 30 he announced that his own civil-rights bill would soon be introduced in the county council, and said that he hoped there would be no public demonstrations at Gwynn Oak or elsewhere because they might hurt his bill's chances. All his bill did was create a human-relations council for the county, which would handle civil-rights disputes. And Agnew seemed to be saying that he opposed demonstrations not only at Gwynn Oak but also at the hotels, motels, and restaurants covered by the new state law. "I urge mature consideration of the desirability of a peaceful transition period . . . we need a calm dispassionate approach to these changes lest there be setbacks to gains that are imminent." Nobody was listening. On July 1, with all the plans for a weekend of demonstrations at the park known to the public, Agnew said that he was "fearful" for the fate of his civil-rights bill, and expressed concern that there might be acts by the demonstrators "inconsistent with the spirit of the fourth of July." To the demonstrators, the inconsistent act was segregation.

It is easy to use this episode as evidence that Agnew was insensitive or overly cautious, but at that time and place he was probably expressing the confusion and uncertainty of most whites. After all, that same summer, when Negroes marched on Washington in an extraordinarily well planned and peaceful demonstration, the capital was aflutter with fear of violence. The omnibus civil-rights bill then pending in Congress was by no means assured of passage. Robert Kennedy was still telling his brother John of the political risks in supporting such a bill, and so on. In white suburbia, there were contradictory swirls and gusts of public opinion. For instance, a National Opinion Research Center poll in September, 1963, in a "white collar suburb" showed 43 percent of the respondents "upset" and "uneasy" about the civil-rights movement. Only 26 percent were "pleased." In a "blue collar suburb" 58 percent were upset and uneasy and 12 percent were pleased. More than half the respondents in both those suburbs opposed restaurant sit-ins. Nearly half in each suburb disapproved of the march on Washington *after* it was over, having been both peaceful and moving.

Agnew was beginning to make a reputation as a man who spoke his mind, without regard to political considerations and he no doubt was doing so in connection with the Gwynn Oak confrontation—but he was also expressing the fears and resentments and befuddlements of his fellow suburbanites. If anything, he was probably slightly more "liberal" than his constituents.

The July 4 demonstrations at Gwynn Oak created an international sensation. Over two hundred protesters were arrested for trespassing, including such church leaders from all over the country as the Reverend Eugene Carson Blake, Stated Clerk of the United Presbyterian Church in the United States. Union officials joined in the protest, as, of course, did many Negroes. On July 5, Agnew made a public pitch for passage of his bill as an emergency measure, so that it could take effect immediately. On the sixth, the council passed it after only fifteen minutes of debate. At the time, some attributed the passage of the bill to the growing tensions. On the day Agnew had made his appeal, spokesmen for the arrested clergymen called for more demonstrations. There were rumors that whites opposed to desegregation were going to show up in force at the next scheduled demonstrations. The threat of violence was very real. The day after the council passed the measure, another large crowd of demonstrators showed up at Gwynn Oak and was met by a larger crowd of counter-demonstrators. There was some harassment, a little violence, and many more arrests for trespassing. In a pique, Agnew criticized the demonstrators for "emotional self-hypnosis," but two days later he was meeting with their representatives and the owners of the park and making progress toward a cooling-off period. Two days after that meeting, the newly authorized human-relations commission met and immediately tackled the Gwynn Oak problem.

Agnew prided himself on his ability to mediate in such matters. It had been his principal asset as a labor lawyer. Now as the commission, the Price brothers, and the civil-rights leaders began negotiating, Agnew kept his hand in. He first angered, then pleased, the liberal commission members by putting public pressure on the negotiators to agree to wait till 1964 for desegregation, and then negotiating an agreement to desegregate the park that summer. Through all this, Agnew's personal relations with the liberal members of his human-relations commission, and with the Negroes in the van of the movement, were only fair and sometimes poor. One reason seemed to be that Agnew consistently operated from the point of view that his determination of what was best was more valid than theirs. It was a form of benign racism.° Most of the union members he had represented in the packing houses and on the menhaden-fishing boats were poor blacks, lacking the articulateness to express their views. Agnew had been genuinely fond of them. But he had perhaps correctly thought that he knew best what they desired, and this attitude seems to have carried over to his dealings with the civil-rights movement—so much so that two civil-rights leaders expressed exasperation and hinted they found this his most salient feature: "It has become increasingly clear that both you and your Chief of Police believe you know what is best for the Negro," Leo Burroughs and W. Maurice Holmes wrote him. Nevertheless, Agnew's view of civil rights in general continued to be somewhat more liberal than that of his constituency or of his Democratic-controlled county council. But not more liberal than that of the human-relations commission. He and Chairman Michael G. Holofcener feuded constantly. Agnew cut the commission's budget in half for its second six months, and publicly rebuked it: "I would like to see the commission come in and sit down with me and get to work on job opportunities and problems in the educational field and get away from these controversial hamstringing problems such as swimming pools and equal housing." He kept after Holofcener until he resigned.

But the currents of the times kept after Agnew, and before he left the county executive's job he proposed, and the council passed, a public-accommodations law broader than the existing state and Federal laws. The vote was 4 to 3 in the council and came a month

° Agnew is not afflicted with that equally common strain of benign racism involving belief in group characteristics. After he became governor, a Prince Georges County judge, William Bowie, remarked during a trial, "It is just a pure fact of life that Negroes and knives go together." Agnew asked a friend what she thought of the statement. "Well, they do carry knives," she said. He gently rebuked her by asking, *"They?"*

before the 1964 elections. These included the Johnson-Goldwater contest which was regarded across the nation as a referendum on the 1964 Federal civil-rights law. In Maryland there was also an actual referendum on the state's public-accommodations law. Marylanders approved the new law by some 340,000 to 301,000, but Baltimore County voters registered opposition to it—and it was milder than the new county law Agnew had pushed—by 77,000 votes to 63,000.

On another touchy civil-rights issue—housing—Agnew was forced ahead of his constituency by his ideals, his judgment, or his ambitions. One of the objections Agnew had against the human-relations commission was its interest in open housing. This was certainly an important issue. As the city filled up with blacks seeking opportunity, and as the jobs moved to the encircling beltway and beyond, the need for black housing in the county became intense. No one pretended that full integration of the suburbs could or would take place. A study in this period by Karl E. and Alma Taeuber came to the conclusion that to achieve "zero" residential segregation nationwide, 86.2 percent of the urban Negro population would have to move to "white" neighborhoods. For Baltimore County to change its racial character in a single decade would have required an unnatural growth pattern. In 1960 its population was 492,000, with 17,000, or 3.5 percent, being Negro. For its 1970 population of 621,000 to reach the national average of 11 percent black, the inhabitants added during the decade would have had to be 40 percent black, 60 percent white. But in view of the differences in income between whites and blacks, and the distribution of housing in metropolitan areas, such a change would be impossible, *even if there were no racism.* Nevertheless, the effort to break down racial barriers is extremely important, as almost everybody who has studied the problem now agrees.

Agnew's earliest statements on the topic certainly reflected his county neighbors' views. His warnings to the human-relations commission were issued at a time when a National Opinion Research Center poll found northern opposition to residential desegregation quite strong. This 1963 poll showed that 52 percent of those with a high-school education, 38 percent of those who had attended college, and 68 percent of those who had only a grade-school education agreed with this statement: "Whites have a right to keep Negroes out of their neighborhood." ° When in early 1964 Baltimore Mayor Theodore R. McKeldin requested that Agnew join with him in working out a metropolitan-wide approach to the problem of open occupancy, Agnew turned him down without even consulting the human-relations commission. Open-occupancy laws "invade the rights of property guaranteed by our federal constitution," Agnew wrote McKeldin. The first indication that Agnew was changing on this issue came later in the year, when he agreed to let the human-relations commission study the idea. He was unsure, as many Americans were at that time. It is one thing to open up parks and cafes. As Congress was learning, opening up neighborhoods is much more difficult. It took Congress four more years after passing the omnibus civil-rights bill to get an open-housing law through. Agnew held up the commission's funds for the study, then criticized a report it circulated as having been prepared by an "incompetent" organization, the private Baltimore Neighborhoods, Inc.

In April, 1965, Agnew had come around to the point of saying, "I am not closing the door to legislation which might require new developments over a certain size to be integrated." He declared that he was for integration, in principle, just as he had said during the Gwynn Oak conflict that he was for desegregation of the park as a moral matter. But in September, 1965, he criticized housing pickets, while reiterating his stand about new developments. He said that a state or Federal law was really needed. In October he said that voluntary desegregation was desirable. Not till January, 1966, did he say publicly that he would support a metropolitan-area open-occupancy law. The law was a limited one, not covering an individual's sale, or resale, and Agnew said that he would work for its passage in the county only if Baltimore city and neighboring Anne Arundel County also passed similar laws. By this time Agnew was definitely looking beyond his Baltimore County constituency to the race for governor. No one knew then, except possibly Agnew himself, that this stand on open housing would be *the* issue in the campaign.

° The results of this and other polls are not to be regarded as information that reached Agnew before he made his decisions. Some of the figures cited here were not published until after he had moved on to other jobs. He never seemed much interested in polls, in any case.

Rights for Whites

In a county as nearly all-white as Baltimore, a county executive must deal with many matters besides civil rights, especially in a jurisdiction like Agnew's, where the county government stands alone, with no city or town governments to provide public services. In Baltimore County, the executive has a lot of power. He drafts the budget, which the council can only cut, not add to. And he runs the departments. There is relatively intense public interest in the governmental process. Both critics and defenders of suburbia have noted the "grass-roots" nature of suburban politics. In Baltimore County one reason for this was that approximately 80 percent of the housing units were owner-occupied when Agnew became executive. Hence the citizens had a direct and obvious stake in many of the political issues that inevitably came up, as they do in all growing, developing counties. Zoning, as mentioned earlier, was certainly one. Taxes was the paramount issue, since so much of the revenue for a county like Baltimore came from the property tax. More than 70 percent of the county's general fund came from this tax, compared to less than 50 percent for the city at the time. Another was the location of public facilities, the need for which grows as rapidly as population. Another was the need for new governmental services. Still another was the problem of how to impose equitably the stronger governmental control of property and habits that rising population densities required. During his tenure as county executive Agnew had to deal with such mundane problems as where to locate incinerators, whether to fund football in the high schools, how to outlaw pinball machines, how to control firearms, how to get rid of deteriorating properties. When he wasn't caught between the suburbanites' desires for a better life, but less governmental control, for more services, but lower taxes, he was caught between his own desire for a more professional government and the political realities.

One of the first bills Agnew proposed was one to forbid political activity by policemen and firemen. Such politicking, which had become traditional in the county, hardly inspired great confidence in the two departments. Agnew objected to this activity not only for that reason but also because it was a good source of political assistance for the Democrats.° The bill came before the council in early March, 1963. Testimony in its favor was given by Agnew's new public-safety commissioner, James Devereaux, the Marine hero of Wake Island in World War II and a former Republican congressman, and by the new county police chief, Robert J. Lally, an ex-FBI agent. The issue was nonpolitics versus politics, and politics won. The council amended the bill to allow the men to politic out of uniform and off duty. Agnew fumed. Two months later he tried again with a new bill, and was defeated again.

His pinball crusade lost to pure partisan politics. There were from three to five hundred pinball machines in the county at different times during his county-government days. State law allowed them as games of chance, provided the payoff for winning was in the form of free games, not money. Federal law required gamblers to pay a tax on the machines. Many in the county did. Agnew had no doubt that the free games were being replaced by cash. He expressed his opposition generally in terms of the outraged moralist, and in 1963 introduced a bill to get rid of pinballs used for gambling. He said, "The machines bring a group of youngsters together in an atmosphere that has nothing to recommend it." The Democrats snubbed him so completely that he later withdrew the bill from the council altogether, saying he wanted to restudy it. In late 1964 he announced he would try again, and in January, 1965, he did so, with another sermon about how children were spending their lunch money to play the machines. He added that the money was financing "gangsters." The bill was defeated. Later attempts in 1965 and 1966 to attack the machine owners by increasing the county license fee of $250 per machine, first to $2,500, then to $2,000, then to $800, also failed. Agnew meanwhile had broadened his attack to include arguments involving politics as well as morality. He publicly accused liquor-license officials of coercing tavern owners to install the machines. There had been rumors of such activities for years, and the Democrats were the natural suspects, since they had controlled the licensing and since the taverns, particu-

---

° During the just-concluded campaign for county executive, Police Chief Gilbert Deyle, Michael Birmingham, and State Senator James Pine had held a meeting at Deyle's home, attended by most police inspectors and district captains. When Agnew blasted this, Deyle answered that no politics had been discussed. Even Democrats in the county scoffed at that reply. Maverick Brooks Bradley said, "This is obviously an untruth."

larly those in the eastern end of the county, the industrial section, were run by men and women close to the Democratic politicians there. Many of Agnew's friends describe this pinball fight as showing Agnew the moralist at work. Unquestionably, he was genuinely opposed to what he saw as a wasting of money by children and working men in such a pursuit, and in part undertook a hopeless fight for this reason. But he also thought it would be of political advantage to himself and his party. He said later in an interview that he believed attacking the link between the pinball interests and the Democratic politicians would hurt his adversaries. It is not unusual for Agnew's friends to describe episodes in his life in nonpolitical terms, and for him to point out a political dimension to the same episode, as in this case. For some reason a number of people close to him think of him as more of an ideologue than a politician. He has done many things that were not "political" in their outcome—in the sense that he lost. But in most cases he himself acted out of honest political motives, which he never tried to hide. Whether or not Agnew is a good politician may be open to question—an objective judgment is difficult to reach—but a politician he is.

In the pinball matter, county and state Democrats charge that yet another layer of political self-interest was involved. Dale Anderson, a Democratic county councilman running for county executive to succeed Agnew in 1966, charged that Agnew tried to get pinball interests to contribute to him and other Republicans in 1962 and 1964, and that when the effort failed, Agnew engaged in a "vendetta" against the men involved. The general public does not appear to have taken the charge very seriously. Anderson said the man who actually approached the pinball people was E. Scott Moore, whom Agnew had appointed county solicitor in 1963, and who was Anderson's opponent in 1966. The story sounded too pat, and made little splash in the newspapers. Later, Agnew aide Robert Marsh wrote that the approach to the pinball operators probably was made, but without Agnew's knowledge.

A second legislative defeat that Agnew suffered in his county-executive days was in his attempt to have a gun-control law passed. This defeat involved no partisan politics. Agnew's desire for a well-managed, well-ordered urban county community just ran into the fiercely held American countryman's insistence that his right to bear arms is as absolute in a crowded civilized setting as in the wide-open spaces. A number of critics of suburban attitudes have expressed particular dismay at the suburbanite's belief that he can be as individualistic and self-sufficient on his frontier as his great grandfather was on his.

Agnew's first gun-control bill was comprehensive. It would have required purchasers of any type of firearm to first get a permit. The Maryland adjutant general led the attack on that bill, terming it "vicious" and saying it had been drawn up by someone ignorant of the need for guns. In the face of this criticism, Agnew withdrew the bill and asked the adjutant general to serve as a consultant in drafting a new one. He did, and in 1965, Agnew tried again. The new bill required purchasers of pistols to get an identity card, after first proving to police that they were not fugitives, addicts, or the like. In the spring, with public opposition still strong, and expressed at council meetings by huge and angry crowds, Agnew withdrew that bill and modified it so that it just forbade the sale of guns to people with certain criminal records. The council turned that down, 4 to 3. Early in 1966, Agnew tried again, but the council was by now fed up. It put the bill aside and never voted on it.

There is unlikely ever to be another opportunity to curtail sales of weapons in such urban-suburban areas as Baltimore. Since the council turned its back on Agnew and responsibility, the mood of suburbia has become even more fearful and the people there have begun buying guns in such numbers (while Negroes in cities have done likewise) as to raise the specter of race war in America. No less a sober and cautious figure than Milton Eisenhower so warned in 1971. What sent gun purchasing in metropolitan areas soaring was the urban rioting of the mid-sixties. In 1963 and 1964, when Agnew first tried to get a tough gun-control bill, urban riots were not yet frequent enough to frighten suburban residents. By 1966, when he made his last try, there had already been riots in many cities, including the dramatically destructive one in the Watts section of Los Angeles. In 1966 the state did manage to enact a mild handgun law that keeps certain dangerous persons from buying pistols. About all this law has accomplished, it turns out, is to give the counties a record of the number of pistols now piling up in private arsenals. Slightly over four thousand pistol permits are issued a year in Baltimore County now, an increase of about 20 percent over the number issued in 1967, the last full year before the epidemic of riots in April, 1968. There was a riot in Baltimore then. What happened immediately thereafter demonstrated what motivates so many county residents to buy pistols. In one week after the riot, 262 requests for pistol permits were filed.

One of the bitterest, most visible fights Agnew got into with the council and his constituents during his term in office was the one regarding urban renewal. As in the matter of gun control, he was beaten not so much by politics as by his insistence on going against the public grain, again in behalf of what he considered necessary, up-to-date county management. Some Democratic officeholders were not above using the issue to hurt Agnew. Urban renewal is not usually associated with the suburbs, but though Baltimore County's slums were relatively tiny, they did exist. The living conditions in many of them were as horrible as anything that could be found in Baltimore city. Furthermore, there was Federal money available, the usual write-down on the cleared land would make it attractive to industry, which could buy it cheap and use it for purposes other than housing (one study estimated the taxable base could be increased something like $50 million)—it was a perfect project for the Man with a Plan. But county residents were fearful that the whole thing was a plot to bring in poor Negroes from the city to live in public housing. At least, county residents were *made* fearful by the well-publicized charges to that effect, originated by people whom Agnew rightly labeled right-wing extremists. Typical of the opposition were the sentiments expressed at a meeting in the Towson American Legion hall in April, 1964. Agnew was publicly scathed, and urban renewal was labeled "malicious, socialistic cancer." Agnew's director of the Redevelopment and Rehabilitation Agency, a Lebanese named Vladimir Wahbe, was criticized for not being an American citizen. A former employee of the House Un-American Activities Committee spoke against the plan, saying that "you don't have civil rights if you do not have property rights." Agnew blamed much of the supercharged atmosphere on the fact that civil rights was then so immediate an issue. The Senate was debating the civil-rights bill, and George Wallace was campaigning in Maryland's presidential primary, running against President Johnson's stand-in, Senator Daniel Brewster.

(Agnew endorsed Democrat Brewster.) There was no question that the atmosphere was heating up. Politically, Agnew probably should have withdrawn his proposal, though it is unfair in retrospect to blame him for what was a decent if impolitic impulse. Typical of the way other county officials were reading the new danger-level temperatures was liberal Democratic Representative Clarence Long's reaction to the issue. He said he was for urban renewal "generally," but he wasn't too sure about urban renewal in east Towson and Catonsville, the two prime sites for it in the county.

Agnew's last hopes were dashed in November when county voters turned down an urban-renewal bond issue by a three-to-two vote. Every other bond issue on the ballot carried. In December the council rejected a proposal for a study of blight in the county. Then Agnew presented a purely local slum-clearance program, and the next February the council killed that. Finally, Baltimore County Democrats in the Maryland General Assembly successfully abolished the Redevelopment and Rehabilitation Agency (after first introducing a bill to create a substitute agency and then dropping that after the Redevelopment and Rehabilitation Agency was unmistakably dead).

The Democrats had the people on their side in the fight and they punished Agnew. At that point, his own prospects were anything but good. He had suffered in the political feuding and in the efforts to lead county voters toward the goals he thought important. Not only had he angered his constituents by his views on guns, civil rights, and urban renewal, he was also making many of them mad by his attempts to tackle another problem that should have been strictly managerial rather than political. This was the question of converting the county's garbage-disposal procedure from landfill to incineration. He wanted to build four incinerators. Every site he and his experts settled on was immediately made controversial by neighborhood objections. Councilmen are elected county-wide but represent a single district. Democrats seized on the objections to the incinerators as another club to beat Agnew with. He stormed at them in a rare appearance at a council meeting, charging them with "misleading" statements and "demagoguery." The county had to do something, he said with exasperation. It was running out of land for disposing of its ten million pounds of refuse each week (two and a half pounds per person per day!). But the council wasn't interested. There were too many names on too many petitions against every suggested site.

Agnew had other reasons for being exasperated. For two years his pet projects had been beaten. (He did get a new conflict-of-interest law, and he had modernized record keeping and brought about other reforms in the management of the government.) The 1964 presidential election had subjected the small county Republican party to great pressures, resulting in cracks in the facade of unity. There was a strong Goldwater element in the party and Agnew had been a bitter-end opponent of the Arizona senator's presidential hopes. Meanwhile, Michael Birmingham had died and the Democrats looked as if they might end their intraparty feuding. In 1965 and 1966 they began to snipe at Agnew with telling effect. The council and other Democrats attacked him when it was revealed that three Republican insurance men had been named brokers for the county employees' million-dollar-a-year insurance plan. The arrangement was legal and apparently would have cost the county no more than a few thousand dollars, but charges were made and well publicized that it would cost an extra $120,000 to bring in Agnew's friends. Agnew tried to defend the plan, but whether he won any public support is doubtful and the council killed it. Ironically, in previous years Democrats had followed a practice of giving business to loyal friends who did no work, but passed it on to another firm in return for a kickback; Agnew's workers would at least have earned their fees. A grand jury had criticized the old practices the year Agnew was elected. He had gone to the firm that had been paying off the county officials' friends and worked out an arrangement to recover some fifty thousand dollars.

In 1965, the council cut Agnew's office budget, depriving him of an aide. Then it even prevented him from promoting his driver, a county policeman, from corporal to sergeant. The next year it eliminated another aide's salary from the budget. This was petty stuff. Some of it Agnew brought on himself, in the eyes of some Democrats, because he was so often not willing to play a political role, or what they considered a political role should be. When it was clearly in his interest to compromise and trade, Agnew would do so. He has said, in fact, that his best political trait was his ability to get conflicts resolved. But too often he did not see any advantage in resolving a conflict. Many of the measures he lost in council might have been saved had he been more of a compromiser, or less combative. "He was the kind of man who would walk a mile to help a friend, and cross the street out of his way to fight an enemy," said Jervis Finney, a Republican on the council when Agnew was county executive, and a member of the General Assembly when he was governor. Even so, Democrats would not have retaliated had they thought Agnew was still popular in the county. He was not, and he and they knew it. His fights had alienated too many conservatives. In addition to all the other conflicts, there was the continuing fight involving taxes. Agnew took a progressively enlightened view of local taxation during his four years of exposure to the problems of government. To the degree that this attitude involved agreeing to the idea of higher taxes, to be spent in part not in the county but the city, such enlightenment was suicidal—at least for a man whose horizons were bounded by the county line.

Paying for Suburban Amenities

What does a county resident owe his city neighbor? In the 1960's this question became central to the whole "urban crisis," for as the suburbanite became increasingly wealthy, the city resident became increasingly poor—and more in need of expensive services. Every time a $10,000-a-year family moved from Baltimore city to Towson, the $3,000-a-year family left behind had fewer resources to draw on to pay for its schools, medical services, street and sidewalk upkeep, garbage collection, and so forth. The poor family also had fewer resources to use in maintaining the streets and buildings and facilities used by the suburbanites when they occasionally came back to town to work or play. Even for a suburb like Baltimore County, with its rapidly growing job market, retail centers, and cultural facilities, a city like Baltimore was essential. During Agnew's service as county executive, the eighty thousand county residents who came to the city to work every day were still more than double the number of city residents who worked in the county. The city's fine and famous Enoch Pratt Free Library, its two large museums, and other facilities were suburban delights subsidized by the city. The problem is nationwide. In 1966, Agnew's last year in the county, Professor William Neenan of Michigan studied the situation in Detroit and its suburbs. He constructed a formula that allowed him to estimate what each suburbanite paid to support the city services that benefited him, and what in fact such services cost. In five of six communities, the suburbanite paid less for the services he received than they cost the city. Dr. Neenan said that this subsidy of the rich by the poor should be reversed, and that it could be, since suburbanites actually assigned a higher value to city-performed services than those services cost. He estimated that the affluent residents of Birmingham, Michigan, who were paying $5.64 per capita for services worth $9.02, would be willing to pay $18.22.

If someone ran for office in Birmingham—or in Towson—proposing such an increase in payments, he would more than likely be defeated. Raising taxes is never popular, and raising them in order to help other people in another place is less popular still. Spiro Agnew did not in his four years as executive lead a fight for this kind of increase, but he did take a much more enlightened view of taxes than did many in his situation. He favored progressive taxation in the county, and the use of county tax funds for city services.

One reason for his attitude was that the need for new revenue-raising arrangements in Maryland was so great that something had to be done. Local governments were so reliant on the property tax, that whether they functioned in a fast-growing area, like the county, or in one not growing at all, like the city, they experienced a continual need to raise the tax rate to meet the rising costs of government. Other sources of revenue were needed. Agnew's first idea was a metropolitan sales tax. He proposed in 1963 that Baltimore and Anne Arundel counties and the city all pass a 1 percent local sales tax. There long had been a state sales tax of 3 percent. In Maryland the sales tax is not as regressive as it is in many states, since food and medicine cannot be taxed. The newly installed mayor, Theodore McKeldin, said he preferred an income or earnings tax. His eye was on the commuter. The city's fiscal adviser, Mrs. Janet Hoffman, argued that as time passed, sales-tax revenues would grow in the counties but not in the city, so some arrangement was needed for the rich areas to share with the poor. Agnew said he was in favor of some sort of sharing, hardly a popular stand for a first-year county executive. (Eventually the state legislature authorized the three localities to levy a sales tax, but they never did.)

In 1964 Agnew explained his position on aiding the city in a long letter to the Baltimore *Sun*. County residents, he declared, owed the city for fire and police protection during the hours they were there, and for their use of the museums and the Memorial Stadium. In an answering letter, Councilman Henry Parks, Jr., asserted that "the basic problem" was that the county had erected barriers to the poor, forcing the city to house the whole area's poor population. He said further that many dirty industries, expensive to support with public services and necessary for the entire region, were located in the city. And he pointed out that hospitals and other vital services that were tax exempt served the area from city locations. Agnew continued the debate with another letter. In it he made the usual rebuttal that growing new communities had enormous capital-improvements costs that older cities did not have, mentioning sewers and schools. In addition, Agnew introduced a relatively new argument for the suburban point of view. He pointed out that there was plenty of heavy industry located in the county and serving the metropolitan areas, along with hospitals, colleges, and churches in the county that paid no taxes and that served residents of the city as well. Many of these facilities had moved to the county from the city, for instance, Goucher College and the Greater Baltimore Medical Center, a hospital complex. Foreshadowing the shape of things to come, Baltimore County had become much like a city by the 1960's, so much like one, in fact, that Agnew mused about designating the county as a city officially. "We are after all a larger homogenous entity than most cities," he said.

The issue came to a head in 1966, Agnew's last year in office. The Maryland General Assembly failed to pass its tax-reform measure, and so had to give Baltimore city special one-year power to tax earnings. The county could have taxed income, too, in such a way as to prevent its residents' taxes from going into the city's bank account. The council passed such a bill, which Agnew vetoed as retaliatory as far as the city was concerned but regressive as far as county residents were concerned. The council overrode his veto, but then backed down when the city devised a scheme to tax county residents regardless of whether they were paying taxes in their home county.

Of all the suburban political leaders in the metropolitan area, only Agnew expressed sympathy and understanding for the city in this period. He had proposed that the counties give the city a one-time lump sum from their general funds equal to the amount the earnings tax would get from the commuters. His colleagues shot that down in a hurry. A more typical suburban attitude was that of a legislator who said the city didn't deserve help. Agnew's 1966 stance was even more "enlightened" than it had been in the three previous years. This was enlightened self-interest to a degree. He was now a candidate for governor. Tax reform was expected to be the number-one issue, after the legislature's failure to act the winter before, and Agnew would need city votes. He got them, but not because of his stand on taxes.

Chapter Six

The Race for Governor

Why Not?

In November, 1962, when Maryland Republicans were celebrating Spiro Agnew's first election victory and the party's principal one of that year, somebody came up to Art Sohmer, the brash newcomer to the county who had managed Agnew's campaign, and said, "Next time, Governor." "I said, 'Why not?' That made a lot of sense to me." It shouldn't have. Republicans seldom elected governors of Maryland. Party registration was as lopsided in the state as in the county—Democratic by about three to one. In recent years, the only Republican to win the governor's job had been the ebullient Theodore R. McKeldin. He was elected twice, as a result of circumstances even more special than the Democratic split in the county that had just elected Agnew. Even when Republicans were elected, they did not come from any of the suburban counties. For years Maryland had operated primaries under a county-unit system that gave the unpopulated rural counties and heavily populated Baltimore city all the power in the state. The general elections were by popular vote, so the party machines in the small counties knew they needed the big votes the city politicians could deliver. A city-rural axis of sorts had evolved. Governors came either from the city or from the Eastern Shore or the far-western mountain area. So Sohmer and his companion were talking through their campaign glow. What they said made no sense. But four years later Agnew was elected governor.

In the summer of 1965 Sohmer wrote Agnew a private memorandum predicting that the Democrats would be split in 1966. He recommended that Agnew run for governor. Agnew responded with interest. In September he said publicly that he would seriously consider making the race if there was a Democratic fight. Actually he was not the most likely party member to take on even the split Democrats. He was relatively new to elective politics, and he was unknown around the state. But in October of that year, a poll of the twenty-three Republican members of the General Assembly put him in second place, behind Congressman Rogers C. B. Morton. Still, the most likely candidate if Morton chose not to run, or even if he did, was the state's other Republican congressman, Charles Mathias. Morton was a transplanted Kentuckian, a wealthy giant of a man who had settled on the Eastern Shore and become a working gentleman farmer. He was hugely popular in that conservative area, yet managed to maintain an aura of moderation that would have allowed him to run fairly well in the more liberal parts of the state. Mathias was a liberal from the western part of the state. He was a member of the Judiciary Committee and had proved to be a hard worker for civil-rights legislation.

Agnew approached each of them in late 1965, offering his support. He said that if both refused the race, he would like to make it. Mathias showed only a flicker of interest, then declared he would prefer to stay in Congress. He had told other party leaders the same thing. Morton showed two or three flickers of interest. The legislative routine was not as appealing to him as it was to Mathias, and he had some ideas about party organization which he thought only a governor could carry out. But he too finally decided not to run. Both congressmen offered Agnew their support. The other Republican high-level officeholders in the party were Baltimore Mayor McKeldin, serving a second term after an interval of eight years as governor; Joseph Alton, executive of Anne Arundel County, a suburb of both Baltimore and Washington; David Scull, of Washington's suburban Montgomery County; and J. Glenn Beall, Jr., the state House minority leader. Agnew touched base with them all. For one reason or another, Agnew had better credentials than any of them. At least his situation was more promising. McKeldin was too familiar a face, Alton too new in the job, Scull had had his chance, having sought the nomination unsuccessfully in 1962. Beall was more interested in the United States Senate. Another name that always came up was that of Milton Eisenhower, the former president's brother, who was president of Johns Hopkins University; but though a party leader, he was never ultimately a candidate. He wasn't interested. "To give Ted his due, most of us were afraid to take a whipping," said one of the Republicans Agnew approached. The conventional appraisal of the times was that the Republicans were down, that 1966 was not going to be a Republican year. In 1964 not only had Lyndon Johnson carried the state in a walk, but a young group of so-called "shiny-bright" Democrats led by Joseph Tydings had apparently captured the Democratic party and the imagination of the state. Tydings had defeated an old-guard opponent in the primary, then swamped incumbent Republican Senator J. Glenn Beall, Sr.

Agnew had something else going for him besides the reluctance of his potential rivals: he had little choice. If he wanted to stay in politics he had to run for something other than county executive. He could never be reelected, and he knew it. He said so outright to Edgar Jones, of the *Sun,* and he told Mayor McKeldin and Anne Arundel Executive Alton that he would have a better chance being elected governor than of being reelected county executive. His four years of battling over civil rights, urban renewal, gun control and so forth had eroded his public support, and his feuds with the Democrats had unified them: they would not let the divisions of 1962 happen again. Also, Goldwater Republicans in the county were cool to Agnew.

So, in April, Agnew announced for governor. In advance of his formal plunge, the newspapers were reporting that the nomination was "his for the asking." When he went to Annapolis to file, he was accompanied by his family and by almost every well-known Republican officeholder in the state. He said that he would campaign hard in the primary, despite the weakest sort of token opposition, because he wanted to get his name known "where the people are, especially the Washington suburbs." He pledged that as governor he would deal more with local officials than with legislators. He said "urban conditions" would be given "special consideration" in his campaign, specified tax revision as the first and foremost issue, and listed these others: transportation, water pollution, traffic and industrial safety, and better hospitals and jails. He was wrong. The campaign boiled down to one issue, not mentioned in that statement, unless "urban conditions" was to be regarded as a euphemism for it.

"Your Home Is Your Castle—Protect It."

There is not another George Perry Mahoney anywhere, and there is not ever likely to be. Nor should there be, probably. The world would be a poorer place without Mahoney, but two Mahoneys would make for an indigestible richness. Mahoney led a life straight out of Horatio Alger. That is of course said about many people, but usually erroneously. The typical Alger hero was characterised not only by shrewd judgment and a willingness to work hard, but also by extraordinary luck; he was always saving the banker's daughter from a runaway horse, or something. In the years before World War I, George Mahoney was heading nowhere much in life, working as a teen-age bellhop at the Waldorf in New York. The eleventh child of a policeman, he had fled there from the genteel working-class poverty of Baltimore's Irish ghetto. One night he came across a forlorn drunk in his hotel. He lectured him and helped him sober up. The man turned out to be a professor of engineering. He got George a job building the subways, and taught him the rudiments of the construction business. Back to Baltimore Mahoney came, still quite young, to begin his own sand-and-gravel firm. He prospered, soon was bold enough to demand successfully his share of the "paving ring's" business with the city, and became a wealthy man. In 1941, at the age of forty, he entered public life as a Democrat, accepting an appointment to the Maryland Racing Commission. Soon he was chairman, and making a lot of two-dollar bettors happy by exposing various shady practices at the tracks. In 1946 a new governor bumped him from the commission, and in 1950 Mahoney ran for nomination as governor for the first time, beginning a track record unmatched anywhere. He lost in the Democratic primary, but his campaign so divided the party that a Republican was elected governor. In 1952 Mahoney ran for the Senate nomination and won it. That was the year of the first Eisenhower landslide, and Mahoney lost to Republican J. Glenn Beall, who was firmly clutching the General's coattails. In 1954 Mahoney again sought nomination for governor; he lost out in a very close, very hard-fought primary, and the inevitable result was that the Republicans kept control of the statehouse in November. In 1956—nothing ventured, nothing gained—Mahoney did get the

senatorial nomination, only to be stopped by the second Eisenhower landslide; though he ran 120,000 ahead of the top of the
Democratic ticket, he lost to John Marshall Butler, Joe McCarthy's
legacy to Maryland. In 1958 Mahoney tried for the Senate again,
came in second, and split the party just enough so that the same
Beall who had won a fluke election thanks to Eisenhower in 1952
was reelected.

There was no statewide office to be filled in 1960, but George
was back in 1962. He lost the gubernatorial primary to the incumbent governor, Millard Tawes of the Eastern Shore. That made six
straight. Unlike that fixture on the American scene, the perennial
candidate who has no following, Mahoney had been a serious candidate with strong voter appeal in every election. But in 1962, politicians noticed that his formerly secure hold on the Baltimore city
vote was relaxing. The country-type Tawes beat him in the city.
The city was changing, for one thing. Mahoney himself had moved
to a handsome 350-acre "model farm" in Baltimore County. His
personal style, his almost determined clumsiness, his insistence on
running one-issue campaigns, and his very record of failures were
doing him in. After 1962 and then the Tydings victory of 1964 (a
family tragedy kept Mahoney out that year), it looked like the
Democrats weren't going to have George Mahoney to kick around
any more. But appearances were deceiving. Some of Agnew's
friends say today that he predicted a Mahoney candidacy before
1966. Mahoney did enter the primary, and just as he had once
raised hell with a one-plank platform—repeal of the sales tax—this
time he rocked his party from the precincts to the White House on
the issue of open housing. His platform looked like backlash's last
stand. Congress in the previous two years had approved first an
omnibus civil-rights bill, then an innovative bill to insure Negroes'
voting rights. It was considering an open-housing bill, fully supported by one of the Democratic candidates for nomination as governor, Representative Carlton Sickles.

According to a National Opinion Research Center poll of June,
1965, three out of four whites outside the South said they agreed
with this statement: "It would make no difference if a Negro with
the same education and income moved into [the] block." Even in
the South there was about a 50-50 split on the question, according
to the National Opinion Research Center. And in December, 1965,
when Mahoney and other Democrats soon to run for governor

were asked about open housing, they all supported the bill that was before Congress. Mahoney later explained during his campaign that when he endorsed open housing, "you must remember, I was not a candidate at that time."

The principal Democratic candidates in the primary were Mahoney; Sickles, a very liberal, labor-supported congressman from Prince Georges County; Clarence W. Miles, an elderly veteran of public service, from the Eastern Shore; and Thomas B. Finan, the attorney general, who was the candidate of the old guard. Most of the Tydings Democrats supported Sickles. It is a sad commentary on the times that, by sticking to his campaign platform, Mahoney forced Finan and Miles to renege on open housing and in the end advocate only very mild forms of legislation promoting it. Sickles gave up his hopeless support of a stronger bill and endorsed the one finally passed by the House, which was written by Representative Mathias, and exempted owner-occupied property of up to four units, land sales, and developers who conducted less than two transactions a year. Irrationally, a Federal law, about which a governor would have nothing to say or do, had become the issue. As Mahoney defined it for his adversaries: "I firmly believe that the bill before Congress concerning open housing is in violent disagreement with our Constitution. One of the basic precepts of our Founding Fathers was that a man's home is his castle." Thus his campaign posters everywhere said, "Your Home Is Your Castle—Protect It." In September, Mahoney won the nomination with less than 30 percent of the vote. Sickles came in second, fewer than 2,-000 votes behind him. Finan came in a fairly close third. Mahoney again did only fairly well in the city, but in Baltimore County he got almost as many votes as Finan and Sickles combined. Actually, Sickles lost the race in his own suburban home county of Prince Georges—that mixture of blue-collar workers, the University of Maryland, lower- and middle-level bureaucrats, and the first growing suburban black ghetto spreading out from Washington. He and Finan ran neck and neck. Finan's backing down on open housing presented him to these suburbanites as an acceptable compromise between the more liberal Sickles and the racist Mahoney.

Within days, the White House passed the word that Mahoney, Georgia's Lester Maddox, and Arkansas' Jim Johnson would not be endorsed by Lyndon Johnson. Senate Minority Leader Everett

Dirksen announced that the Maryland primary was a straw in the wind that suggested the open-housing bill now before the Senate should be killed. At his urging, it was. And so George Mahoney headed for a showdown with Spiro Agnew, with one scalp already on his belt.

Your Kind of Guy

Robert Goodman is a native Baltimorean who opened his own advertising agency in the city in 1959. He was just thirty years old, and his experience at other agencies included much work on political advertising. Political advertising agencies, and consultants who specialized in campaign advertising, were going to spring up everywhere in the 1960's, and Goodman's agency was to be one of the most successful by the beginning of the following decade. Among his clients were Governor A. Linwood Holton, of Virginia, Senator Robert Taft, of Ohio, Governor Winthrop Rockefeller, of Arkansas, and many other Republicans. They came to him after he took his first client from relative obscurity to the governorship of Maryland with one little song. The client was Spiro Agnew. In 1966 Goodman had his choice between handling Agnew's or Thomas Finan's campaign. He chose Agnew's, perhaps in part because it represented a challenge. He later told an interviewer, "[Agnew's] record was kind of undistinguished . . . so we didn't have a good record to run on, but we did have what we thought was a really beautiful guy and we ran a sex campaign. The song was a sex appeal type of song."

"The song" began, "My kind of guy, Ted Agnew is . . ." and to the tune of "My Kind of Town, Chicago Is," extolled Agnew's virtues. It concluded by describing him as "your kind of guy." On television the tune was often played while films showed Agnew at work behind his desk, or just striding manfully into a building. The first thing the tune was supposed to do, sex appeal aside, was to let Maryland voters know that a guy named Agnew existed. All summer, radio and television stations broadcast the song. Though Agnew's opposition in the primary was only nominal, though the real race would not start till after the September primary election, at Goodman's recommendation the strong advertising campaign was begun right away, and Agnew stumped the state as if he were in a real primary contest. There was no talk about issues. Agnew said publicly that this would come in the general-election campaign. In early September, he told a reporter, "My principal problem so far has been identification outside the Baltimore metropolitan area. I was delighted when I walked into a crab plant in Crisfield [on the Eastern Shore] and five or six women started singing the song." By primary day, the second week in September, Agnew had spent more money on his non-campaign (he got over 80 percent of the primary vote) than any of the Democrats except Finan in their hotly contested primary. Agnew's outlays totaled a little over $360,000, Finan's approximately $450,000, Sickles' $306,-000, Mahoney's a bargain $124,000. Like Lester Maddox in Georgia, who was running a shoestring campaign that would cost only about $50,000, Mahoney was learning that a little racism stretches a dollar a long way. Mahoney's expenditures amounted to less than a dollar a vote. Agnew's amounted to about $3.50, so small was the turnout in the Republican primary.

But Agnew got his name spread before the public statewide not only by means of the song and the expensive campaign but also because of his involvement in what his critics called a flagrant conflict of interest.

The Bay Bridge Property

A long, curving two-lane bridge soars high over Chesapeake Bay just above Annapolis. It provides metropolitan Washington's only access to the Eastern Shore and the beach resorts of Maryland and Delaware, and serves as the most direct access to these areas for metropolitan Baltimore residents. By the mid-1960's summer weekend use of the bridge was so great that state highway officials began to plan for a second bridge. There was some debate about where to put the new span, with most state officials favoring a parallel bridge beside the existing one. In early 1965 this route seemed assured, with the governor and legislature supporting it. In the summer of 1965 nine Baltimore County men together bought 107 acres on the Revell Highway approach to the bridge in Anne Arundel County. Eight were wealthy businessmen and the ninth was Agnew. Agnew's share was worth $34,200, of which he put up only $5,000. He borrowed the rest, presumably from the other men or from the Chesapeake National Bank. Agnew was a director of that county bank, as were three other members of the nine-man group. One of these was an old friend, J. Walter Jones.

The Baltimore *Sun* reported that Jones had other interesting involvements with Agnew as well. His appraising firm had received $24,135 from the county since Agnew took office, half the total county bill for appraisals. Furthermore, the paper's county reporter said, two other members of the nine-man investment group were Lester Matz and John C. Child, and their engineering firm had received $315,061 from the county during Agnew's term of office. But the implications of these and other similar ties to the bank and to county businessmen were largely ignored. They were publicized after Agnew, himself, revealed in July, 1966, that he was involved in the land deal. Instead, attention was focused on the very heated and often emotional debate that was churning up about Agnew's association with the bridge itself, even though, as he logically pointed out, his investment was perfectly proper. As county executive he would have been in an obvious conflict-of-interest position if he had bought land speculatively in Baltimore County, but this land was not in the county. Also, he now promised to sell the land if he were elected governor, and thus placed in a position where he could take official action regarding it.

His critics saw the situation differently. Hyman Pressman, the Baltimore city comptroller, charged Agnew with being a "wheeler and dealer." Baltimore County's Democratic Representative Clarence Long, who was the leading opponent of the parallel bridge, said a conflict of interest existed even while Agnew was a *candidate* for governor. He challenged him to sell the property or get out of the race. On July 8, two days after Agnew made the revelation of his investment, he announced that he would sell. On balance, the story probably helped him. It got him a lot of headlines in connection with an issue of interest to the public. Two years later, the matter came up again in the vice-presidential race, and again Agnew probably benefited by the publicity.

The whole Bay Bridge issue had come up in a perverse way, and its aftermath was perverse, too. To begin with, Agnew had been pressured into disclosing his interests by Representative Long's insistence that he take a stand on *where* the bridge should be built. Though the legislature had authorized the parallel site,

Long had led a fight to place the matter on the November ballot. Maryland is referendum-crazy. Long wanted the bridge built north of Baltimore, to serve his constituents more directly. Other enemies of the parallel bridge wanted it farther south, to serve Washington's suburbs. Long used the issue masterfully (in part, he later said, to divert Baltimore County voters' attention from his suddenly Mahoney-exposed position on civil rights: he was quite liberal). In November the voters did turn down the parallel site by a slim margin. But the next year, Governor Agnew and the General Assembly displayed some real sleight of hand. They authorized all three bridges, then announced they'd build the parallel bridge first. Agnew's partners were delighted, of course. They had bought back his interest in the property. (But so far the property has not been zoned for development.) Agnew also arranged for his friend and adviser George White to become the "local attorney" for the underwriting firm that handled the bridge bonds. The arrangement was unprecedented, worth an estimated $55,000 to White's law firm.

No Maddoxville

When Agnew opened his state headquarters in the Lord Baltimore Hotel in June, he declared that the city's "crisis" was the number-one problem in Maryland. His goal as governor would be tax reform, to save the city and other local governments. If he expected that this number-one problem was also going to be the number-one issue, he learned better after Mahoney finished tearing up the Democrats. Though Agnew and the independent candidate Hyman Pressman did talk a great deal about taxes and other issues, and though Mahoney also did so on rare occasions, the civil-rights questions of the day, as exemplified by open housing and crystallized by Mahoney's slogan, completely dominated the race, just as they had the Democratic primary. The contest was between Agnew and Mahoney; Pressman, who wound up with only 10 percent of the vote, was never a factor. Pressman and Agnew appeared on television for debates on the issues, but they were shadowboxing, and everybody knew it. The shadow was George Mahoney, who refused to appear. He was having more fun with his own highly individual, hug-here-kiss-on-the-cheek-there type of person-to-person campaigning. He also knew that he could not cope with Agnew's presence or Pressman's bulldog grip on details. "I wouldn't dare go on television with those two nuts," Mahoney said when asked about his absence. His supporters loved it. He called Agnew "the big slob." They loved that, too.

Mahoney attacked Agnew personally several times during the campaign. He tried to make Agnew's ethnic heritage an issue, in a clumsy, heavy-handed way. He noted that Greek shipping men, including the son of movie magnate Spyros Skouras, had helped Agnew raise money.° "I'm frightened by this . . . will he do anything to destroy the port of Baltimore?" Mahoney asked from the stump in Elkton. On another occasion Mahoney told a women's club in blue-collar Dundalk, in Baltimore County, "The Greeks in New York and some of the worst characters in the world sit around [together]. If [Agnew] gets too nasty, I will be compelled to talk about it."

Agnew for his part was running a high-level campaign. It was his—and his advisers'—idea to emphasize his image, as he had in the 1962 campaign in the county, as the cool, calm, intelligent, compassionate, professional citizen, above politics. When the state Republicans met, about three weeks into the campaign, Agnew showed his disgust with Mahoney by referring to him as "a vulgar opportunist," but for the most part he stuck to the issues.

On *the* issue, he was worried. He went out of his way to stress that he supported only a mild open-housing bill. "If an open housing bill affecting the right of the individual homeowner to sell to whomever he wished passed, I'd veto it," he said in early October. Negro leaders did not like that, but they believed they had to go with Agnew. Pressman's more liberal views were more attractive to

---

° Of the approximately $700,000 Agnew's financial committees raised for his two campaigns, less than 5 percent was traced to his proud fellow Greeks inside and outside the state. Many of the large contributions came from businessmen in Baltimore County. Real-estate-related business interests were a good source of money. The biggest contribution was from I. H. Hammerman II—$10,000 from himself and his wife. One of Agnew's partners in the Revell Highway property, with his wife and son, gave $7,500. J. Walter Jones gave $2,000. But, as everywhere, engineers and road builders were the biggest contributors. Agnew's campaign was far more costly than Mahoney's. Mahoney spent a total of only $329,000 in the general and primary campaigns. In 1968 Greek-American friends of Agnew raised over $100,000 in Maryland for the Nixon-Agnew campaign, and much more elsewhere.

them, but they knew he couldn't win. Baltimore City's leading
Negro businessmen and public officials began endorsing him. The
wealthy black businessman-councilman Henry G. Parks, Jr., announced the formation of Democrats for Agnew. Other black and
liberal leaders began to do the same. The state AFL-CIO committee on political education endorsed a Republican gubernatorial
candidate for the first time in history. The black state senator Clarence M. Mitchell III announced that his organization was solidly
behind Agnew. The state Americans for Democratic Action endorsed Agnew and urged Pressman to get out of the race. "It is important that liberals unite behind Mr. Agnew," the Americans for
Democratic Action statement said. Maryland resident Dean Ache-
son, a Democrat, wrote the Baltimore *Sun*, "I shall vote for Mr.
Agnew." The states' two Democratic senators implied that they
supported Agnew. Both the *Sunpapers* endorsed him. So did *The
New York Times*. Clergymen in rural counties, thirty-one members
of the Baltimore Colts, the Maryland Conference of Social Welfare,
and Oriole third baseman Brooks Robinson, a county resident and
local culture hero—all endorsed Agnew as October came and
went. Robinson's support may have been more important than it
seems. The last half of the governor's race was conducted in the
heady, happy afterglow of the city's first World Series. The Orioles
defeated the Los Angeles Dodgers in four straight games. Balti-
more-area residents were in just too good a mood that fall to go for
Mahoney's meanness. In 1969, the fact that the New York Mets
won their first World Series during the mayoralty campaign is said
to have contributed to the reelection of Mayor John Lindsay in a
contest somewhat similar to the 1966 Maryland governor's race.

Despite his lukewarm support for open-housing legislation of
any kind, and his opposition to any meaningful legislation in the
field, Agnew was beginning to campaign in a way that gratified
Negroes and civil-rights supporters. In a speech to the Frontiers
Club of west Baltimore in mid-October, he said that the eyes of
Negroes all over America were on Maryland, to see if that border
state would become "Maddoxville," a reference to Lester Maddox.
About the same time, he toned down his disapproval of a tough
open-housing bill by saying that maybe he wouldn't veto one after
all "if it were passed by a strong vote and if there were public sentiment for it." He began to campaign more in black neighborhoods.

On one occasion he and Mayor McKeldin walked along Pennsylvania Avenue, the old ghetto's main street of bars and small businesses. McKeldin, much more outgoing and much more at home, stole the show with his enthusiastic shouts to "my people" and "my brother." McKeldin suggested another such expedition in Baltimore's huge Lexington Market, a collection of dozens of small food stores under one roof. Much of its clientele was black. Agnew refused, and some in the campaign organization thought he did so because he felt uneasy around Negroes. But after telling McKeldin he wouldn't be there, Agnew went by himself. He felt more uneasy around the scene-stealing McKeldin than around Negroes. The two men had other differences. A week before Election Day, McKeldin sailed off to the Caribbean. In 1968 Agnew saw to it that McKeldin—twice mayor, twice governor, the nominator of Eisenhower in 1952, and the seconder of Rockefeller in 1964—was not a delegate to the Republican National Convention.

Agnew's commitment to civil rights was seemingly being made stronger by his support in the Negro communities and by his growing frustration and disgust with Mahoney. His challenges for a debate were never answered. He began to perceive that Mahoney's competence and his slogan were themselves issues, apart from everything else. With three weeks to go, he began to take on Mahoney. On October 20 he told a Baltimore County audience that Mahoney was against the constitutional rights of freedom of speech and freedom of the press, against the right of the people to know the workings of the government (Mahoney had said he wouldn't deal with reporters if he were elected). "He is threatening our rights," Agnew said. Still, his attacks on Mahoney were restrained. He seemed to feel it important to establish a stark contrast in demeanor. But on October 23, the day after Agnew and McKeldin visited Pennsylvania Avenue, key members of the Agnew staff held a meeting in the Lord Baltimore Hotel headquarters suite with some outside advisers, members of a liberal-Republican consulting firm, Campaign Consultants, Incorporated. The meeting was held at the request of Ormsby S. ("Dutch") Moore, a campaign aide. He and some others were deeply concerned over their latest polls, which showed Mahoney approximately six points ahead of Agnew. Campaign Consultants' recommendation, after a long session of reviewing the campaign, was for Agnew to take a much harsher line with Mahoney in the closing weeks. Agnew and some of his advisers were somewhat reluctant to make changes so late in the game, but apparently the recommendation was accepted after a chance meeting between Agnew and Mahoney two days later.

The candidates were both guests at a cocktail party and dinner for the chairman of the state Public Service Commission, held in a synagogue in Baltimore County. Agnew walked up to Mahoney. Mahoney ignored him for a long thirty seconds, while the room became electric with anticipation. Finally, Mahoney pursed his lips in irritation and extended his hand.

"How are you, Mr. Agnew?"

"Fine, George. How are you?"

"This certainly is a relief from campaigning, isn't it?" Mahoney said. Then he turned to leave without waiting for an answer. Agnew pursued him.

"Let's talk about the issues, George," he said to his back. "There are reporters here. Let's hold a press conference and discuss the issues. We can talk about education, taxes, and other important problems facing the people."

Mahoney stopped, and lips quivering at the challenge, said, "Let's talk about your friends up in New York who are giving you all that money."

Agnew was firmly in control now. "Come on, George. I've finally caught up with you. You can't keep running away from me forever. People want to know if you're qualified even to be governor [or not]." Agnew turned to the crowd that was watching in fascination. "Why is this man afraid to talk about the issues?" he demanded.

An angry Mahoney said to him, "You run your campaign and I'll run mine," and left. Agnew apologized to his hosts, but said he felt frustrated.

The next day he told Baltimore Republicans that Mahoney supporters were members of the National States' Rights party and the Ku Klux Klan. "It is nothing but bigotry that man is appealing to," he said. The same day he went to a rally in Anne Arundel County to charge that Mahoney was "giving comfort to the forces of evil." The following day, at a Kiwanis meeting in downtown Baltimore, he spoke of "political vultures . . . setting fires of hatred, fear and uncertainty . . . flocking like moths to the flame of the fiery cross."

Mahoney cried out in wounded rage that this was the "lowest of the low in the history of Maryland" and that he, an Irish Catholic, would hardly support the Klan. The Klan met on October 28, and while it did not endorse a candidate, the Grand Titan did single out Agnew for attack, calling him a socialist.

Whether it was the calculated execution of Campaign Consultants' recommendation, or the result of frustration or of honest disgust with Mahoney, Agnew's closing campaign worked. Mahoney went further and further to the right and began to make blatant racist appeals. If the polls of mid-October were accurate, Agnew made a miraculous recovery. Maryland voters gave him 50 percent of their ballots, with 40 percent to Mahoney, and 10 percent to Pressman. Agnew's margin over Mahoney was 82,000 votes, which is about the margin he piled up in Baltimore city and Montgomery County. He got nearly three-fourths of the liberal Montgomery County suburbanite vote, almost all the Negro vote in the city, about 55 percent of the vote in the mixed-economy suburb of Prince Georges County. He lost Anne Arundel County and the remaining suburb, his home, Baltimore County. None of his running mates did well. On the state ticket, Charles Bresler and William Doub, the Republican candidates for comptroller of the treasury and attorney general, each lost, receiving less than 40 percent of the vote. In Baltimore County, E. Scott Moore, for whom his old boss did not campaign, lost the race for county executive. Only 8 of the 43 state senators elected were Republicans, and only 25 of the 142 state delegates.

More significant than the alignment of parties was the fact that 70 percent of the newly elected General Assembly would be newcomers. This was Maryland's first legislature since reapportionment. The four suburban counties would have 20 senators instead of 4, 63 delegates instead of 40, almost half the membership of each chamber. In his first post-election interview, Agnew took note of the fact that the legislature was going to be new in more ways than one, and expressed the belief that he would get along with it well.

Chapter Seven

Governor of the Free State

America in Miniature

THE ONLY MARYLAND GOVERNOR before Spiro Agnew who seriously aspired to national leadership was H. L. Mencken's friend Albert C. Ritchie. Ritchie was an urbane Baltimorean who after World War I was elected to the office four times in a row. Mencken was always boosting him for the presidency, in part because of his enlightened attitude toward prohibition. Ritchie refused to enforce it. He and one of Mencken's colleagues popularized the notion and the slogan that Maryland was "a free state," to the outrage of some of the Southern members of Congress. The most outspoken drys of the South in the 1920's found it scandalous for a governor to take such a stand, particularly the governor of a state that was, if not truly Southern, at least located on the correct side of the Mason-Dixon line, at least a former slave state, at least a state in which public institutions were segregated. Had Albert Ritchie ever been nominated for vice-president, no one would have accused his party's presidential candidate of adopting a Southern Strategy. In truth, of course, Maryland was not a free state, particularly for its black citizens, as the existence of legal or official segregation and discrimination into the 1960's suggests. Nor was it southern. The state did not join the Confederacy, and escaped Reconstruction and the South's subsequent rigid one-party politics. Maryland Negroes had exercised the franchise ever since the end of the Civil War. Maryland was divided during the Civil War and continued to be divided thereafter. Its Eastern Shore was as Southern in its economy, history, and mores as the Eastern Shore of Virginia. Western Maryland was like West Virginia, loyalist, Republican as a consequence, a poor area of small farms and Appalachian coal mines. It was oriented more toward Pittsburgh than toward Baltimore. And Baltimore, itself, the sixth-largest city in the country, was not particularly oriented toward the South. It had grown to be an important port because its rail-heads were closer to the Southern markets and resources than were those of the ports of New York and Philadelphia, but also because it was closer to the markets and resources of the West. Baltimore looked west at least as much as it looked south, partic-ularly after World War I increased Europe's demand for water-borne American grain. In the 1960's a black civil-rights advocate said the state combined the features of North and South, that it was the "worst" Northern state. Perhaps the only reply to this observation would be that it was the "best" Southern state.

Marylanders usually respond to criticism of their state by com-paring it to the nation. They assert that whatever faults and virtues Maryland has, are the faults and virtues of the nation, and indeed they often refer to the state as "America in Miniature." What they mean is that Maryland has a rural Southern area—the Eastern Shore; a bustling Northern metropolis with steel mills and every other sort of industry and commerce—Baltimore; all sorts of farm-land, mountains, and seashore; and a varied population. It is also typical, in fact more than typical, in another respect: it has a sub-urban population that is larger in proportion to the whole than can be found almost anywhere else. In its demographic character Maryland has been a decade or so ahead of the national trend. It became an "urban" state by census definition in 1910, while the United States did not become an urban nation until 1920. In 1970, the Census Bureau found that, for the first time, more Americans were classified as suburban than as either urban or rural. That is, more people lived in the noncentral portions of metropolitan areas than lived in the central cities or entirely outside the metropolitan areas. In 1960, Maryland's four suburban counties—Prince Georges, Anne Arundel, Montgomery, and Baltimore—already contained some 45 percent of the state's population. In addition, since certain parts of some of the more sparsely populated counties are also included in the Baltimore metropolitan area, altogether more than half the state's population could be loosely classified as suburban. By 1970, the four suburban counties alone contained 52 percent of the population. America in Miniature was also America Anticipated.

The reason for Maryland's suburban character is that whereas most states have one central city for each suburban ring, Maryland has two suburban rings and only one city. Washington, D. C., with over a million Maryland suburbanites in its orbit, is not a part of the state. If Washington's 700,000 citizens were counted as Marylanders, the state's population distribution would not be so skewed. Maryland is not the only state so favored with suburbanites. New Jersey has an even more pronounced suburban character, since it contains a large number of the suburbanites encamped outside two of the nation's largest cities, New York and Philadelphia, while the cities themselves, with their urban populations, are in other states. It is even more the state of the future than Maryland. An old joke has a man returning from a visit to New Jersey with the remark, "I have seen the future and it doesn't work."

Properly for this governor in this state, Agnew assembled a team of top-level aides that was striking for its suburban tone—the predominance in it of men from Maryland's suburban counties, many of them relative newcomers to the state. Agnew's staff was larger than previous governors' had been. A study commission had just proposed a reorganization of the executive department, and Agnew was the first governor to have a full-fledged "cabinet" of staff aides. His principal assistant was Secretary of State C. Stanley Blair, a thirty-nine-year-old lawyer who had been born in Baltimore County but had practiced law in Bel Air, in neighboring Harford County. He had also represented Harford in the Maryland House of Delegates. The county was part of the Baltimore metropolitan area, but Bel Air was twenty miles from downtown Baltimore, a long commute by Maryland standards. A more likely destination for commuters from that county was Baltimore County. John G. Lauber, as director of the Governor's Task Force on Modern Management, was in a position of influence second only to Blair's. Lauber, a New Yorker, was a former finance director of Montgomery County. Arthur Sohmer, who had managed Agnew's campaigns in 1962 and 1966, came with him from Baltimore County to be his appointments secretary; also from the county was Mrs. Cynthia Rosenwald, a housewife who had the title of administrative assistant, but whose principal responsibility was to write Mr. Agnew's speeches, a chore that would eventually make her famous in her own right.

Agnew installed six "program executives" to deal with the state bureaucracy. Four of these were old friends or associates from the county. Ormsby S. Moore, a real-estate man who had worked on Agnew's county-executive staff, was in charge of commerce, labor, and state administration. B. Melvin Cole, formerly a school official in the county system, was in charge of education. Vladimir A. Wahbe, the public-works official who caught so much lightning in the Towson-Catonsville urban-renewal fight, was program executive for urban affairs. Robert J. Lally, Agnew's police chief in the county, a Pennsylvanian who had lived about the country, was program executive for public safety (briefly, then he became state superintendent of police; he was replaced by another former FBI man, Edward J. McCabe, who came from New York). The other two program executives were Russell H. McCain, a veteran state employee from western Maryland, who was in charge of transportation matters, and Dr. Gilbert Ware, thirty-three, who handled "health, welfare, and human relations." Dr. Ware was the first Negro ever named to a Maryland governor's staff, and the first of several very high-level black appointees Agnew was to assign to executive and judicial posts. Ware was a graduate of Baltimore's Morgan State College and did his graduate work at Princeton. He came to the Agnew staff from the United States Civil Rights Commission. Another important Agnew aide was Charles Bresler, named to the newly created post of national-relations officer. He was a flamboyant millionaire developer from Montgomery County whose plans to put new apartment buildings in the old, New Deal experimental town of Greenbelt had so outraged residents there that Agnew made it a point to explain that *their* national relations would be handled by someone else. One of the most important of all Agnew's appointments was the selection of Jerome Wolff of Baltimore County as director of highways and chairman of the state roads commission. Wolff was a transplanted Chicagoan, a consulting engineer and one-time assistant director of public works in Baltimore County. He became the personification of the city-be-damned suburbanite highway builder to many in Baltimore when he pushed for an interstate route through the city's historic waterfront. "Who's Afraid of Jerome Wolff?" buttons were a brief fad—and the highway wasn't built. The two other top officials on the Governor's team were Herbert Thompson, who was named public-relations officer, and Robert Montgomery, Jr., a former teacher, who was named legislative officer. Both were originally from North Carolina; Thompson had most recently been the Associated Press bureau chief in Annapolis, and Montgomery a lobbyist in Washington.

Unlike the New Jersey of the joke, the Maryland of 1967 still worked, and worked well, but there was a problem which the campaign had never been able to focus on, despite some efforts by Agnew to do so. That was the matter of fiscal affairs. The state was not collecting enough revenue, and was not properly distributing the funds it did collect. An attempt to rewrite and reform the basic tax laws had been narrowly defeated in the General Assembly in 1966. As soon as he was elected in November, Agnew asked the leader of that unsuccessful fight to try again in the coming year. But a different result was not likely. The reform had been bitterly opposed by the legislators from the suburban counties in 1966— and their number was greatly increased in 1967.

Hughes-Agnew-Lee

The fiscal crisis Maryland faced in the mid-1960's was a familiar one for states. Local governments were starving for funds, primarily because the broad-based and growing taxes, such as the sales tax and the income tax, had been preempted by the state. Localities depended for the most part on property taxes, which grow rather more slowly as a source of revenue. Maryland's income tax at the time was not a progressive one, being a flat 3 percent. The state's formula for distributing state-collected taxes was also not very fair. The double result was that *no* localities were getting back enough money from the state, and that those with the most poor people, those that needed the money the most, were getting less than their share of what money there was.

In mid-1965 a study commission headed by Harry Hughes, a state senator from a small county, and Dr. Paul Cooper, director of the state's Fiscal Research Bureau, recommended sweeping reforms, based on two principles. One was that the income tax should be graduated, to range from 3 to 6 percent. The other was "equalization," the principle that the state's revenues should be distributed on the basis of the local governments' need and effort.

High-taxing, poverty-stricken Baltimore city would get about 40 percent of the tax money to be returned, while Baltimore County, affluent and a relatively light taxer, would get only 14 percent. Half the city taxpayers would pay only ten dollars more a year or less, but only a third of the county taxpayers would be that lightly touched. Back in mid-1965, County Executive Spiro Agnew said, "It smacks of outright socialism to me. It sounds like communism." Since so many of his county constituents would be hit by what in effect would be a doubling of the tax rate, Agnew's statement was not surprising. Others in the county government were even more critical. As the reform proposal was changed in one particular or another, in an effort to win for it greater favor in the suburban counties that it would hit hardest, Agnew began to come around to mild support. This shift took place after he had about decided to seek nomination as governor, and some of his critics believed his decision to run was a reason for his new attitude. If the General Assembly passed the tax bill in 1966, as most observers anticipated, and thus settled the matter, Agnew could probably expect not to have to concern himself with it during his campaign or after election. When in 1966 he said he could support the proposal, Agnew was attacked by county Councilman Dale Anderson, who called the tax plan "legalized larceny." Anderson spoke for a large body of his constituents when he said he wouldn't mind so much if the new taxes were going to the state instead of the city. That attitude sums up the urban crisis of our times.

The Cooper-Hughes plan was passed by the state Senate, despite opposition from three of the four suburban senators. It appeared that it would succeed in the House of Delegates, despite a parliamentary maneuver by opponents that made a two-thirds vote necessary for passage. Lobbying was intense. Several of the city's thirty-seven delegates were hesitant about voting for even so beneficial a tax rise in an election year. The president of the Baltimore city council, Thomas D'Alessandro III, came to Annapolis with a list of relatives of delegates on the city payroll, and explained to the delegates how many firings might result from a failure of the bill. All but three members of the city delegation came around. The vote for the bill was 70 to 64, a majority, but not the required two-thirds. Baltimore County delegates voted against it, 12 to 1;

the Montgomery County vote was 8 to 0; the Anne Arundel vote was 6 to 1. Only Prince Georges, of the suburban counties, favored the bill, by a narrow 6 to 4.

So the state gave the city earnings-tax authority for one year, as a bail-out, and the showdown on taxes was put off another year. In November, 1966, Governor-elect Agnew called Senator Hughes and asked him to try again to devise a reform plan. He hinted strongly that he thought the suburban counties should not be hit as hard as they had been in the first Cooper-Hughes plan. Harry Hughes could read the results of the last election. He knew that in the Senate, for example, there would be a fivefold increase in suburban representation. "Everybody knew the first plan could not be passed," Hughes said, meaning everybody on the special committee set up at Agnew's request, with minimum city representation. Everybody also knew that some plan had to be passed. The committee worked out a compromise, called at first "Hughes-Agnew." In January, before he took office, Agnew described the new proposal as a "good compromise," one that would be easier to pass than Cooper-Hughes had been because it imposed less "penalty" on the rich counties.

Here indeed was the essential difference between the two plans —the new one involved less "penalty," or cost, to the middle-class wage earner, and dramatically less cost to the middle-class strongholds in the state. The Baltimore *Sun* commented, "The impression is inescapable that Hughes-Agnew is much less of a balanced tax program than the previous Cooper-Hughes plan and that it has been padded in key places to win favor among suburbanites."

But though middle-income wage earners would pay slightly less in taxes under the new plan than they would have paid under the original one, they would still be paying much more in taxes than they were at present. One newspaper survey concluded that Hughes-Agnew would "saddle medium income families with the highest income tax on the Atlantic coast and the fifth highest in the nation." The plan called for an income tax ranging from 2 to 6 percent as the basic revenue-raising device. The equalization formula had been changed from that of the original plan so that more money would be returned to the rich counties. Mayor McKeldin of Baltimore said he would prefer a different reform plan. Some rural county legislators threw their support to an even less ambitious plan, with a 2-to-4-percent tax.

Caught between all these opponents on the one side and the unquestioned need to raise taxes on the other, Agnew threw his full energies into the fight. In January, he told the Maryland County Commissioners Association, "Montgomery and Baltimore counties know they will have to pay more than they will get back." Of course they knew it, and Agnew was only whistling in the dark when he expressed the belief that those counties were not going to be "parochial." Parochial they were, and it is a measure of how much he needed their votes that he sent his top financial aide, John Lauber, to Montgomery County to make no fewer than twenty-five speeches in favor of the proposal. Agnew himself campaigned hard for it in Baltimore County. He told a Lincoln Day dinner there of prison revolts, rising crime, traffic deaths, pollution, and crowded state hospitals and said, "Can we afford the luxury of those grim statistics in order to hold the line on taxes?" But it began to look as if the state could indeed afford the luxury, or at least was willing to try. Despite the modifications designed to win suburban support, Hughes-Agnew was in trouble in the General Assembly—so much so, in fact, that in March, Agnew agreed to the suggestion of Montgomery County Senator Blair Lee for a further compromise—the reduction of top-bracket taxes to 5 percent. Lee said a 6-percent-tax would be too much of a burden on those with income of over $11,000, of whom there were many in his county. At last the Assembly went along.° The result was not the salvation needed by the city and the poorest counties, but the plan did bring in an extra $100,000,000 to be used for public services that the previous governor and General Assembly had been unable to raise. Even Agnew's critics in Annapolis gave him grudging credit for that.

His critics went even further and gave him credit generally for a good start as governor. When the legislature adjourned, the record showed that the Republican governor and the Democratic General Assembly had not only passed the ambitious if watered-

---

° The vote was 109 to 17 in the House of Delegates, 35 to 8 in the Senate. All but two of the No votes in the House, and all but one in the Senate, were cast by legislators from the suburban counties.

down tax bill, but also had achieved several other triumphs. The machinery for calling a constitutional convention had been approved.° An office of consumer protection had been approved. Criminal sanity had been redefined. A 306-year-old ban on interracial marriages had been abolished ("a blot on Maryland's escutcheon," Agnew called it). The state's public-accommodations law had been expanded to conform to the 1964 Federal act. A limited open-occupancy bill had been passed. Baltimore *Evening Sun* columnist Bradford Jacobs, who had predicted trouble between the Governor and the legislators, wrote that the former had displayed "courage and canniness" and the latter willingness to cooperate. "Both look better now than we had much reason to expect as the year began."

The open-occupancy law was the first of its type to be enacted by a Southern or Border state. It was a mild law, exempting housing built before passage, owner-occupied single housing, owner-occupied apartment buildings of less than eleven units, condominiums, coops, and church-owned properties. The Maryland Commission on Interracial Problems and Relations praised it as "epochal" since it "firmly established that discrimination in the sale or rental of housing accommodations is unlawful and against the public policy of the State of Maryland." Several real-estate and business organizations and the mayor of Baltimore asked for a more meaningful law. Agnew refused to support a bill also covering existing apartments, a decision which Baltimore County civil-rights leader Eugene King, Sr., called a betrayal of his campaign promise to sign any law the General Assembly passed. It is highly unlikely that the Assembly would have passed a tougher law. Even the weak open-occupancy law went against the Maryland grain. It was petitioned to referendum, and in November, 1968, was defeated by a vote of about 343,000 to 275,000. Of the four big subur-

° The convention drafted a model modern state constitution that drew praise from every quarter. Agnew, every living former governor, every high-level officeholder, every segment of business and labor leadership, endorsed the new constitution. The only opposition that attracted much attention based its argument on the fact that consolidation of cities and counties might become more likely. In a stunning and unexpected result, voters turned down the constitution 367,101 to 284,033. The Washington suburbs voted for it, but Baltimore and Anne Arundel counties voted against it by a ratio of two to one. Perversely, Baltimore city voted No by a slight margin.

ban counties, only Montgomery County gave it substantial support. Baltimore County went against it by 15,000 votes; Anne Arundel by 14,000; and Prince Georges was evenly split, 50, 317 to 50, 617. Even the city vote went against it, partly because of black despair. Fewer citizens voted on the issue in the city than in Montgomery County, half its size. It is conceivable, though not likely, that in the winter of 1967 there had been public support for a mild open-housing law in the state, but by the time the referendum occurred in November, 1968, a greal deal had happened, including the widespread rioting that followed Martin Luther King's death. The voting in the referendum on the housing act may also have been affected by the fact that in the spring the Federal government too had passed an open-housing law, so that the survival of Maryland's law made no difference. Lyndon Johnson had signed that law on April 11, 1968, a date we shall soon pay close attention to.

East-Coast Version of Ronald Reagan

Not everybody was satisfied with Governor Agnew's first year. His critics were usually city-oriented. For instance, one of the first criticisms of the first Agnew budget came from Raleigh Hobson, director of the Department of Social Services. He said that the Governor was in effect cutting the food and housing allowances of welfare recipients, the overwhelming majority of whom lived in the city. A young state legislator from a downtown district, Paul Sarbanes, was most critical of all. He complained that too many of the Agnew proposals were financed in ways that would prevent the poorer localities from participating: the alcoholic centers and community mental-health centers were authorized in such a way that the more taxes people paid, the more state aid they received; this arrangement seemed backward to him and to others in the city. Another problem that Agnew had to face was the rise in the cost to the state of the new Medicaid program. Again, a high percentage of the people who depended on this lived in the city. The costs were outracing estimates, so Agnew announced he would cut back the program.

By the beginning of Agnew's second year in office, his conflict with the city was so far out in the open that Sarbanes issued an unusual twenty-two-page indictment, charging that the budget

Agnew had submitted to the General Assembly was "an austerity budget in a time of prosperity . . . the East Coast version of the Ronald Reagan budget." This budget was the first to be truly Agnew's. The fiscal 1968 budget had been set in many ways before he took office; this 1969 budget was his from start to finish. Furthermore, to what apparently was an unusual degree, it was "his" in the sense that his new team of program executives and his modern-management group did more than the state-agency heads to determine the apportionment of funds. In July, 1967, Agnew had informed agency chiefs in a routine letter that he wanted "necessary services . . . at the lowest possible cost . . . budget analysts and program executives will ask you to rigorously rejustify all expenditures . . . I am holding you personally responsible for uncovering all areas of inefficiency, waste and duplication." He said with emphasis that he wanted a "minimum" budget. The result was an increase in the general fund from fiscal 1968 to 1969 of only 6.1 percent, in one of the fastest-growing states in the nation. That was the lowest increase in twenty years. And the worst was yet to come.

Part of the reason for Agnew's hold-the-line attitude was that revenues had not been rising as fast as had been expected by him and others responsible for keeping close touch with this vital matter. Agnew's honeymoon with the Democrats had ended not long after the 1967 session of the General Assembly adjourned in March. That summer the first of a series of clashes with a Democratic warhorse, Louis Goldstein, the comptroller, made things worse. When the Governor's staff told him that income was falling off, Agnew announced to the public that he would therefore have to cut some state programs. Comptroller Goldstein followed the next day with an income estimate much higher than the one Agnew had used. Agnew had said, "The future looks extremely bleak." Goldstein said, "The future looks bright." Almost everybody could see the political dimension here, and Agnew made it perfectly clear. He asserted that his staff estimates were based on data supplied by Goldstein's office, and that this was not the same material Goldstein was using in making his prediction. He accused Goldstein of withholding the information he needed "so that it can be used as a political springboard for the Comptroller." If Agnew had trusted Goldstein before, he did not seem to do so afterward.

He based his 1969 budget on his own figures, which turned out to be nearer right than Goldstein's.

That was the "Reagan" budget that Sarbanes objected to so vehemently. Sarbanes recognized that there were problems with raising the personal income tax again, however, and recommended increasing the business tax. Agnew refused, and instead followed the recommendations of a joint executive-legislative committee to "reform" business taxes by lowering them. Even had Sarbanes won his fight, even had Agnew been willing to shift priorities, nothing much would have been accomplished. In May, 1968, state officials suddenly discovered that there would be a shortfall in income of $30 million that fiscal year and of $36 million the next year. Agnew immediately announced that he would invoke special powers (requiring top Democratic officials' cooperation) to cut some budgetary allotments by as much as 25 percent. He blamed the crisis on inflated estimates by Comptroller Goldstein and the Board of Revenue Estimates, which included Goldstein, the state treasurer, and the state budget director, all Democrats. A shaken Goldstein met Agnew and said that they ought to stop blaming each other and work together: "We've got a problem."

Agnew replied testily, "My friend, I don't have a problem now. You have a problem." Through it all, Agnew steadfastly maintained that no matter what, there would be no tax rise. Democratic leaders went along with him—reluctantly, some said later; they probably could have forced a tax hike if they had wanted to. But it would not be popular. Two months later Agnew cut $3 million from funds for the Department of Mental Hygiene, $2.8 million from the Department of Health, $1.3 million from Welfare, $1.8 million from Education, $1.3 million from Public Safety, Resources, and Recreation. There would be more cuts in mid-August. By then, his remark to Goldstein that "I don't have a problem" had taken on a new meaning. He had sweated over his first and last state budget. The 1970 budget, submitted the following January, after he had left Annapolis for Washington, was a thrown-together job. It was balanced by arbitrarily increasing the revenue estimate provided by Goldstein and the Board of Revenue Estimates. No governor had ever rejected this estimate. If Agnew had reason to be distrustful of Goldstein, it was because of errors resulting in overestimates; for Agnew himself to increase Goldstein's estimate was to risk compounding the error. The next administration called the budget phony, rewrote it, sped up tax collections to provide for a windfall —and still had to increase taxes.

A Very Bad Year

Until the vice-presidential nomination came in August, the year 1968 was looking like a very bad one for Agnew. He was having political troubles with the Democrats, troubles that had started in 1967. In his naïveté when he first came to Annapolis, Agnew had run afoul of political imperatives. One difficulty added to another until by 1968 there was a real question as to who would run the state. Whether the Democrats in the legislature would have forced this same result with a more complaisant Republican governor is hard to say. Previous Republican governors had found that only by giving the Democrats more or less all they wanted could they get anything done. Agnew and others who knew this history still anticipated that he would have a little more leeway with the newly apportioned General Assembly of 1967–1971. Agnew's first clash— and first defeat—concerned the appointment of a state treasurer. This is a powerful job. The treasurer, the comptroller, and the governor sit as the Board of Public Works, with immense authority. Agnew wanted to name a Republican to the job. But it was a legislative not an executive appointment, and the Democratic legislators were not about to give him a Republican. Then he tried to change the practice of giving scholarships to state colleges through state senators. The Governor preferred loans. In the eyes of many disinterested observers, his plan was a better one, but the state Senate was not disinterested, and defeated it. He vetoed a bill which would give Democrats control of the Prince Georges Board of Election Supervisors, and was overridden. He vetoed a bill which would give Democrats patronage power over the Baltimore County Liquor Board. Overridden. Much of this sort of thing could not have been avoided; he could have avoided using the veto in lost causes, however. The Democrats in the General Assembly wanted a role in policy making, and said so. They even set up a Democratic Policy Committee to operate when the General Assembly was not in session.

Agnew still had enormous powers despite the heavy Democratic majorities in both chambers of the legislature. He could veto a bill after the session ended, thus postponing passage even if his veto was later overridden. He alone could add to the expenditures projected in a pending budget. He had patronage powers. He had greater access to the public than any member of the opposition party. But he felt frustrated almost from the start. It was like the job of county executive: power had to be shared to be realized. Besides, he had come to the conclusion that he didn't like being governor. The ceremony bored him. He didn't like to meet with state officials. The president of the university system fought for a year to get to see him on an urgent matter. The state budget director never did see him. The head of one major department met him for the first time a year after he had taken office, in an elevator—and Agnew did not make conversation. Individual members of the General Assembly, especially Democrats, said they seldom saw him or talked to him. Only the leaders met with him with any regularity.

In addition, there were his defeats on political matters. The never-ending fiscal problems. The demands on his time. In August, 1967, less than a year into his term, he told friends he was tired of it all, wanted to go back to the practice of law and make some money. He correctly believed that he would command higher fees and obtain different types of cases as a former governor than he had as a former chairman of the board of zoning appeals. When a story of these private conversations made the papers, Democrats pounced on them. An old foe, Senator James Pine of Baltimore County, prophesied that Agnew would not be able to govern any longer. These and similar reports to him caused him finally to announce that the story was "premature," that along with the disappointments there had been some accomplishments, too, and that he had not yet decided whether to seek reelection.

At about the same time, Agnew's interest turned away from Annapolis to politics elsewhere. Suburban Republicanism was of a peculiar nature in Maryland. It rarely required real, old-fashioned precinct-style organization. The middle-class white-collar workers and housewives who, while not the whole population of the counties, constituted the largest group and were more issue-oriented and personality-oriented than had been their storied forefathers in the big cities. They required less from government and the party in the way of direct assistance. However, some party structure was needed. Agnew was responsive to the county chairmen to a far greater degree than the previous Republican governor, McKeldin, had been. He even took a slight interest in helping the party in the city, where it was little more than a ghost. In 1967, Arthur Sherwood, a young lawyer, ran for mayor of Baltimore against the very popular City Council President Thomas D'Alessandro III. Though Sherwood's was a lost cause, Agnew offered him some support, unlike McKeldin, then the outgoing mayor. When the predicted deluge came in November, 1967, Agnew seemed to take the results personally. He met with city Republican leaders and chewed them out, saying that he personally would lead the party back to power, with the help of some activist young blacks, who flirted with the party for a while. Nothing came of it, because electing mayors is nothing compared to electing presidents, and Agnew suddenly burst on the scene as a leading spokesman for the moderate-liberal Republicanism of an improbable candidate for the 1968 presidential nomination, Governor Nelson Rockefeller. More of that later. Agnew understood the issue-orientation of the new politics in the suburbs better than most, but even those Republicans who gave him high marks for his efforts in behalf of the party thought him a little too personally aloof, a little *too* taken with issues. The small favors that the party faithful always expect were beyond his understanding or concern. Just as he held bureaucrats at arm's length, so he was aloof to party workers. The national committeewoman lamented after Agnew left Annapolis that she never saw the inside of his office and that it took months of effort to convince the governor's staff to throw a party for volunteer party workers whose only rewards were such affairs.

In 1968 his frustrations grew worse, as the General Assembly moved to take over more and more initiative. Democratic leaders openly chided him for what they thought was inattention. And one Republican said publicly, "He is spending a lot of time on other things." Others grumbled privately. For his part, Agnew took the offensive. He said in public that Democratic leaders were just smarting from his successful first year. In a private breakfast meeting with those Democratic leaders at the handsome old governor's mansion in the center of Annapolis, Agnew chewed them out. He lambasted them even more severely than he had the Republicans in Baltimore after Sherwood's defeat. He said the Democrats were playing party politics with him, were refusing to cooperate, were shutting off lines of communication. He gave them a lecture on good government. The speech was harsh, and its tone angered some of the Democrats there. "He talked down to us," one said. "He chastised us as if we were children." There were a few angry retorts, and when the meeting broke up, some of the delegates and senators were convinced that the next two years "were going to be very interesting," as one put it, menacingly. During the rest of the legislative session, Democrats went out of their way to put their own stamp on programs. The *Sun* summed up the session as a good one, citing business-tax reform, an expansion of the public-ac-commodations law, a water-pollution bill for the bay-conscious state, and other acts as proof of "a constructive balance of rural and urban interests." The paper said these accomplishments had been made with "only nominal leadership from Governor Agnew," and the editorial concluded that the greatest criticism that could be made was "the continuing failure of the state to recognize in full its obligation to meet the urban problems that plague Maryland's one large city."

That was in March. One other new law received scant notice. It gave the governor new powers to bring in militia and police in the event of a riot or other civil disturbance. In April, he used them.

Chapter Eight

Riot

Forest Park and Oldtown

FOREST PARK HIGH SCHOOL was desegregated in 1954, as were all the city's schools. Baltimore was prompt in obeying the Supreme Court's epochal ruling of that year. Throughout the decade, the school was still practically all white. The neighborhood had become a Jewish ghetto by the mid-fifties, reaching a destination toward which it had been moving for thirty years. It was still definitely middle class, but not settled and stable; no sooner had it become one type of ghetto than it began the transformation into another kind.

Robert Emmett Curran has written a memoir of the desegregation of his southwest Baltimore neighborhood in the 1950's. It began when an elderly widow who was leaving the city sold her home to a young Negro couple with two children. The neighborhood was largely Irish-Catholic, and the Negroes were not welcome. The church decreed that only children *born* in the diocese could attend the parochial school. Nevertheless, within a few years there was a large influx of Negroes. The Currans, like many of their neighbors, moved to Catonsville, in the county. Very soon the whole neighborhood was black. In northwest Baltimore, Agnew's Forest Park and the neighboring communities of Ashburton and Windsor Hills were a little more hospitable, but not much. The first Negro moved into the 3700 block of Sequoia, Agnew's old haven, in 1958, when a widow who no longer lived in the area sold her home to a broker, who sold it to a Negro. Ashburton, a neighborhood of more expensive homes, was the site of a determined battle in which whites who had long lived there and newly arrived blacks, both affluent, joined in the effort to maintain a truly integrated community. Teams were set up to attract whites into the area. Even quotas were discussed. Real-estate firms that had the reputation of preying on such changing neighborhoods were openly opposed. A similar effort went on in Windsor Hills, also largely Jewish.

But the pressures were immense for black housing and there were few neighborhoods in which Negroes could buy homes and feel relatively comfortable. So once a neighborhood began to "change," it became a haven for those Negroes who understandably did not want to be the first to enter new territory. Such neighborhoods also became a target for a new type of operator—the "blockbuster," appropriately named after a World War II aerial bomb of great destructiveness. Once a block ceased to be 100-percent white, it was soon "busted," with all the previous white residents gone as completely as if they had been bombed. A typical example of this phenomenon, as it occurs in the Northern and Border states, took place in Windsor Hills. A real-estate firm put 2,400 circulars in the mailboxes of residents on several streets, advising them to sell their houses right away, while they could still get a good price. There were follow-up telephone calls, often anonymous, to make sure everybody got the unstated point—Negroes were soon going to be moving in in numbers, causing a dramatic fall in property values even if they didn't bring the social plague with them. A typical street in Ashburton in the late 1950's might have For Sale signs in front of twenty out of twenty-three homes. The practice was always roundly condemned, but it also always worked. Representative for the period and the place was the case of a white man who in panic sold his $42,000 home for $20,000, to a real-estate firm. Often in such instances, and perhaps in this one, the firm then resold the home to a black customer at more than the original value. That practice still continues in Baltimore and elsewhere.

When the home involved was expensive, it was not unusual for several families to move into a formerly one-family dwelling, imposing an extra load on community facilities without increasing community tax resources, and thus starting the community on a slow spin down toward becoming a slum. In Ashburton and Windsor Hills there was little of this multiple occupancy, but parts of Forest Park did not escape. Most of the sales were to members of the rising urban black middle class of post-World War II, but not all. In the early 1960's, Forest Park was poised between its old status and its new. A study then of the population around the cross-roads where most of the neighborhood stores, churches, and fire department clustered offers a statistical snapshot of a time between eras: 71 percent white; 56 percent owner-occupied dwellings; median income $6,500; median age 35.6 years; 3 percent unemployment. The population had grown slightly from 1950 to 1960. But the central fact about Forest Park in this period—not visible in the stop-action snapshot produced by the study—was that it was changing rapidly. In the course of a year or two, it would become almost all black. "It just seemed as if the Jewish population picked up and moved to Pikesville overnight," said a Jewish teacher at the high school. Pikesville is in Baltimore County. By the end of the decade, enrollment in the high school was predominantly black. The same thing was happening in almost every other northwest Baltimore neighborhood.

The whites who left had varying emotions, thoughts, and motives. Many saw no racism in their act. An oft-repeated story by some of the white families who still live in Windsor Hills is that of the woman who sold her home without informing either of her two next-door neighbors, both friends, of her intentions, then called them from her new county home while the movers were still at work and asked them to sign a petition demanding that the local department stores hire more Negroes.

There was never any question about the motives of the blacks. They wanted desperately to get away from the miseries and dangers of the older, increasingly crowded slums in what was coming to be known as the "inner city." Between 1950 and 1960 the number of Negroes living in Baltimore increased by 100,000, yet the number of housing units increased by only 13,000. Obviously, neighborhoods were going to change. The slums were becoming such nightmares that middle-class and affluent Negroes were more than willing to pay the blockbusters their inflated prices. The working poor among the Negroes were just as desperate, and their ransom took the form of so-called land-installment contracts, under which they paid rent on the homes they were purchasing until every cent of value had been drained, then were saddled with the financial responsibilities of the full mortgage.

The black slums of any big city have to be seen to be believed. In fact, all the senses are required, and imagination as well, for the

visitor to understand what life there is like. Statistics offer the mer-
est guide, but they can be helpful. Here are the figures for a typical urban slum in 1968—Oldtown, in east Baltimore—as determined by official city surveys: 2,000 residents, all Negroes, in 655
dwelling units; occupancy had declined by one-fourth since 1960.
Though only one-fourth of all heads of households in Oldtown were
elderly, over half of the homeowners were. Only half the heads
of households were in the work force. Even fewer worked full time.
Only one family in eight had a car. The median annual family income was $2,835. One head of a household in ten had finished high
school.

Out of similar pits of hopelessness had come the sparks in
urban riots in every previous summer since 1964, and it should not
have surprised anyone that on April 6, 1968, at 4:45 P.M., in the
500 block of Gay Street in the heart of Oldtown, a bottle soared
out of a large crowd of black teenagers who were roaming the
street, and broke a window in the Fashion Hat Shop. A riot had
begun. Four nights later, six persons were dead, seven hundred
had been injured, a thousand businesses had been destroyed or
damaged, with a loss of 14 million dollars, five thousand persons
had been arrested, the National Guard had had to come to the aid
of the police, and the United States Army had had to come to the
aid of the Guard.

Seven Days in April

Rioting seemed to be on the way toward becoming a way of
life in America's black urban slums in the late 1960's. In one spasm
in July, 1967, three riots occurred that brought about changes in
America whose extent has yet to be determined. It is possible that
the extraordinarily bloody and expensive riots in Newark, New Jersey, and Detroit, Michigan, so accelerated the migration of whites
to the suburbs that the survival of big cities as biracial communities is no longer possible. Early evidence of the 1970 census seems
to indicate that population projections—of race and residence—
made in the mid-1960's, disturbing as they were in their implications of a developing metropolitan polarization, actually under-
stated the coming whiteness of the suburbs. The Newark riot,
which began on July 12, resulted in twenty-six deaths, 1,500 inju-

ries, and property damage estimated at 15 to 30 million dollars. It was the worst riot yet; then on July 23, Detroit went up in flames that were brighter, higher, and hotter. Property damage there was some 75 million dollars, forty-three persons were killed.

Alongside these spectacular events, the riot that occurred on July 24 in the sleepy little Eastern Shore town of Cambridge was nothing. No one was killed. Property damage was estimated at only $200,000. But the episode introduced the Governor to the likes of H. Rap Brown, a self-styled black revolutionary, and set Agnew on a fixed course that would lead to his name becoming a household word, as he was identified as the personification of polarization and separateness. Brown spoke in Cambridge on the night of July 24. He told Negroes in the segregated town's black district that their school was a firetrap and "you should've burned it down long ago," and made a number of other incendiary comments, all recorded on tape by the state police. When he finished speaking, he led a march to the business district. It was repulsed by policemen firing pellets from shotguns. Brown himself was nicked, at about 10 P.M. In the next couple of hours there were several incidents involving white and black youths, including some in which whites drove through the ghetto firing guns. After midnight the school caught fire. Local volunteer firemen refused to fight the fire or even lend their equipment to the Negroes; otherwise the damage would have been much slighter. Brown was indicted for arson and inciting to riot. Subsequently, the location of his pending trial was moved to another county in the state. The day the trial was to begin, a bomb killed a colleague, and Brown disappeared. He was not found until the fall of 1971. The evidence seemed to indicate that the dead man had been transporting the bomb when it exploded.

Brown's July 24 speech outraged Agnew. He often played the tape of it for visitors to his offices in Annapolis. Rabbi Israel Goldman, of the state human-relations commission, was quoted as saying after one such performance that Agnew paced up and down "in great distress, and said, 'How can we put up with agitators like this?'" Agnew and his staff were shocked when a playing of the tape did *not* shock Negro State Senators Verda Welcome and Clarence Mitchell III of Baltimore. The staff was outraged when another playing of the tape, at Agnew's Baltimore office for a group

of black ministers, brought no response. Agnew could not understand the ministers' position—which seems only properly Christian
—that "no one is all bad." He did understand, but strongly disagreed with, the argument of Senators Welcome and Mitchell that
attacks by highly placed whites and blacks on people like Brown
only increased their visibility and their appeal to youthful radicals
and potential radicals. Agnew had gone to Cambridge the day
after the fire. Right from the start, his statements showed how he
was being torn by opposing forces. He expressed indignation at the
"sick" enforced segregation of Cambridge, but he blamed the erup-
tion solely on Rap Brown.

And many forces were at work which made it easier and easier
for men like Agnew to see the actors in the drama while ignoring
the setting. There was repeated "intelligence" from his top police
aide, Lally, about agitators roaming the state. Even more impressive were similar warnings coming from the Federal Government,
particularly the Department of Defense. The Army in early 1968
was alerting state law agencies about antiwar and antidraft leaders
who were inciting crowds in line with instructions from Communists in foreign governments whose countries they had visited.
Some civil-rights leaders, too, were so characterized; Stokely Carmichael was mentioned specifically. As governor, Agnew often singled Carmichael out for attack. A reporter who covered Agnew in
Annapolis and later investigated the Army role in the surveillance
of civilians said he thought it "likely" that Agnew received reports
on Carmichael, Brown, and others during the period leading up to
the Baltimore riot.

Governor Agnew was ready to believe the worst even before
the Baltimore riot. He was also prepared to take fast action. The
riot was one of over a hundred that swept the nation that April following the assassination of Dr. Martin Luther King, Jr., but only
Washington had a riot that week similar in its awful dimensions to
Baltimore's. Washington's started almost immediately after word of
the assassination arrived. The Governor first reacted to the threat
of riot in response to the fears of suburban Prince Georges and
Montgomery counties. On Friday afternoon, April 5, the day after
the shooting of Dr. King, Agnew ordered the Maryland National
Guard into a state of complete readiness. The highly professional
adjutant, Major General George M. Gelston, hastened back to

Maryland from a meeting in Georgia. An operations center was established for the troops at the armory in Baltimore. Troops were sent to armories in Hyattsville and Silver Spring, near Washington. The Governor's Baltimore office, in the same general building complex as the armory, was staffed on a round-the-clock basis. The Governor signed the new law giving him expanded powers in an emergency. He accepted an invitation to meet with the Baltimore mayor the next morning.

The meeting was held in Annapolis. The Mayor was newer in his job than Agnew, having been in office less than a year. He was Thomas D'Alessandro III, son of a former mayor, at thirty-eight already a veteran in city hall, a former city-council president. He had moved from Little Italy to the suburbs inside the city line, while his father stayed in the old neighborhood. "Young Tommy" represented the kind of mayor many liberals saw as the salvation of troubled big cities—the liberal, white "ethnic," political operator, dedicated to his city. His Mediterranean good looks and his malapropisms enhanced his reputation as the "real article." As it turned out, real articles were no more able to solve urban problems in the 1960's than such aristocrats as John Lindsay of New York or such black dynamos as Carl Stokes of Cleveland. In 1971, after only one term, D'Alessandro retired.

In April, 1968, D'Alessandro thought Baltimore could escape the fires that were then burning in Washington, thirty miles away. At the meeting in Annapolis he and his advisers argued that what Baltimore needed were signs of concern from top officials, not curfews and increased military firepower and manpower. Agnew and his staff argued that agitators from Washington could easily start massive trouble in Baltimore. D'Alessandro and his staff suggested that the Governor demonstrate his concern for the black community by making an appearance at a black organization or institution, or by declaring a state holiday. Agnew and his staff called for city police intelligence reports on suspected weapons caches and guerillas. If ever a conversation between two groups of officials was carried on at two levels of comprehension, this was it. D'Alessandro and Agnew were talking about two entirely different things. Members of each side were ever after dismayed by what they regarded as the failure of those across the table to understand what was involved. Some on each side later said they thought some of the devestation could have been avoided if their own realism had prevailed. Two observations typify how far apart the two were. An Agnew aide said, "They bragged that they knew exactly where Molotov cocktails were being made, but thought nothing of it. We were stunned!" A D'Alessandro aide said, "Agnew told us he didn't think Martin Luther King was a good American, anyway!" There was a dismaying symbolic aptness in the choice of aides. The Mayor depended on Baltimore attorney Eugene Feinblatt, a former urban-renewal chief, a future co-director at the Johns Hopkins Center for Urban Studies, and a brilliant lawyer deeply committed to the city, who had been an outstanding athlete and student leader in the very Forest Park class that Agnew had been a member of. He was the principal advocate of calming the city. The Governor depended on Charles Bresler, the millionaire suburban developer, who wanted to confine the blazes of rebellion to Washington before they spilled or were carried into the suburbs of the capital and then to Baltimore. The Governor's other aide at the meeting was the Southerner Herbert Thompson. The mayor's other aide was a young and active member of Baltimore's Greek community, Peter Marudas. The implicit symbolism of that should not be followed too far. The most important symbolic aspect of this meeting on the fate of the city, the most obvious one, was the absence of any black man.

By nightfall, Gay Street was burning, and many other areas soon followed. The rioting spread all over the inner city, east and west, but arrest records show that it was localized in the sense that most rioters seem to have rioted in their own neighborhoods. Before midnight of Saturday, April 6, National Guardsmen were patrolling the streets. Their presence was a shock to the city and the state, and a worse one came two days later. On April 8, Agnew had to ask President Johnson for help; the disorder was out of hand and could not be controlled by the city police and the 5,500 National Guardsmen. For the next three days, the United States Army was in command. The President nationalized the Guardsmen and sent in 4,895 regular Army troops.

The Governor figured in one bit of unpleasantness. The troops were forbidden to shoot looters, and Agnew made known his agreement with the order. He received a heavy volume of calls and other communications opposing this policy. Hyman Pressman attacked it publicly. Many of Agnew's closest friends and supporters expressed the view then, and were still doing so three years later, that Agnew was the "good guy" in those riots, that his policemen and Guardsmen had not displayed the trigger-happiness shown by their colleagues in other states, that he had kept his own remarks throughout the disturbances far more temperate than those of other governors under similar stress—and that he had never received credit for his restraint. There is some truth in their claim. In one of the two riots of the year before, for example, Michigan Guardsmen and Detroit police were blamed by the Detroit *Free Press* for killing twenty-eight people, only seventeen guilty of any crime, fourteen of those guilty only of looting. And in Chicago in 1968, the liberal Democratic Mayor Richard Daley called for the shooting of looters. The reason Agnew's liberal record during the riots has since been overlooked was that on Thursday, April 11, the sixth day after he first ordered the National Guard alerted, with the city at last quiet and Army troops beginning to leave, Agnew let himself go, with a speech heard round the world.

No, Governor

Racial tensions had been building up in Maryland, as in the nation, during the first part of 1968. Early in February Agnew took over the health and welfare responsibilities from Dr. Ware and assigned him full time to civil rights. In March, the first crisis arrived, at Bowie State College, in a suburb of Washington. The predominantly Negro student body boycotted classes for three days to protest "102 years of neglect"—that is, the condition of the school's facilities, which was equivalent to that of a near slum. The boycott was followed by a takeover of the campus. Agnew ordered state police there to regain control for the administrators, which was accomplished without resistance by the students. The protest leaders were a moderate lot, drawn mostly from the conservative National Association for the Advancement of Colored People.

The following week, 227 students, some 200 of them black, went to Annapolis in four chartered buses to conduct a "study-in" at the statehouse. They said they would stay there till the Governor met with them to discuss faculty salaries and the condition of buildings at the school. They did not see Agnew or Dr. Ware. Instead, the

Governor's assistant for education, Melvin Cole, relayed a message from Agnew: They had no appointment; if they weren't out of the statehouse by 5 P.M., the regular closing time, they would be arrested and the college would be closed down. They sat under the watchful eye of state troopers, some with cattle prods, beyond the time limit, were arrested, and were marched to buses for a drive to the county detention center. Then Agnew appeared to tell a press conference that at that very moment troopers were closing the college, sending the other four hundred or so students home. Agnew said the trouble was the result of "outside agitators," specifying a non-student official of the NAACP and students from Washington's Howard University. And on that night, Martin Luther King, Jr., was killed.

Dr. Ware played little or no role in formulating civil-rights policies during that incident, nor during the rioting that erupted in Baltimore two days later. Nor in the composition of the speech of April 11. Agnew wrote that himself. It was delivered at a meeting with Negro leaders in Baltimore, a meeting that had been arranged before the rioting broke out. Bowie State had caused Agnew to decide to arrange the meeting on his next regular day in the Baltimore office. He dictated his remarks to his secretary, Mrs. Alice Fringer, on the night of April 9, and the next day showed the draft to Bresler, to Thompson, to Sohmer, and to Mrs. Rosenwald—but not to Dr. Ware. The next day, Agnew drove to Baltimore for the meeting. The Army was still in the city; things were just settling down. Only that day did Agnew lift the curfew he had earlier imposed. While in the Baltimore executive offices, he met with military and police officials to discuss the withdrawing of the military forces, scheduled to begin the next day.

While those conversations were going on, Bresler went to the meeting room, where a hundred Negro leaders were gathering. He warmed them up with some my-immigrant-parents-never-rioted stories. Then, and this almost certainly was just bad staff work, not a calculated bit of stage business, the Governor walked in with General Gelston; the state police superintendent, Lally; and the city police chief, Donald Pommerleau. All of them sat at the table facing the crowd. With the bright lights of television making the scene even more stark, Agnew began to read his speech to the startled Negroes. Before he was half through, some seventy of them had walked out, including the director of the city human-relations commission, the director of the Morgan State College Urban Studies Institute, the director of the Community Action Agency, the president of the Baltimore Teachers Union, and a member of the Republican central committee for the city.

Agnew and his staff said later that the walkout was staged, that several politically oriented members of the audience had seen advance copies of the speech and had agreed to walk out as soon as he started. Such an organized walkout would have had to be hastily planned. Copies of the speech reached Baltimore, where they were distributed by Herbert Thompson, the press-relations aide, only shortly in advance of the delivery. (Civil-rights adviser Ware saw the speech only then.) Those walking out were clearly in various stages of outrage, preplanned or not. One of the first to leave was the Reverend Marion C. Bascom, who said in the hall, "He is as sick as any bigot in America. He is as sick as anything I have seen in America." ° Most of the Negroes went to a nearby church, where after a long meeting they drafted a statement in answer to the Governor.

The essence of the Agnew statement was that they, the moderate leaders of the "black community," had refused to speak out against extremists and that therefore the city had been burned and looted. The essence of the black reply is to be found not in the formal response, but in the plea to him from one who did not walk out, Mrs. Juanita Jackson Mitchell, an aristocrat of the civil-rights movement and of black politics in Baltimore. She told him that violence had worked where nonviolence hadn't and that though she deplored it, "this city, this government have made our children what they are . . . have made our children burners and looters." Agnew asked insistently, "Do you repudiate Rap Brown and Stokely Carmichael? Do you? Do you?" It was like the Annapolis meeting of the previous Saturday morning all over again. He was talking about one thing and she was talking about another.

Public reaction to the speech was instantaneous. Mayor D'Alessandro quickly called a press conference to deplore it. "This is a bad time to say what he said." He termed the Agnew remarks

---

° Bascomb had been involved with Agnew in the Gwynn Oak negotiations in 1963. According to one printed account of those meetings, Agnew had said to him, "Every time I see you I am repulsed." No explanation was given.

"somewhat inflammatory." Reporters pressed him. Did he want to withdraw that word? "On second thought, yes, it *was* inflammatory." He went on to urge "reconciliation, harmony, not divisiveness." Telephone calls and telegrams to the state capital the next day were solidly in Agnew's favor, according to staff tabulations— 117 to 69 in telegrams, 312 to 7 in calls. Most were from Maryland, but some were from as far away as Texas. The speech was widely quoted, in news articles and on television news shows, and drew several critical comments in the editorial pages of Baltimore and Washington newspapers. Agnew later told a friend he was surprised by those. He was particularly galled by an editorial in the establishment-y Baltimore *Sun*. Under a headline that Agnew's lawyer George White still quoted with bitterness three years later —"No, Governor"—the paper said that Agnew had insulted the Negroes and they *should* have walked out on him. White dates Agnew's feud with the *Sun* from that point. Press aide Thompson said Agnew had expected the black reaction but not that of liberal whites.

At one point in the meeting with the Negroes (it lasted two hours), Agnew had said, following a reference to his having been elected with the help of the black vote, "Don't you think I know I'm committing political suicide when I sit here and do this? I know it." His staff agreed. Driving home to Baltimore County that night, highway-chairman Wolff told speechwriter Rosenwald, "We just saw a man kill himself politically." They both said that just this kind of candor and courage was what had attracted them to him. Not everybody regarded the speech as harmful politically. Several of the Negro leaders accused Agnew of using the race issue to advance himself with the conservatives in the party. And ex-Mayor McKeldin, who thought the speech was "pretty good" except in tone and arrangement, said, "That speech made him the darling of the Strom Thurmond set. If he hadn't made it Thurmond would have never heard of him and he wouldn't have become Vice President." Senator Thurmond, the South Carolinian who was to lead the fight for Richard Nixon in the South, said later that he did not recall seeing the reports of Agnew's speech at any time. One person who did see a text of the speech in the papers and who did remember it later was a young former editorial writer named Patrick V. Buchanan. He cut the speech out and sent the clipping to his boss, Richard Nixon.

Chapter Nine

Rockefeller for President

The NonCandidate

AGNEW'S INTEREST in national-level politics had surfaced almost as soon as he was elected to office. In the spring of 1963, while still in his first half year as county executive, Agnew had read with pleasure a news story about a speech by California Senator Thomas Kuchel. The Senator, who was the assistant Republican floor leader, was widely regarded as one of the more progressive members of his party. In his speech he attacked right-wing "zealots who defile the honorable philosophy of conservatism." He specifically indicated the John Birch Society and ridiculed several current rumors about Communist successes in the United States. Agnew went to Washington to meet Kuchel and praise him. He returned to begin talking him up as a presidential nominee. "He talks like I think," he said of the Californian. "He's terrific." In Agnew's opinion, New York Governor Nelson Rockefeller was too liberal for rank-and-file Republicans, and Arizona Senator Barry Goldwater was too conservative. Kuchel was just right, with neither a liberal nor a conservative "brand name." Rather, he was "a leading exponent of the moderate viewpoint of Dwight Eisenhower that was twice acceptable to a majority of the electorate." Agnew or someone on his staff ordered copies of Agnew's remarks sent to leading Republicans around the country and to California newspapers. Kuchel sent an aide to Towson to get him to stop. "We're for Rockefeller" was the flat message.

Agnew was not yet ready to go with Rockefeller, but he did stop campaigning for Kuchel. In late 1963 he went to Albany, New York, and met the New York governor. If Rockefeller tried to win his allegiance, he failed. In January, 1964, Agnew said the party needed "a candidate who shuns the liberal or conservative label . . . so far it seems that man has not entered the race for president." The next month he went to Harrisburg, Pennsylvania, to see how Governor William Scranton looked.

Meanwhile, in the one arena where he had influence, the county Republican organization, he was being challenged. Fife Symington supported Goldwater, and wanted the state delegation to the convention pledged to the Arizonan. Agnew at that time wanted the delegates to be uncommitted. He barely won his point; the outcome was a slightly larger number of delegates and alternates backed by Agnew than backed by Symington. By the time the Maryland state Republican convention was held in June, Scranton had more to recommend him to moderates and liberals. By then, Rockefeller's hopes had been ended, with his defeat by Goldwater in the California primary. Scranton came to Baltimore to announce to the convention that he was challenging Goldwater for the nomination. Agnew was named his state campaign-committee chairman. But in the next month of searching the nation, Scranton gained practically no contested delegates. Maryland's Milton Eisenhower nominated him anyway in San Francisco, in an appropriately funereal black suit. Mayor McKeldin seconded the nomination of Governor Rockefeller, another futile gesture. The convention was tumultuous; the divisions in America had never been more apparent. The Maryland delegation stuck with Scranton, 12 to 7, with 1 vote for Rockefeller. When Goldwater's nomination was assured, Mrs. Katherine Massenburg, the Maryland national committeewoman and a Scranton supporter, sobbed openly. Marshall Jones, a black delegate from Baltimore, shouted "No, no" and was assaulted verbally by a white Goldwater delegate from Florida. He would have been assaulted physically if calmer delegates had not intervened. The state's five black delegates strode out of the hall, announcing they were "walking out on the candidate for president, Mr. Goldwater, and his weak civil rights plank." That issue had been a principal divider of moderate and conservative Republicans. The omnibus civil-rights bill had just been passed that summer, over Goldwater's No vote in the Senate. Republicans who tried to get an endorsement of the bill into the platform failed. Milton Eisenhower said he would have to think about the plank and study it before he could support Goldwater, and he left San Francisco uncommitted. McKeldin also left without endorsing Goldwater. Before the balloting he had said, "I don't act when I'm angry. When I'm angry I count to ten. When I'm very angry I count to a thousand. If Goldwater gets the nomination, I am going to Baltimore and count to ten thousand." He caught a slow train and never got to ten thousand and an endorsement of Goldwater. Agnew voted for Scranton but then reluctantly supported Goldwater. Casting about for something to reconcile the Senator's positions with his, he lamely settled on saying that, well, the acceptance speech was at least "gung ho."

Agnew was busy with his own career in 1965 and 1966, but as soon as he became governor, he lifted his eyes to the horizon again. In April, 1967, he spoke out in support of Rockefeller, urging him to seek the presidency. Just as he had supported Kuchel when Kuchel was a Rockefeller booster, now he supported Rockefeller when the New Yorker was a George Romney booster. Romney, the Michigan governor, was far and away the leading Republican candidate. He was already campaigning hard for the nomination. Agnew's speech was immediately interpreted as the opening gun in a Stop Romney campaign. "No," said Agnew, Romney was "a good candidate," but he personally just preferred Rockefeller. He had not been prompted to speak out by Rockefeller. They had their first discussion of the matter the following month. Agnew and other Maryland officials were in New York on bond business. He visited the Governor at his Manhattan office, and they chatted for an hour and a half. Rockefeller gave him an unequivocal No. Agnew told reporters after the meeting that "I'm giving up [on Rockefeller] to the extent that I'm looking over the moderate candidates that remain." He said he was not ready to endorse Romney. Rockefeller issued a warning that if the moderates didn't unite behind Romney, the party's candidate might turn out to be somebody they couldn't support. Whether in reference to this remark or not, Agnew said that he didn't consider Governor Ronald Reagan too conservative.

In June, Romney invited Agnew to Mackinac Island for a weekend of golf. Other Republican governors would receive similar invitations in the weeks ahead, a Romney aide said; Agnew was the first. On his arrival in Michigan, Agnew declared that he still thought Rockefeller was the best Republican to beat President Lyndon Johnson. He praised Romney, but said he saw signs that

Rockefeller was rethinking his refusal of May. He was referring to a Rockefeller statement that he might become a favorite-son candidate. While in Michigan, Agnew also praised Richard Nixon. Romney wondered why he had invited him.

By September, Agnew had come up with a "dream ticket": Rockefeller for president and Reagan for vice-president. He explained that his continued drumbeating for Rockefeller was prompted by the record the New Yorker had made in dealing with the massive urban problems in his state. Agnew said that the war in Vietnam, which was the focus of most national attention, was a secondary issue to the urban crisis. This was not an unusual viewpoint for a Republican. In New York that December, Richard Nixon told the National Association of Manufacturers that a "[racial] war in the making" was the most important issue before the nation.

Nixon was away and running. Romney's campaign had sagged badly after he told reporters he had been "brainwashed" by American officials in Saigon into supporting the war policies. When the Republican governors met at Palm Beach in December, Agnew campaigned hard among his fellows for his man. Agnew and Governor Tom McCall of Oregon announced jointly that soundings showed a majority of the governors preferred Rockefeller, but that his noncandidacy was allowing Nixon to pick up momentum. Agnew was optimistic to the end. Even a noncandidate can be drafted, he announced. The more realistic McCall said with a shrug, "It's beginning to look like we'll have to reconcile ourselves emotionally and ideologically to Nixon."

Draft Rockefeller

Agnew could not reconcile himself. In February, Romney learned the results of the latest of a series of disconcerting polls dealing with his campaign to gain support against Richard Nixon in the New Hampshire primary. He decided it would be futile to continue, and according to some members of his campaign team, he also felt that if he were to be defeated by a landslide, as seemed inevitable, the Nixon momentum would become too great for any liberal Republican to withstand. So he dropped out of the race.

(His name was still on the ballot and the landslide still took place, but liberals could claim that this primary was not a true test, since Romney had stopped campaigning.) On February 27, while flying to another governors' meeting, this one in Washington, D. C., Nelson Rockefeller and his companions listened on earphones to Romney reading his drop-out statement. As soon as news of the Romney decision reached him, Agnew started a new drive to get the governors to endorse Rockefeller. When the Rockefeller entourage arrived in the national capital, Agnew was invited to Rockefeller's Foxhall Road home. There Agnew, Rockefeller, Governor Winthrop Rockefeller of Arkansas, and New York Republican national committeeman George Hinman discussed the situation. Agnew emerged from the meeting to announce that he was calling off his effort for the time being. The Romney decision had caught all Republican governors too much by surprise for them to act, he said, and he thought it would be better for everybody to go home to think things through and to talk to people at the grass-roots level.

Agnew himself had done plenty of talking at the grass-roots level. He had already organized Marylanders for Rockefeller, a state-level committee to draft the New York governor, which was composed of many old Agnew associates, including Democrats. The most noticeable group of members consisted of bankers; officers of the biggest banks in the state were among those joining Agnew in this venture. The Democratic leader in the House of Delegates had noted this, and issued a statement suggesting that these men did not have many reasons for supporting Rockefeller, but did have many reasons for placating Agnew. He read out a list specifying each banker and the amount of state funds deposited in his bank. "[So and so] has 4,500,000 reasons . . ." he announced to the House, and so on.

In the confusions of the rest of that month, the committee was not active, but in March it met and heard Agnew say he was certain that Rockefeller would announce in a week or so. Rockefeller, meanwhile, was having trouble. Other Republicans were urging him to make a decision. A few days before the Maryland group met, Agnew and six other Republican governors, three Republican senators, New York Mayor John Lindsay, several veteran Republican professionals, and some other interested parties met with

Rockefeller in his Fifth Avenue triplex.° In shortly over two weeks, unless Rockefeller filed a disclaimer of candidacy, his name would go on the ballot for the Oregon primary. He told the gathering he was thinking of filing that disclaimer. The consensus of the meeting was that Rockefeller should run. Rockefeller said he'd give it some thought.

The problem for him then became to get the pressure eased so he could make up his mind more rationally. Accordingly, it was decided to shift attention elsewhere. The next day George Hinman called a former Rockefeller campaign aide in Washington, Albert Abrahams, to come up and talk with him and Pennsylvania's William Scranton about forming a Draft Rockefeller organization that would draw all the pressures away from New York, giving Rockefeller the time he needed to reconnoiter the situation. Abrahams arrived, but not Scranton; political complications made it impossible for him to head the draft movement. Hinman's next choice was J. Irwin Miller, an Indiana industrialist. But Abrahams, who would do the day-to-day work, of course, told Hinman he would rather see a political figure in the top job, one who would understand what was going on. Hinman agreed but had no suggestions. Abrahams lived in Maryland, he respected Agnew, knew of his Marylanders for Rockefeller group. Abrahams suggested Agnew; Rockefeller approved the choice; and Agnew, approached by Hinman, accepted the job. Thus in early March, with the Democrats in his state beginning to take control of the government away from him, Agnew took the next step upward. Where he had been just the respected governor of a small state, he now became a nationally known figure. Though not yet a household word, his name was suddenly a fixture on the front pages of the nation in that frenzied political season. It was a figurehead job, with the work done at the staff level. The choice was a matter of luck for Agnew in that Abrahams happened to be a resident of his state, but it should be recognized that in his own right he was suitable for the job—he was a long-time advocate of just such a draft, he was a substantial enough figure to give the committee some legitimacy (and this was

° Another famous Republican was in the building but did not attend the meeting. Richard Nixon, who lived there, left while the meeting was in progress for the windup in New Hampshire.

not a legitimate draft in the eyes of Hinman, Rockefeller, or Abrahams), and he was astute enough to leave the staff alone. In short, the appointment can be regarded as another case of Agnew luck only if one considers luck to be something one earns.

On March 19, *The New York Times* reported flatly that Rockefeller would be a candidate, and would announce on the twenty-first. Also on the nineteenth, Abrahams got around to opening an office in Annapolis. At noon on the twenty-first, Hinman telephoned Abrahams and told him to call if all off. Abrahams asked if Agnew had been alerted, and Hinman said Yes. But he hadn't been. Rockefeller's secretary had called Agnew to say there would be a message *after* the announcement, but hadn't said what the announcement would be. An Agnew aide had suggested to him that morning that he watch the Rockefeller announcement on television, with the statehouse press corps in attendance. It was to be a rare triumph for Agnew. He had started campaigning for Rockefeller when nobody thought his candidacy was a likelihood, and now his man was going to announce. As has since been well recorded, to Agnew's humiliation, Rockefeller said he was not a candidate but might accept a "true and meaningful draft." He not only had not thought enough of Agnew to warn him in advance of what was coming, he even seemed to be blowing the cover on the Agnew draft effort. It may be that Agnew matured politically at that moment. He made a brave statement about his disappointment, and declared he was still convinced Rockefeller was best for the country. Then in the weeks ahead he stepped carefully through a mined field of political explosives as Rockefeller got back in the race, as Nixon began to "roll up the governors," including Agnew, as one Nixon man later put it, and as his own state delegation split apart over the Nixon-Rockefeller competiton.

Agnew later explained his disappointment with the Rockefeller bow-out in these terms: "It put me in an awful situation with my own power base [Marylanders he had convinced to come out for Rockefeller]. I wasn't able to cushion their shock. My political livelihood was on the line with those people. All a politician has is his credibility. Nelson had put me in a position where my credibility was open to serious question." When Abrahams met with some members of the Agnew staff for a farewell drink in an Annapolis hotel bar a few days after Rockefeller's dropout, one of them put it another way. "We've been had," he said, declaring that he was speaking for the staff and for Agnew. Agnew told his wife he was "embarrassed" by the Rockefeller performance, and he told his secretary just after the television announcement by Rockefeller, "I feel like I've been hit in the stomach with a sledgehammer." A few days later, Stewart E. Mott of New York formed a Committee for a Republican Alternative (to Nixon), and asked Agnew to help. Agnew refused, characterized the committee as one whose "aims accentuate ideological divisions within the Republican party," and praised Nixon as a "loyal and experienced party leader."

On March 31, President Johnson withdrew from the race, and Rockefeller decided to reenter it. In mid-April, the "true and meaningful draft" was launched. This time J. Irwin Miller was national chairman. Senator Thruston Morton of Kentucky, brother of Maryland's Rogers Morton, was the moving force. Abrahams and Hinman were of course back in action. One of the first orders of business was to "remove the knife" from Agnew's back, as one Rockefeller man put it. Rockefeller came to Maryland to a party affair at a handsome estate located between Baltimore and Washington. With hundreds of hastily invited Republicans milling around, in a setting of rolling pastures complete with romping thoroughbred horses and grazing blue-blooded cattle, Agnew and Rockefeller made little speeches. Everybody was in good spirits. Everybody said nice things. But Agnew was almost certainly lost to Rockefeller by then. He had become a favorite-son candidate and refused appeals to let Maryland delegates vote for Rockefeller on the first ballot. Then and later, Rockefeller workers tried to regain Agnew's support, but without much hope. One said, "We never really thought Nixon didn't have him." At Miami, in desperation, there were hints that Agnew would get a good position in a Rockefeller administration, and there may even have been an actual specific offer, in the manner in which these things are handled. Agnew said later that he had expected all along that Rockefeller would give him a job, just as he began to expect one from Nixon after he cast his lot with him. A Republican officeholder who had several looks behind closed doors during the second Draft Rockefeller movement said of overtures to Agnew made in this period, "Nelson groveled." He would not specify what he meant, and Agnew, when informed of the statement, denied it.

Whether he groveled or not, Rockefeller learned during those weeks between the launching of the second draft and the nomination of Richard Nixon in Miami that he and his part of the Republican party had finally been placed in the position where they might have to grovel to get their way—they were out of power.

There may have been a element of personal vengeance in Agnew's motivation. There have been several instances in his career where he had a chance to get revenge and took it. In 1963 he reprimanded a county policeman who had refused to shake his hand during the campaign for executive. In 1968 he saw to it that a state employee who talked back to him in the April 11 meeting in Baltimore was fired. In one of his very first brushes with newspapers, a weekly criticized him in the county, and he blocked its legal advertising. But if in 1968 retaliation was a motive, he hid it well, making his performance all the more professional. He never showed his desire for sweet revenge.

Agnew would soon move into power, but that spring, few anticipated this development. Probably no one but Agnew knows what Agnew thought of his future at that time, but an editorial writer for the Baltimore *Evening Sun* summed up what many Marylanders were thinking the day Rockefeller bowed out: "Had Governor Rockefeller run—and won—who knows what rewards might have showered on Mr. Agnew? There would have been in the forecaster's language, about an 80 percent chance of political precipitation. The directorship of some prestigious federal agency? A diplomatic post perhaps? Even a cabinet job. The reading has changed, of course. Mr. Nixon assumes an almost unassailable front running position. Chances of political precipitation? Near zero tonight, tomorrow and on into the foreseeable future, for Mr. Nixon is unlikely to forgive. Certainly he will never forget."

Chapter Ten

A Bolt Out of the Blue

Nixon's the One

THEY MET IN 1964. Richard Nixon came to Maryland to campaign for Barry Goldwater, and the county executive and the former vice-president exchanged brief pleasantries. Nixon probably did not remember Agnew when they met again in January, 1968, though, of course, he knew who he was—knew that he was a liberal Republican governor of a Democratic state, a spokesman for the Rockefeller wing of the party, and an advocate of Rockefeller's nomination as a presidential candidate. He also knew that Agnew had not invited him to Maryland in 1966 to campaign for him when he ran for governor. The 1968 meeting was at a small party in the Manhattan apartment of Maryland State Senator Louise Gore, a wealthy Montgomery County socialite-politician. Nixon and Agnew were the only two men present; Judy Agnew and several other women were there. The party soon became a forum in which Nixon could hold forth about himself, his ideas, the party, and the country. He and Agnew talked, with the ladies silent and serving almost as an audience. After the meeting, Nixon is supposed to have told Senator Gore that he was impressed with Agnew and that he hoped she would encourage him to speak out more on national issues. Agnew was impressed, too, but not as much as his wife had been. On the trip back to Maryland, Judy told her husband she hoped Nixon would be the next president. Agnew's plans to draft Rockefeller were already firm. He said he liked Nixon, but Rockefeller was still the one.

Both the memory of his favorable impression and the fact that Agnew was a very visible Rockefeller supporter made him a real prize in Richard Nixon's eyes when Rockefeller bowed out of the presidential race in March. The day Rockefeller announced his withdrawal, Nixon told his staff they had better get to work immediately "to pick up the Republican governors." Patrick Buchanan said later that the feeling was that Rockefeller was not gone for good, so it was necessary to take strength away from him before he got back in the race. Robert Ellsworth, a former liberal Republican congressman from Kansas and a leading Nixon-for-president operative, went to see Agnew with an appeal that is reported in two different versions. Agnew says Ellsworth told him that "we're still around," and nothing more. Buchanan says Ellsworth's mission was to seek a negative commitment, that is, some expression from Agnew that he would not go back to Rockefeller.

Without asking for an ironclad positive commitment, Nixon began to put a good bit of pressure on Agnew. A week after Rockefeller dropped out, Agnew announced that he was going to New York to "explore Mr. Nixon's views." He said, "I'm not against Mr. Nixon. He may be my number-two choice." On this day, March 28, he was still, for the record, a Rockefeller man. On March 29, after almost two hours at lunch with Nixon in his Fifth Avenue triplex, Agnew said he wasn't ready at that time to support Nixon—or anybody. He and Nixon both told reporters after the lunch that politics was not discussed, that Nixon did not request, and Agnew did not volunteer, support. They talked of the problems of the cities and the relationship of rural poverty to urban ills, they said. "I was especially impressed by the way he let me give him my ideas on running the country," Agnew declared.

The pressure and the flattery continued. (It was not *just* flattery. Nixon told several close friends and aides that he was genuinely impressed with Agnew's views.) In early April a young Nixon aide, Martin Anderson, was sent to Annapolis "to pick his brain," as he put it. Anderson spent an hour interviewing Agnew in the governor's mansion, with the conversation focusing on Agnew's two favorite ideas, standardized welfare payments to keep the rural poor from migrating to big cities, and Federal encouragement for the building of new towns, which would include housing and jobs for the poor. Anderson also talked with several members of Agnew's staff, then returned to New York to prepare a long and highly favorable memo for Nixon. Neither Anderson nor any other member of the staff thought of this activity as any sort of investigation of a potential vice-president. If the idea of Agnew as a running mate for Nixon was alive anywhere then, it is safe to say it existed only in the inner thoughts of Nixon himself.

By May, after the riots and the return of Nelson Rockefeller to the contest, Agnew was expressing more of an interest in Nixon. Rockefeller had given Agnew no more advance notice of his reentry than he had of his earlier exit. Agnew was vacationing in Hawaii (as the guest of private businessmen who did business with the state, a fact which gave his critics another opportunity to bewail his insensitivity to conflicts of interest) and learned of Rockefeller's decision just like everybody else, from news broadcasts, on April 30. He had no comment. On May 4 Agnew announced that while he still liked Rockefeller, he had become "considerably more enthusiastic" about Richard Nixon. And that wasn't all. He was thinking about becoming a favorite-son candidate himself, and did so soon afterward. Rockefeller needed every first-ballot vote he could get. Maryland traditionally sent a liberal delegation to the convention, so a favorite-son candidacy would deny Rockefeller support he could normally expect. Agnew was keeping a cool head. The political initiative he was showing undoubtedly impressed Nixon—who was not, so far as can be learned, directing any of these moves. Says John Sears, a young lawyer working on the Nixon team at the time, "Delegate need was always in the background of our dealings with Agnew in this period, but there was never any pressure, never any talk of a *quid pro quo*. With some Republicans we were talking that way then, but never with Agnew."

Nixon was campaigning in Oregon in May, against the challenge of the conservative governor of California, Ronald Reagan. A new theme had begun to dominate politics—law and order. Nixon was proving day after day that he was not soft on that issue. (And in the Democratic contest between Senators Robert Kennedy and Eugene McCarthy, the same issue was taking over, with Kennedy especially stressing his toughness as attorney general.) On May 17, David Broder of the Washington *Post* reported that Nixon was considering Agnew as his running mate. Agnew was emphasizing his hard line on law and order, too. The week before the Broder story appeared, Agnew had won headlines with a speech in New Jersey blaming "permissiveness" and the silence of Negro leaders for April's riots. His now-familiar theme was that there were evil men as well as evil conditions and that the former were the greater menace. As for campus riots, he called them the result of "permissiveness run rampant." It was in this period, too, that Agnew criticized the march on Washington of the caravans of the poor, led by Martin Luther King's successor, the Reverend Ralph D. Abernathy. The poor had set up a "Resurrection City" on the Mall in Washington to dramatize their poverty and their desire for Federal legislation and other Federal action to help them. Agnew said that in the handling of such demonstrations, and of racial disturbances, Nixon would be "more forceful" than President Johnson had been.

When Agnew saw the Broder story in the *Post*, he got in touch with Nixon by phone and asked him if the story was true. Nixon said it was, and Agnew said he was very flattered. He had a high regard for Nixon the politician. When reporters asked Nixon about the story that day, he confirmed it. Agnew told reporters at his regular press conference in Annapolis that he was taking the reports lightly. But though at that point he probably did not believe he had a chance for nomination as Nixon's running mate, he couldn't have been taking the possibility too lightly. Not many people had yet been proposed for this position, and Nixon and his staff did seem to be giving him a lot of attention. Agnew may also have known that he had been mentioned to Nixon as a potential vice-presidential candidate as early as anyone else. Back in February, Nixon had asked many party leaders for suggestions about a running mate and Representative Rogers Morton had responded with one recommendation—Agnew. In mid-June, Agnew visited Nixon in New York again. The meeting was meant to be secret, but reporters recognized Agnew when he left. Word was relayed to Annapolis and he was questioned about it there. He said it was just "a private in-depth discussion of the issues and politics." For the first time he conceded that he might not serve out his term as governor if offered the number-two position on the ticket. His mind was very nearly—if not completely—made up.

About this time or shortly thereafter, Agnew told Nixon he was for him and would deliver as many of the state's delegates at the convention as possible. Both men agreed that there was no need for a public announcement of support at that time. Agnew, meanwhile, was not fighting to keep Rockefeller supporters off the delegate list. "We thought in this period that he was still a possible Rockefeller supporter," says national committeewoman Mrs. Katherine Massenburg, "because he let known Rockefeller people become delegates." During this time Agnew did confide to a few Maryland Republicans that he was shifting over to Nixon, but in a way that kept his options open. He and Representative Charles Mathias discussed the situation in June, or perhaps as early as May, neither remembered the date later. "It could have been May, because we had peelers [soft-shell crabs] for lunch, the first of the season," Mathias recalls. "He made it clear that he had decided Nixon would make a better president." Mathias, however, thought that Rockefeller would make a better president, and would help him in his upcoming race for the Senate—and so argued. Agnew didn't actually say he was committed, but Mathias left the lunch believing he was.

In July, Agnew went to a governor's conference in Cincinnati. Politics was all anybody talked about. Agnew did not reveal to anyone that his decision had been made. He even proposed to two other favorite sons, Ohio's Governor James Rhodes and Michigan's George Romney, that the three of them join their forces—totaling 132 delegates—but *not* behind any candidate. Rhodes was not interested. Also in July, Nixon paid a last preconvention visit to Maryland. First he met with the delegates behind closed doors at Baltimore's Friendship Airport. He made a standard candidate's speech, telling them why he thought they should vote for him, and why he thought he would win, but not offering any reason to believe their governor would also be on the ticket. (Rockefeller had paid a similar visit the week before, bringing Spyros Skouras down to talk to Agnew. He was much too late. The day the New Yorker arrived, Agnew's speechwriter began preparing the announcement in which Agnew would release the delegates and endorse Nixon.) The Agnews and the Nixons motored to the governor's mansion and a party for members of a group of "business and professional people who believe in good government" known as the "Executive Assembly." Each of these people had contributed a thousand dollars for Agnew's "political" expenses. The arrangement was a strange one, in that the Republican state central committee managed the fund, but Democrat J. Walter Jones, Agnew's old friend and benefactor from the county, was the real inspiration behind it.

Several other Democrats had paid their thousand dollars to join. Other Democrats pounced on the revelation of the existence of the Assembly, called it a "slush fund," and thought they had the final straw to finish off Agnew in the state. As it turned out, Agnew's later sudden move up overshadowed the Assembly as a topic of conversation.

A week after the visit, as Republicans were gathering in Miami Beach for the convention, Agnew got a call from the Nixon camp. He was invited to place Nixon's name in nomination. Surprisingly, Agnew hesitated, according to Marvin Mandel, then speaker of the House of Delegates, later governor of Maryland. Mandel reports that the night before going to Miami, Agnew told him of the just-received offer, saying that he was for Nixon but wasn't sure he ought to nominate him. It is hard to understand why he would feel that way. Perhaps he thought such a close association with Nixon would be the last straw for the party in Maryland, already straining under the weight of having among its leaders one of Nixon's chief supporters, Rogers Morton (now the convention floor manager for the candidate) and also several very strong supporters of Rockefeller—including the state chairman, two members of Congress, and both the national committeewoman and the national committeeman. This is pure speculation. Agnew has never explained his hesitancy, or even confirmed that it existed. In any event, he did agree to nominate Nixon, and went even further, pressuring the Rockefeller delegates to join him in supporting Nixon.

Agnew arrived in Miami on August 2, the Friday before the convention was to begin. He told the Rockefeller delegates then, in private and requesting secrecy, that he was for Nixon. His speechwriter, Cynthia Rosenwald, his former paid advertising consultant, Robert Goodman, and two Nixon aides, Raymond K. Price, Jr., and Leonard Garment, were even then working on the nomination speech. Agnew urged them to concentrate on the idea of Nixon's stability and centrist position. Price and Garment, two of the more liberal members of the Nixon team, wanted Nixon's humanity and warmth praised.

Publicly Agnew was still uncommitted, but the game was about played out. The papers were full of speculation that he was with Nixon now. Rhodes and Romney were still favorite sons, and Rockefeller was now hoping Angew would remain a favorite son: it was more important to deny Nixon the Maryland votes than to pick up any for himself. Nixon was very close to having the necessary majority of delegate votes to win the nomination. Some observers were beginning to consider his closest rival to be Ronald Reagan, rather than Rockefeller. Reagan was popular with the Southern delegates and with some Western delegates, and he had his California delegation behind him. He announced that he was a candidate on August 5, the day Richard Nixon flew to Miami. That same day, Agnew announced that he was bowing out as a favorite son to support Nixon.

For the Maryland delegation, and for the other delegations as well, it was apparently all over. Representative Mathias, not a delegate but in Miami as a member of Congress and to introduce former candidate Thomas E. Dewey to the convention, held a midnight press conference to announce that he was still for Rockefeller, and urged Maryland delegates to support him. Agnew said publicly that he was releasing the delegates with no urging as to how they should vote, but then went to work to pressure those reluctant to support Nixon. He won over 17 of the 25 (not counting himself). Nixon was nominated on the first ballot with 692 votes, 25 more than he needed. Nixon had other votes held in reserve in Kansas and Hawaii. Still, it was a close enough thing so that Rockefeller supporters in and out of Maryland are not likely ever to forget that at one time Agnew was on their side, and they misused him.

On the evening Nixon was nominated, rioting broke out in Miami's ghetto and four people were killed. It was almost as if there were some supernatural imperative to emphasize the growing polarization and divisions in the country. But the riot diverted attention from something much more significant that was happening in America that night, the final shifting of the control of the Republican party from its traditional masters to its new ones. The shift had begun at the start of the decade, and was now complete. Theodore White in *The Making of the President—1968* describes the scene that night in Nelson Rockefeller's hotel suite. Rockefeller and two of his brothers, Winthrop Aldrich, Mrs. Vincent Astor, Mrs. William Scranton, Mr. and Mrs. Maurice Moore, Gardner Cowles, J. Irwin Miller, Mr. and Mrs. Thomas Braden, Henry Kissinger, and

Emmet Hughes gathered to watch the nomination speeches. White called it "a tiny cross section of what there is of an American elite. . . . Thirty years ago men such as these controlled the Republic Party, could compel Midwestern and Far Western delegates to do their bidding, force the nomination of Wendell Willkie against the will of the primitives. But American politics had matured beyond their control, and this convention was beyond them. There was, one recognized, no Establishment. Or, if there was, the junior Jaycees of the Nixon staff were at least as potent in America today as any other establishment." As much as any other single man, the Governor of Maryland, there on the television screen nominating Nixon, was responsible for that night's being the night of the triumph of the new establishment of suburbia and South and West and "junior Jaycees" over the old one.

Agnew was the one that got away, and with him went hook, line, sinker, creel, boat, and maybe even the boathouse. The old establishment's trouble was that its members never took Agnew seriously enough, as a man, as a politician, or as a symbol of modern times. It is hard to fault them. Few people did, Richard Nixon being almost alone in prescience. Only a day before, the Maryland delegation had held a luncheon for all presidential candidates. Nixon didn't come. Reagan didn't come. Rockefeller and Harold Stassen came. At one point during the meal, Rockefeller expressed his frustration to a Maryland supporter. "What do I have to do to get Ted's support? Offer him the vice-presidency?" He was grinning, and everybody had a good laugh at that. Richard Nixon had been thinking about the same thing for some time by then. To him, it had never been a laughing matter.

"Guess Who's the Other One"

While the presidential balloting was going on that Wednesday night, a confident Nixon sent messages to leading Republicans on the floor, inviting them to his penthouse in the Hilton-Plaza. The purpose: to choose a vice-presidential nominee. During the next several hours, beginning about 1 A.M. Thursday morning, there was a series of meetings devoted to narrowing down the choice. This was an unusual process. The selection of a running mate is an individual decision, seldom undertaken by committee, much less by committees. The process was remarkable in another respect, too. By the time the meetings began, Nixon had already decided who his running mate would be. Almost all available evidence points to the fact that the decision was made a week or more before he even arrived in Miami. Two of his top aides, John Sears and Patrick Buchanan, believe that is so. Vice-president Agnew himself told a group of reporters in 1971 that the decision to select him was made prior to the opening of the convention.

But the meetings beginning after midnight Wednesday are interesting for what they tell about the conflicting elements in the Republican party at that time, and about the desire of Richard Nixon to resolve those conflicts in a way that would do no harm to his candidacy. The first group with whom Nixon discussed the vice-presidential nomination consisted of those on his staff who were in the penthouse while the presidential balloting was still going on. While they waited for the conclusion of the balloting and the arrival of the first group of dignitaries, Nixon and twenty-four members of his campaign staff discussed the question for about forty-five minutes. Among those at that meeting were campaign manager John Mitchell, H. R. Haldeman, Robert Ellsworth, Richard Kleindienst, Peter Flanigan, Leonard Garment, Frank Shakespeare, Herbert Klein, Maurice Stans, and Walter Hickel—all of whom would win high-ranking positions in the Nixon administration. Nixon told them he had "brought no names to Miami Beach." He asked the staff for suggestions. The names of those who had been speculated about so much in the press immediately filled out a list: Reagan, Romney, Volpe, and Agnew among the governors; Senators Howard Baker of Tennessee, Mark Hatfield of Oregon, Charles Percy of Illinois, Robert Griffin of Michigan, John Tower of Texas; Representative George Bush of Texas; Mayor John Lindsay of New York City.

Nixon said he thought that above all the vice-presidential nominee should be capable of becoming president and should not divide the party's liberal and conservative wings. He had already given a pledge on that last point in several meetings with delegates during the two previous days. It is probable that this was the consideration uppermost in his mind. As he told a friend at about this time, after all the years he had spent winning the nomination, he was not going to make it worthless by splitting the party apart with his first act as the nominee. This desire also explains the elaborate charade of meetings for the purpose of arriving at a decision which he had already made. He wanted everybody in the party to feel that his point of view had been taken into consideration in the selection of number two. (As of course it had, but long ago.)

At the very least, the suggestion that the candidate have a unifying effect was limiting. It was meant to bring the choice right on target. Memories of the meeting are not all exact, and do not all jibe, but some who were there recollect that Nixon himself suggested Agnew when no one else did. He praised his nominating speech. As that meeting broke up, Nixon said, "So you suggest I pick a centrist?" He had made that suggestion, not the staff. At 2:30 A.M. the men invited off the convention floor arrived. There were twenty-one of them, including former Arizona Senator Barry Goldwater and five conservative senators: Strom Thurmond of South Carolina, Jack Miller of Iowa, Karl Mundt of South Dakota, Paul Fannin of Arizona, and Hiram Fong of Hawaii. The state Republican chairmen of Florida and South Carolina were also there, as were four conservative representatives. Nixon's friend Robert Finch, the lieutenant governor of California, was there, as were Thomas Dewey and former Attorney General Herbert Brownell. There were a couple of others of liberal persuasion, but the group consisted essentially of Southern and Western conservatives. Billy Graham was there. After a little victory celebration and a round of drinks, the group heard Nixon charge them. He wanted a moderate, with national acceptance and with a background that was urban and maybe ethnic as well. Despite this straitjacket, some in the room still argued for their previous favorites. But Thurmond vetoed Lindsay, the choice of Rhodes, Brownell, and Miller; and Finch eliminated Reagan ("He won't take it"). Senator Mundt objected to Percy as too ambitious. (Nixon had eliminated Percy months before, when a poll showed him costing him votes in Illinois.) Shortly before dawn the meeting broke up, the participants having arrived after some two hours of debate back where they started from, with only two men who fit the original Nixon description: John Volpe, moderate, governor of an urban state, of Italian ancestry; Spiro Agnew, moderate, governor of an urban state, of Greek ancestry. The twenty-one men left the penthouse, and Nixon went to bed.

At nine that morning, a third meeting was held, in the Jackie of Hearts Room of the Hilton-Plaza. This time the real political operators were in attendance: the House minority leader, Gerald Ford, and the Senate Minority Leader, Everett Dirksen; Rogers Morton; the National Committee chairman, Ray Bliss; the chairman of the Republican Senatorial Campaign Committee, George Murphy; the chairman of the Republican Congressional Campaign Committee, Bob Wilson; the Texas and Wisconsin Republican chairmen; Senator John Tower of Texas; and—once more—Robert Finch. These were largely men who had been invited to the 2:30 A.M. meeting but hadn't made it. They started all over again, with the long list. Nixon left. This was where he had come in. At 11 A.M. this meeting ended, and a final one was held by Nixon with the closest of his advisers: Finch, Mitchell, Haldeman, Morton, Ellsworth, and Tower. Edgy, weary, confused, they suddenly found themselves starting all over again, with new names. Meanwhile, the time for the scheduled press conference to make the announcement came and went. According to several reconstructions of this final meeting, Nixon offered the vice-presidential nomination to his friend Finch, who refused because he was not nationally known except as a Nixon crony. It wouldn't look good, he is supposed to have said. Some Nixon aides who were not at the meeting find it difficult to believe that he made this offer. "It just does not sound like R. N., and I don't care what anybody says," says Buchanan. Sears concurs.° The group decided they could not start checking out new names and could no longer delay. There were two candidates left who had survived every challenge: Volpe and Agnew. They agreed on Agnew at 12:25 P.M. Nixon finally had his centrist. Morton was told to get his fellow Marylander on the phone.

Nixon had been able to handle the selection meetings smoothly because he had been through an almost identical process once before—had rehearsed it, so to speak. In the last days before the convention opened, Nixon was resting and thinking at Montauk, on Long Island. He got Buchanan to call conservative columnists around the country and ask for their suggestions. James J. Kilpatrick wanted Reagan. William F. Buckley wanted the liberal John Gardner(!). And so on. Nixon said those weren't the sort of names

° Finch had turned Nixon down months before, and interpreted Nixon's bringing it up again at Miami as a reminder of that, not an offer.

he was looking for, and had the columnists re-polled, telling them to "stick to centrists." This time the list included only Romney, Baker, Bush, Volpe, and Agnew. Romney was out because his press relations had been so poor during his presidential run. Bush and Baker were too inexperienced. Volpe just wasn't regarded as a "heavyweight"—among other things, he had lost his own state presidential primary to a Rockefeller write-in. This poll is probably what Agnew had in mind when he said later that Nixon had made his decision before coming to Miami Beach. When Nixon said he brought "no names" to Miami Beach, he meant that he brought only one name.

When the phone rang in the Agnews' twelfth-floor suite in the Eden Roc Hotel, Stanley Blair answered. The Governor, two of the children, Judy, Blair, Charles Bresler, and two other aides had been waiting for a call all morning. Superstitiously they had talked of all the reasons why Agnew would *not* be selected. The idea that he would be had been conveyed to Agnew some time before. He had dismissed the Broder story of May, but for some reason he had changed his mind in June or July. He told Judge Lester Barrett while playing golf at Baltimore County's Turf Valley course late in July that he thought he had a fair chance for the nomination. And then in Miami Beach just two days before this day, John Mitchell had called on him at his suite after midnight to ask if he would accept the nomination. Agnew said Yes, and asked if this meant that he was definitely on the list, that he was really a "possibility." Mitchell said that there was no longer a list, that Agnew was "probably" the nominee. By the time Mitchell left, Agnew knew that unless something extraordinary interfered, he would be his party's next nominee for the second-highest office in the land.

When Blair answered the phone, Morton told him to put Agnew on. "Are you sitting down?" he said to Agnew, and handed the phone to Nixon. Agnew didn't say a word into the phone, but turned to Judy and said, "I'm it." Then they went to the Hilton-Plaza, where Nixon held a press conference to talk about his choice. He said that he had wanted a man qualified to be president, able to campaign everywhere, and willing to assume new duties in the field of state and local operations. Then Agnew held his own press conference. He told the reporters the selection had come "like a bolt out of the blue." He also said he knew "the name Spiro

Agnew is not a household name. I certainly hope it will become one within the next couple of months."

The announcement was certainly a bolt out of the blue to other people. Baltimore *Evening Sun* political columnist Bradford Jacobs expressed disbelief under the headline "Guess Who's the Other One." The Cleveland *Plain Dealer* expressed "disappointment." The Suffolk *Sun* said, "Mr. Nixon could have done better than that." Many liberal Republicans didn't think Agnew was a centrist at all. Nelson Rockefeller expressed his shock and displeasure, and when a reporter told him Nixon had said he had checked the choice out with 100 top Republicans, Rockefeller replied scornfully that he must be 101st in the party. Republican delegates from Ohio, New York, Michigan, Pennsylvania, Massachusetts, Minnesota, Wisconsin, Kansas, and Iowa quickly agreed to back a Lindsay-for-vice-president revolt, but Lindsay refused. He was going to second Agnew. So a few disheartened big-state Republicans supported George Romney in a minirevolt. Rogers Morton nominated Agnew. Lindsay, Percy, Tower, and former Senator William Knowland, a Reagan backer, seconded him. Nevada chairman George Abbott nominated Romney, who claimed his foredoomed candidacy would serve to unite the party and would convince Nixon to give as much attention now to industrial-state Republicans, in order to win the election, as he had given to leaders of the "Southern and Southwestern" states in winning the nomination. Agnew got 1,119 votes to Romney's 186.

His acceptance speech set a pattern for the campaign ahead. Instead of taking a centrist position, he presented balancing views: on the one hand, "Racial discrimination, unfair education and job opportunity must be eliminated no matter whom it displeases"; and on the other, "Anarchy, rioting, and even civil disobedience have no constructive purpose in a constitutional republic."

The next day, a relaxed Nixon tried to calm the swell of opposition to his so carefully chosen noncontroversial centrist. He sat and drank iced coffee, played the piano, joked with reporters and the ubiquitous Billy Graham, who was radiant in an orange shirt and yellow slacks. Agnew was "the most underestimated politician in America," Nixon said, and was "the best available man" for the nomination. He said he liked Agnew on "city stuff," but it was really Agnew the man, not Agnew the expert, that appealed to him. He had been an Agnew fan since their first meeting in January. "There can be a mystique about a man. You can look him in the eye and know he's got it. This guy's got it. If he doesn't, Nixon has made a bum choice." Nixon could not know that the choice would become a major campaign issue, presented in those very terms. Not even the Romney revolt of the night before foretold what was ahead.

Chapter Eleven

Southern Strategies

Southern Strategy I

ONE OF THE MOST persistent stories to come out of Miami Beach was that Spiro Agnew's nomination had to be "cleared" with Strom Thurmond. Nixon was pursuing a "Southern Strategy" in the convention, it is claimed; he had to have the Southern delegates, and bowed to kingmaker Thurmond's desires on the issues and on the vice-presidency. After the convention, Nixon followed a campaign plan which recognized that victory was attainable by winning votes in the South, the Southwest, and the Plains-Mountain areas, and this plan too was called by some a Southern Strategy. Nixon, Agnew, campaign manager John Mitchell, and almost everybody else connected with the Nixon enterprise then and later denied, often vehemently, that such a thing as a Southern Strategy ever existed. Yet it did exist. Indeed, there were two separate Southern Strategies, one for gaining the nomination and one for getting elected to the presidency itself. When Republicans, or disinterested journalists, deny their existence, as many have, it is because they mean one thing by the phrase "Southern Strategy," while the people who believe there was (and is) such a strategy mean another. Definition can be cumbersome in this area. A good way to approach it is to look at the history of the party, at the region that gives the strategy its name, and at what happened in 1968.

For nearly a hundred years, Southern Republicanism was a sad joke played on Negroes and a few "spoils systems" whites in the states of the old Confederacy, whose loyalty was rewarded with Federal jobs. The Republican party was the party of union, which made it alien as well as unpopular in the South immediately following the Civil War. Then it became the party of Reconstruction, which made it even more unpopular with the whites who dominated local politics in the era. The fact that it became the party of Negroes was another reason for it to be regarded as an outsiders' party, especially after Democrats began to exclude blacks legally from party voting and other affairs following Reconstruction. The white Democratic primaries came to be the only elections that counted in most of the states of the old Confederacy. Republicans soon stopped running candidates for office at all. In Georgia, for one example, the party did not even nominate a candidate for governor from 1884 to 1966. In presidential elections, as we shall see in more detail shortly, the Democrats were just as supreme.

The unimportance of the Southern wing of the party was reflected in the national conventions. Candidates for president courted delegates in ways that had nothing to do with personality or issues, both sides knowing that there would not be any Southern Republican votes in November. What the delegates from Alabama thought about the tariff or whatever was of no consequence. Not a single Republican convention was held in a Southern city—until 1968. Of all the convention chairmen, temporary and permanent, only one hailed from a Southern state in the years from the end of the Civil War through 1968, and that exception was way back in 1884. No national party chairman ever came from the South.

Southern delegates to the Republican national conventions seldom voted in blocs in modern times. Typical splits occured in 1940, with Robert Taft gaining 88 votes to Wendell Willkie's 77 (other Southern votes were scattered) on the sixth and final ballot. In 1948 Taft won 95 votes to 90 for Thomas Dewey and Harold Stassen on the second and last ballot. In both cases Taft won the South barely, but lost the nomination. In 1952 Taft got 93 delegate votes to Dwight Eisenhower's 119. In that contest Eisenhower won the nomination because he successfully challenged Taft slates in three Southern states and picked up practically all their votes.

Eisenhower also ran well in the South in the general election, and this success foreshadowed an end to the old-style Southern politics, in conventions and out. There were no contests in the 1956 and 1960 conventions. In 1964, for the first time Southern delegates *en bloc* became not just an important resource for a presidential candidate, but the most important resource. Senator Barry Goldwater's pre-nomination campaign was so pitched to the newly issue-oriented politicians of the South, specifically to the most conservative ones, many of them traditional Democrats, that someone (Goldwater thinks it was columnist Joseph Alsop) coined the phrase "Southern Strategy" to describe it. That was in 1962 or 1963, well in advance of the convention, while Goldwater speeches were wooing the South, and Goldwater lieutenants were sewing up the Southern-state delegates or delegate selectors. (There were few primaries in the South then.) Goldwater later said this campaign was the result not of a "strategy," but of the recognition of "a fact of political life," as of course it was. Here was a region that had always been more homogeneous than the others and was becoming more so every year as it retreated under a growing pressure to desegregate its public facilities. It was ripe for the plucking by a candidate who offered a kind word on race conservatism. Goldwater's vote against the civil-rights bill in 1964, shortly before the convention, won the South over. One of his speeches in Georgia was characterized by a Negro civil-rights leader as a demonstration of Goldwater's "opposition to slavery—in principle." And the South —angry and homogeneous—was a large entity. The eleven states of the old Confederacy had 283 votes, or 43 percent of the number needed for nomination. Goldwater got 271 and was nominated with ease.

Because in the general election he carried only Arizona and five Southern states, and because performance in a presidential election affects a state's delegate strength at the following convention, the South was even more influential in 1968. Of the nine states that had larger delegations at Miami Beach than they had had at San Francisco, six were Southern: Alabama, Arkansas, Georgia, Louisiana, Mississippi, and South Carolina. The other three were Maryland, Nevada, and Hawaii. Only one Southern state lost strength—Virginia. The result was that the South could supply a candidate with 47 percent of the votes needed for nomination. Though Nixon did not do quite as well as Goldwater had done, he did manage to gain 227 Southern votes, better than two out of three, and enough.° But getting them took a fight, and Strom Thurmond was a key figure.

Thurmond had become a Republican in 1964, a "Goldwater Re-

° Nixon won only 26 of the 300 votes of the biggest states, New York, California, Pennsylvania, and Ohio. This showing was predictable from the start, and another reason why there was a Southern Strategy.

publican" it was called at the time. He campaigned hard for the Arizonan, and his state of South Carolina, which had been *the* most Democratic of states in the earlier days of his career, followed him. After the Johnson landslide of that year, Thurmond began to consider the prospect of the South's electing a Republican president, who would respond to the historic change in party allegiance with some historic changes of his own. According to Thurmond, and to those who know him best, he did not want a president who would make a deal on civil rights: he knew that a truly Southern position on civil rights, like Goldwater's, was a liability no national leader could overcome. Goldwater couldn't be elected and neither could anyone else of similar views. But Nixon could be elected. Thurmond respected Nixon as a presidential prospect and as a politician. He particularly liked his strong stands on cold-war issues. Thurmond, an Army general and a member of the Armed Services Committee, was as militant in his anticommunism as in his opposition to civil rights for Negroes.

He became a Nixon ally, stumping the South for him, promising potential delegates that Nixon had assured him he would do nothing in choosing a running mate, or as president, that the South could not live with. He would have to do some things that the South would not like, but he would be fair. Nixon's aides had decided (or Thurmond had decided and convinced them) that this position was the key to unlocking the South. So Thurmond trekked from state to state, crisscrossing the path of other Nixon supporters, conferring with the new Southern Republican leaders, who were frequently amateurs in politics. A great many were amateurs in the bad sense, and never displayed any understanding of, or inclination for, organization or work. They were even more issue-oriented than the typical suburban voter. Most Southern Republicans had a choice of their own for vice-president—Governor Ronald Reagan. He was as conservative as Goldwater, and probably as unelectable. But as governor of the most populous state he seemed to the Southerners to be qualified at least for the number-two spot on the ticket. All Thurmond and the other Nixon men would reply was that Reagan hadn't been ruled out. Nobody was ruled out who was in the "mainstream," they would say, making it clear that what the Southerners thought was the mainstream was indeed the mainstream.

A few Southerners felt that Reagan could win at the top of the ticket, and that they would be happier with him than with Nixon. Reagan was not a declared candidate before the convention met at Miami Beach. He was a favorite son, but that was all. It was enough. The California delegation's eighty-six votes would make a handsome base if combined with a sizable number of Southern votes. The specter of a Reagan challenge hovered in the background of the Nixon Southern Strategy in early 1968, until the primary in Oregon in May. Though he denied that he was a candidate, Reagan spent some money in Oregon, and there was a write-in effort. Had a Reagan candidacy been truly a substantial idea, he should have done well. He didn't, winning less than 10 percent of the vote, while Nixon was rolling up over 70 percent.

Nixon left Oregon believing he probably had the nomination won. Since Reagan had precluded a California primary contest for the Republicans, Nixon and his staff were finished with the primary phase of their campaign. En route to Florida for a rest, he added a few finishing touches to his Southern campaign. He stopped in Dallas for a fund-raising date, then flew to Atlanta to meet on May 31 with Republicans from all over the South. The next day he met with a single Southern Republican, Thurmond. It seems certain in retrospect that the things Nixon said in that meeting with Thurmond, and repeated in another meeting of the two in Miami Beach in August, kept the South Carolinian, and through him the Southern delegates, on his side. But what did he say? According to several reports Nixon promised Thurmond a veto over the vice-presidential nomination. If such a commitment was made, it undoubtedly took the form of a promise that the nominee would not be unacceptable to any region of the country, a sensible and surely honorable pledge. But Thurmond has been quoted as saying that at that meeting he neither requested nor was given any right to veto the vice-presidential nomination. Another report says the meeting was issue-oriented: "Richard Milhous Nixon, now President of the United States, sat in a motel room in Atlanta in the early spring of 1968 and made his political deal. Senator Strom Thurmond was there. There were others. The essential Nixon bargain was simply this: *If I'm President of the United States, I'll find a way to ease up on the federal pressures forcing school desegregation—or any other kind of desegregation.* Whatever the exact words or phrasing, this was how the Nixon commitment was understood by Thurmond and other Southern GOP strategists."

That report puzzled such Nixon aides as John Sears, who thought that at this time Thurmond was emphasizing national-security matters. Sears says that the briefing memorandum given Nixon before his meeting with Thurmond was limited to these. Thurmond himself denies that he got any indication that Federal pressure would be relieved. He says Nixon said "only" that he favored freedom of choice in the schools. That is a big "only." By 1968, freedom of choice, which Nixon advocated publicly later, had come to mean in the South legal segregation—or only token integration. Federal courts had consistently ruled that despite their high-sounding label, most freedom-of-choice school plans were subterfuges. Even if Thurmond thought that Nixon could offer no more than rhetoric regarding the schools, since the question of school integration was or would soon be in the hands of the courts almost everywhere in the South, and even if he thought that this rhetoric did not constitute a relaxation of pressure (though the pressure of presidential exhortation for integration was itself unpleasant to many segregationist Southerners), it is likely that some Southern Republicans did interpret Nixon's remarks in Atlanta, as relayed by Thurmond, as an indication that Federal pressure against school segregation would be decreased. Some such belief and the energies of Strom Thurmond served to keep those 227 delegates in Nixon's corner in Miami Beach.

Nixon arrived at Miami Beach on the day Reagan announced he was a full-fledged candidate. Reagan's campaign staff was headed by F. Clifton White, who had been the brains behind the Goldwater presidential movement. Men whom White had worked with in 1964 were his opponents now—Tower, Thurmond, Peter O'Donnell, the Texas Republican chairman. In many Southern states he ran into Nixon pledges, and where there were no pledges, there often was Thurmond, urging the wavering delegates to go with a winner. Thurmond had been at this since leaving Nixon in Atlanta. His own state's Republicans had been for Reagan when they met in late June, and Thurmond talked them around to Nixon by arguing political pragmatism: Nixon could win and Reagan couldn't. Thurmond said he was talking about winning in the convention as well as afterward. A Southern vote for Reagan would deny Nixon and not nominate Reagan; instead, Rockefeller would eventually win. This viewpoint was not easy to sell to many of the Southerners whose ideological vein was thick as fat in bacon. Many of them had luxuriated in the new Lost Cause of Goldwaterism for four years and would rather vote for Reagan even if doing so meant Rockefeller would profit. In their hearts they knew he was right. But Thurmond and his former administrative assistant, Harry Dent, then the South Carolina party chairman, and a few others continued to preach winning, and they prevailed.

Thurmond says his choices for vice-presidential candidate during this period were Reagan, Tower, and Baker. He met Agnew for the first time that he could recall in Miami Beach after the nomination. The first time he heard of Agnew as a possible vice-presidential nominee was at a meeting with Nixon in his penthouse at Miami Beach, he said later. That may have been the Thursday-morning meeting, after Nixon had won the nomination. Or it may have been a private meeting on Monday night at which only he, Dent, Nixon, and Mitchell were present. That was one day before Mitchell called on Agnew to tell him he was the probable nominee. According to some secondhand reports about that Monday-night meeting, Thurmond told Nixon that there were signs of Reagan inroads in the Southern delegations, and that continued rumors of a liberal vice-presidential nominee were harmful. Nixon again promised that he wouldn't pick a man who would be offensive to the Southern delegates. Either then or later, he asked Thurmond if Agnew met that test in the South, and Thurmond said Yes.

The next morning Nixon met in a private briefing session with delegates from several Southern states. He assured them that he was against the busing of school children, was for state control of housing (rather than a Federal open-housing law), and would select a running mate who wouldn't divide the party. His need for the Southern delegates was still great enough for him to pursue this strategy. The nearest he came to losing the Southerners was the next day when the Miami *Herald* reported that it had learned Nixon was going to pick Oregon Senator Mark Hatfield as his running mate. Hatfield had his own Southern strategy. He is a Baptist, and he thought his religious affiliation would balance out his liberal views in the scales of the Southern delegates. It didn't. Thurmond, Dent, Nixon's man in Georgia, Howard ("Bo") Callaway, and other Southerners were able to knock down the *Herald* story with *assurances* that it was not true; the 227 delegates stuck, and the nomination went to Nixon.

Was there a Southern Strategy? No other section of the country was dealt with as an entity at the convention or in the months leading up to it. No other section of the country expressed so much interest in the vice-presidential nomination, or received the kind of assurances given the South. And for the first time ever—at this first Republican convention in a Southern state—a Republican vice-presidential nominee was chosen from a state south of the Mason-Dixon line.° Maryland is not a Southern state, but Republicans had so ignored the South in the 104 previous years that not even a Border-state nominee had ever been chosen. One might have expected Republicans to boast of at last making the attempt to become a national party, instead of denying special concern with the South or pretending there was no such thing as a Southern Strategy. Democrats have never ignored or played down the reality of their strength in the South. Their vice-presidential nominee was a Southerner in 1960, 1956, 1952, 1936, 1932, 1928, and in several earlier years.

Nixon's anointment of Agnew represented two things—a bid to seal the nomination, and a bid to compete in the old Solid South for electoral votes.

Southern Strategy II

"The bright Republican hope for making a major breakthrough in the South has been greatly dimmed by the strong position we have taken on civil rights. I believe this is a temporary setback. It means we cannot expect to crack the South on a broad scale in the near future. But over a period of time I believe responsible Southern leaders will come to recognize that there are other issues which are more important to the best interests and to the future of the South than that one. They will also come to realize that their extreme position is, in the long run, untenable, and it would be best for all to have a two-party system. But even now we should

---

° Lincoln chose Andrew Johnson of Tennessee as his running mate in the wartime election of 1864. Johnson was not a Republican, but a "War Democrat."

certainly make an effort to attract into the Republican Party Southerners who find our economic philosophy closer to theirs than the philosophy which has been imposed upon the Democratic Party by its national committee, the Americans for Democratic Action and certain national labor leaders—a philosophy which both the President and I have properly described as radical rather than liberal." The last half of that statement sounds as if it came from Spiro Agnew around 1970, but it was made by Richard Nixon sometime "between 1957 and 1959," in an interview with his biographer, Earl Mazo. The first half is more important, for it indicates the pessimism of the Republicans in the late 1950's. This pessimism came just at the moment when the party thought it had finally cracked the Solid South. In 1952 and 1956, Eisenhower had proved that it could be done, despite the predictions and advice of his political advisers. But then came 1957, the first civil-rights bill since Reconstruction, and Ike's sending of Federal troops to Little Rock, Arkansas, to desegregate Central High School. Eventually, to be sure, Nixon and others in the party would change their minds about the party's prospects in 1960. But before we trace this change, let us look at the near-revolution in voting behavior in presidential elections that occurred in the South in the 1950's.

As we have seen, the South was solidly Democratic throughout the century after Appomattox. Republicans rarely received any electoral votes at all from Southern states during the years of their party's national ascendancy. Even after World War I, when the party became identified with such Southern views as anti-Catholicism and an opposition to immigration, the South stayed solidly with the Democrats until they nominated for president a Catholic, and an antiprohibition Catholic at that, Governor Alfred E. Smith of New York. That year, 1928, Herbert Hoover carried Florida, North Carolina, Tennessee, Texas, and Virginia, five of the eleven states, and won a total of about 48 percent of the Southern popular vote. Such success was unprecedented for a Republican. In the preceding election, President Coolidge had carried none of the eleven states, and had received only some 30 percent of the popular vote. In 1932, running against Franklin D. Roosevelt, Hoover won less than 20 percent of the vote in the South, and he carried no states. Roosevelt's popularity always remained especially high in the South. In 1944, his last election, he received three out of four votes there. In Strom Thurmond's South Carolina, the vote count was F. D. R. 90,601, Thomas Dewey 4,547. The Palmetto State was always lopsidedly Democratic, even in 1928, giving Hoover barely 4 percent of the two-party vote. In 1936 Alfred Landon got just over 1 percent!

The depression, World War II, and the accelerating Negro desire for equal rights slowly changed the Democratic party, however. In 1936 for the first time a majority of Negroes voted Democratic in a presidential election. In the 1940's the white primary was declared unconstitutional. By 1948, the year of the first postwar, postdepression presidential election, civil rights had become enough of an issue within the Democratic party to cause some Southerners to walk out of the convention in Philadelphia. The leader of the fight for a civil-rights plank at that convention was Minneapolis Mayor Hubert Humphrey. The leader of the unreconstructed Southerners was South Carolina Governor Strom Thurmond. That year, Thurmond ran for president on a third-party ticket, and carried four states in the Deep South, South Carolina, Alabama, Mississippi, and Louisiana. Dewey was once again the Republican nominee, and he once again got about one vote in four in the South. But Thurmond and Dewey together received approximately half the votes cast in the eleven states.

Most political observers considered that election unique, with no particular meaning for Republicans. Some, however, saw it as a transitional election, indicating a movement away from old one-party methods and loyalties, toward no one could be sure what—a two-party South? a three-party South?

The next election proved that a two-party South was a real possibility. Eisenhower, the Republican nominee, insisted on campaigning in the Southern states even though his political advisers were, in his words, "flatly opposed." After winning the nomination from Taft, Eisenhower met with his top aides and advisers in Denver in August, to plan the coming campaign. Eisenhower overruled the politicians with what may be considered typically Eisenhowerian logic. "My reasons," he later wrote, "were simple but, I thought, logical. The first were purely personal. I had lived for years among the Southern people and liked them. I refused, as my party's nominee, to visit all other sections and ignore the South. Another reason stemmed from my concept of the Presidency. The man in the White House, I believed, should think of himself as President of all the people." He campaigned in every Southern state but Mississippi, and carried Texas, Virginia, Tennessee, and Florida in the fall, receiving 48 percent of the total vote cast in the South. In 1956 he did even better, carrying Louisiana as well and getting more than half of all the Southern votes cast. His was a landslide victory, of course, in which he even carried such Democratic strongholds as Chicago, but he had definitely proved that Southerners who had only so recently regarded Republicans as enemies would vote for a candidate of that party.

Two tides were rising in the South. One was the growth of an urban middle class. Samuel Lubell calculated that Eisenhower's total margin of victory in the four Southern states he carried in 1952 was smaller than his margin in the urban-suburban counties in those states. The residents of these were property-owning, newly prosperous, younger voters, who had both more of a stake in conservative government (or less in liberal) and fewer ties of memory to the party of their fathers than did Southerners as a whole. The second rising tide was associated with Strom Thurmond's third party movement of 1948. Lubbell said that "in the 157 'black belt' counties which are most sensitive to the race issue—where Negroes outnumber whites but are not permitted to vote—Eisenhower jumped the Republican tally to eight times over 1948." Nixon expected that racist tide to go down after 1957, and since a falling tide lowers all boats, the Republican prospects in the South appeared to him not good for 1960.

Nixon proposed to campaign in every Southern state after winning the nomination, but only to fulfill his pledge to visit all fifty states. However, on a visit to Atlanta early in the campaign he was so warmly received that he began to think that he could win substantial support in the South, at least as much as Eisenhower had won. Flying back to Washington from Atlanta he communicated to his staff the belief that the South was not lost after all. The late Mayor William B. Hartsfield of Atlanta, a Democrat, claimed after the Nixon visit that he had carefully arranged the parade route and the speaking site so that the crowd would look bigger than it was, thus deceiving Nixon into thinking he had more support than he in fact had. Why Hartsfield would want to do that is difficult to understand. Besides, the crowd undeniably *was* large and *was* friendly. That fall, Georgia gave John F. Kennedy 60 percent of its vote, but in Fulton and De Kalb counties, where Atlanta is located, the vote was split almost down the middle. Kennedy led in the former by fewer than 2,000 votes, and in the latter by fewer than 100.

Kennedy received many Negro votes in the South, partly as a result of an incident during the campaign that changed the view held by many voters—particularly Negroes but also a good number of whites—concerning the attitude of each of the two parties toward civil rights. During the campaign Dr. Martin Luther King was jailed following a minor traffic incident. Aides of John F. Kennedy, without his prior knowledge, came to King's defense in the press and in the Georgia court. A typical reaction was that of Dr. King's father, himself a Baptist minister. He said that until then he had been unable to bring himself to vote for the Catholic Kennedy, but now he would. It is often forgotten in discussions of race relations that until very recently at least, most blacks were very Southern, culturally speaking, in their prejudices as well as in their virtues. The shift back to the Democrats of many black votes which had gone to Eisenhower meant the difference, according to some studies, in South Carolina's election, for the popular vote there just barely went to Kennedy. In some Northern states where the vote was close, the escalation of Negro Democratic vote from about 60 percent to 80 percent meant a victory for Kennedy. Election analyst Richard Scammon wrote in 1960 that had the Negro vote not shifted so dramatically, Nixon would have won. It is conceivable that in the postmortems on the 1960 election, the warm Nixon reception in Atlanta and later in other Southern cities, the voting results throughout the South, and the rush of the black vote to Kennedy, all combined to bring to the minds of many Republicans the possibility—the unavoidability—of a Southern Strategy. Nixon expressed bitterness at the Negro vote defection. He claimed in his memoirs that the Kennedy role in the King case had also been recommended to him and he had rejected it as unethical. Lawyers are not supposed to pressure judges. There was more to Kennedy's appeal than just the King incident, however. His campaign speeches went further than any candidate's ever had in appealing for black votes. The uncertain trend of black votes toward the Democratic party became certain in 1960, and was so reinforced by events thereafter that more than nine out of ten Negroes voted Democratic in the presidential elections of 1964 and 1968.

Nixon's results in the white South were impressive. Although Georgia voted overwhelmingly Democratic, although only three Southern states were carried—Florida, Tennessee, and Virginia— Nixon's total vote in the region was approximately 4,000,000; the decline of approximately 5 percent from Eisenhower's 1956 total in the South was in line with the decline from the Republican high-water mark of 1956 nationally.

In the following presidential election the write-off of black votes was made obvious to the Republican party and the appeal of the party to conservative Southerners made even more obvious. In that election the Republican candidate, Barry Goldwater, received over 6,000,000 votes in the Southern states, a 50 percent increase, while losing in a record landslide nationally. It is significant that the "Southern Strategy" of Goldwater in 1964 was quite similar to the strategy of Nixon in 1960 in terms of campaign scheduling. The amount of time the two candidates spent in each of the states differed "only marginally," political scientist Stanley Kelley, Jr., concluded after a detailed study.

So Nixon and his party arrived at 1968. The decision to follow a Southern Strategy was almost unavoidable. Negroes were by then almost equally distributed in the Southern and non-Southern states and were solidly Democratic. Not only had Kennedy become a sainted figure to many blacks, but his successor had pushed through three tough civil-rights bills in the four years. There had been the stark symbolism of the Republican party's running a presidential nominee against him who had opposed the first of those bills (and was gone from the Senate when the other two were voted on). And there had been the strategy Nixon had felt it necessary to follow to win the nomination. If Reagan had won the nomination, the Republicans would have found even less profit in seeking black votes or in trying to win an election by depending on the industrial Northern states, where liberal politics prevailed. And if Rockefeller had won the nomination he probably would have had to make a bid for party unity by accepting a running mate far more appealing in the South than Spiro Agnew, and then would have had to campaign in a manner that would write off the black vote. For, as Barry Goldwater explained in his appealingly crude manner in 1962, "We have to go hunting where the ducks are."

The development of a Southern Strategy was complicated in 1968, however, by the fact that George Wallace, the fiery, segregationist former governor of Alabama, was on the ballot of all fifty states as a third-party candidate. His pitch, which he dressed up as an appeal for "law and order," was that both parties were too liberal on the civil-rights issue. His appeal was widespread in the South. All signs pointed to his carrying several Southern states, and indeed he did. He won absolute majorities, despite the three-way vote split, in Alabama and Mississippi, and pluralities in Louisiana, Arkansas, and Georgia. Both Democrats and Republicans ran anti-Wallace campaigns, led by their vice-presidential candidates. As we shall see, Agnew spent as much time urging voters to ignore Wallace in speeches outside the South as in it—but wherever he was, he was speaking to the South, and he did make one important Southern tour. The Democrats feared Wallace would entice hard-hat votes away from Hubert Humphrey principally in the states of the Great Lakes area. "Law and order" was, like "Your home is your castle," a slogan with multiple layers of meaning, and to many Democrats in places like Chicago and Milwaukee and Cleveland it sounded good. In the South, however, Nixon was the one who would be hurt by the Wallace strength. The people who had voted for Goldwater would hardly vote for Humphrey. One of Agnew's assignments was to convince them that a vote for Wallace was a vote for Humphrey.

The fact that the South has been important in the eyes of Republican presidential candidates in five consecutive elections should indicate that this judgment is not a passing fancy. Real historic shifts in voting behavior are taking place in the region, and are being recognized in the Republican party's highest councils. The South looms as even more important in the future of the party. The most fearless advocate of this point of view is columnist Kevin Phillips. Phillips worked for John Mitchell during the 1968 campaign as a voting analyst. He was then twenty-eight years old. He also worked for Mitchell after he became attorney general. When his book, *The Emerging Republican Majority,* was published, he resigned to become a columnist. Phillips provides a scholarly endorsement of the view of national politics that Barry Goldwater once expressed, and that seems to have become Republican gospel. Goldwater said he thought it would be a good idea to saw off the northeastern seaboard and let it float away from the continent. Phillips says, "Expanding on the pattern of Richard Nixon's 1968 victory, the South, Heartland and California together can constitute an effective *national* political majority."

"The Heartland" to Phillips consists of all of the United States except the South, the Pacific states, and the Northeast. He visualizes future Republican domination as based first on a combination of most of the South (*all* of it if third-party challenges such as Wallace's can be defeated), with all of the states west of the Mississippi River except Missouri, Iowa, Minnesota, and those bordering the Pacific. These states yield 136 electoral votes without the Deep South, and 189 with it. For election to the presidency, 270 votes are required. Phillips predicts that a conservative Republican could win the remaining votes by carrying some of the states in the rest of the Heartland, the Pacific, and "the non-Yankee East." His map in blank where Rand McNally shows Michigan, New York, Connecticut, Rhode Island, Massachusetts, New Hampshire, Vermont and Maine.°

Of all the components of this winning coalition, the South is the most exploitable. It provides 128 electoral votes to the Republicans in a straight Republican-Democratic contest, according to the Southern Strategy prediction, and becomes, Phillips says, "a GOP core area once it abandons third party schemes." In 1968 Nixon carried Florida, South and North Carolina, Virginia, and Tennessee. Wallace carried every other Southern state except Texas, which went to Humphrey. Nixon got slightly more than a third of the total Southern popular vote. Wallace did too, running about a half million votes behind him. Humphrey came in third in the South, with just above 30 percent of the total. Richard Scammon and Ben Wattenberg in their study of voting trends, *The Real Majority*, estimate that in a two-candidate race in 1968, the Wallace

° In 1963 a national Draft Goldwater committee map conceded West Virginia, Delaware, New Jersey, Rhode Island, Massachusetts, Michigan, Minnesota, Missouri, Nevada, Oregon, Alaska, and Hawaii to the Democrats. California was shown as a doubtful state on the map. Goldwater conceded to his then expected opponent, John Kennedy, some states in every region *except* the South.

vote would have split about 80 to 20 in Nixon's favor in the South (60 to 40 elsewhere). That means Nixon would have defeated Humphrey in Texas, too, and won 62 percent of the total Southern popular vote. If this conclusion is accepted (it is based on a scholarly study by the University of Michigan Opinion Research Center), the shift away from the Democratic party in the South is seen as having been completed. Not since 1944 has a Democratic presidential candidate received an obvious mandate in the South in terms of the popular vote. In 1964, Johnson beat Goldwater by some quarter of a million votes, less than half the margin he won by in his native Texas alone. In 1960 the total vote for Nixon and for third-party candidates (in other words, for all anti-Democratic candidates) was only some 200,000 votes below Kennedy's total—and that total included Alabama popular votes that, because of a complicated ballot situation, Kennedy may have been given credit for without deserving. From 1948 to 1964 the national Democratic party could win no more than a bare majority in Dixie in presidential voting. In 1968 it received less than a third of the popular vote and probably would not have obtained as much as 40 percent even in a two-way race. The Solid South has become solid again, but not solidly Democratic.

The 1968 outcome had been delayed by a *Democratic* Southern Strategy of sorts. In 1960 the vice-presidential candidate on the Democratic ticket was Lyndon Johnson, a Southerner with appeal then even in the conservative areas of his native region. In 1964 Johnson was the presidential candidate, with great appeal in the moderate and liberal precincts of the South. His messages in the two years were not all that different, however. The strength of the Democratic party in the South has been its ability to follow a Southern Strategy that operates on two levels of awareness and on two levels of political strength. Because Democrats have controlled politics from the courthouse up to the statehouse and the Congress in the South, and have recognized the importance of the party's controlling the White House, even the most conservative of Southern Democrats have been willing to support the most liberal of presidential candidates. The late Senator Harry Byrd, Sr., of Virginia was a rare exception. He followed a policy of "golden silence" in presidential years, which amounted to endorsement of the Republican candidate. A more typical conservative Southerner was the late Senator Richard Russell of Georgia. He campaigned for the Democratic ticket in 1960 at Lyndon Johnson's urging, but he usually expressed his views by saying that he intended "to hold my nose and vote Democratic." That attitude is not very flattering to the party's leader, but it is helpful. If Dick Russell can vote for Adlai Stevenson, who can't? So the institutional strength of the party allowed Democratic presidential candidates to follow a Southern Strategy that at the same time aimed at uniting the South's electoral vote and the South's voters. The healing and coercing words about civil rights could be spoken without fear of losing the whole region, because the party structure at the grass roots would prevail.

That policy could succeed as long as any Republican or third-party alternative was not too out of line on the civil-rights issue. In 1948, 1964, and 1968, as noted, parts of the South broke away because there was a "Southern Conservative" candidate. But the Republicans still had no institutional strength in the South in 1968. It is significant that the power broker was Strom Thurmond, a failed third-party leader, a failed Democrat—a man more loyal to an issue (or to issues: segregation, preparedness) than to party. Because the party was so weak in the South, the only way it could appeal to the voters was on the overriding issue of race relations. In attempting to unite the region's electoral vote to traditional Republican electoral votes, the Republican candidates for the top office had to divide the people of the South along racial lines. If there were a real two-party system in the South, if the Republicans were strong in all the state legislatures, then Republican candidates for president and vice-president could take the high road, too, in the debate on the civil-rights issues.

But the Southern Strategy of Barry Goldwater, of Richard Nixon and Spiro Agnew, of John Mitchell and Kevin Phillips, is not concerned with grass-roots Republicanism. Nor are the Southerners who vote for a Republican or third-party presidential candidate every four years much concerned with electing Republicans to other offices, as is demonstrated in such off-year elections as those of 1970.

In 1960, when Lyndon Johnson stumped the South and helped win most of it for John Kennedy, he performed a very rare feat. Vice-presidential candidates usually are practically invisible and have little or no influence on the outcome of elections. That was *not* true in 1968.

Chapter Twelve

The Agnew Strategy

Caligula's Horse

IN 1968 SPIRO AGNEW had the rare distinction of playing an important role in the campaign plans of both major parties. His own Republican party featured him in the bid to keep disgruntled voters from swinging to George Wallace (the same role assigned to the Democratic vice-presidential nominee, Senator Edmund Muskie), and the Democrats featured him in an effort to show that he was so unqualified that no one should vote for the man who had selected him to be vice-president and thus just a heartbeat away from the presidency. No vice-presidential candidate in modern times has been the object of so much of the enemy's attack, not even Richard Nixon. Nixon was attacked in 1952 and 1956 for what his opponents charged was deviousness and viciousness. Agnew was attacked for viciousness *and* for what his opponents said was a lack of stature. The second charge is decidedly harder for the target to take. George Ball summed up the difference in the two attacks when he resigned as United Nations ambassador in late September, to work for Humphrey: "It's important that people not forget that [Nixon] was called Tricky Dick. I've known him for 20 years and I remember why he got that name. The very cynicism with which he selected his running mate is a grave indication of his narrow principles. He was willing to choose a fourth rate politician and a hack to a position which could be only a heartbeat away from the Presidency."

Washington *Star* columnist Mary McGrory called this remark "unfair to fourth rate politicians." Columnists and editorial writers were by this time bearing down hard on candidate Agnew. Clayton Fritchey wrote, "Anybody who ever saw the late Joe McCarthy or the 'old' Richard Nixon can now identify Agnew at a glance." On another occasion Fritchey said, "When Richard Nixon chose

Agnew as his running mate, he said, 'This guy has got it!' True—
and there is no known mouthwash that can cure it." "TRB," in the
New Republic, lumped Agnew, Mayor Richard Daley, and President Johnson together and said, "[He] exemplifies the old politics
that the young people are so incensed about. The political pod-
snaps with their irrelevant rhetoric, fundamentally satisfied with
themselves and with things the way they are." Carl Rowan accused
Agnew of "shortsighted emotionalism." Even conservative columnist Richard Wilson said, "He has just that margin of knowledge of
complicated subjects which seems reassuring up to a point and
then he stuns his auditors by calmly stating conclusions that speed
the parting guests in a huff." The *Wall Street Journal's* Vermont
Royster said, "The heart of the matter is that he can't hit big
league pitching." Royster was kinder than most, and concluded
that vice-presidents had surprised people before by growing in the
job. A few conservative columnists were pro-Agnew. William F.
Buckley praised his "toughness, sincerity, decent-mindedness, deci-
siveness."

Among the many editorials that criticized Agnew in the first
month of the 1968 campaign, one stood out in his mind as particularly stinging. It appeared in the Washington *Post* under the heading "The Perils of Spiro."

"I know Ted Agnew well. We have had long and tough discussions.
We have examined each other's ideas, debated issues and tested each
other. He has real depth and genuine warmth. Having watched his performance as Governor of Maryland for two years, I was deeply impressed
by his tremendous brain power, great courage, and unprejudiced legal
mind. He has vigor, imagination and above all he acts. Under pressure,
he is one of the best poised and controlled . . . he has the attributes of a
statesman of the first rank . . ."—RICHARD M. NIXON.
    Well, there is no doubt that Ted Agnew has genuine warmth and
there should be no question by now that he acts. But the Governor's
performance over the past month leaves little doubt about anything else,
except perhaps his capacity for imagination. Given enough time, Nixon's
decision ("I seriously considered more than a dozen able men") to name
Agnew as his running mate may come to be regarded as perhaps the
most eccentric political appointment since the Roman emperor Caligula
named his horse a consul.

What had led to all this? It started in Mission Bay, San Diego,
California, where Nixon invited Agnew to a strategy session in Au-

gust, just after the convention, and before the Democrats held their disastrous convention in Chicago. Agnew and George White, whom he had asked to be his campaign manager, met with Nixon and John Mitchell and discussed the coming campaign. Agnew was to be given the routine vice-presidential assignment. He would go to those places too small to receive a presidential candidate's party (with its much larger staff and press complement), and would make second visits to cities in target states that Nixon had already visited. In a general way, the vice-presidential candidate's job would be to keep the faithful happy, those conservatives pretty sure to vote Republican, while the presidential candidate reached out to the independents and to potential Democratic defectors.

At the meetings in San Diego, first with Nixon and Mitchell, then with just Nixon, then with John C. Whitaker, a geologist with a Ph.D. who was the scheduling chief for the campaign, Agnew and White were told that the campaign would be fairly loose, that they would be given no hard guidelines. Whitaker told them he was assigning him a tour director, Roy Goodearle, and a scheduler, Nicholas Ruwe, not because the Nixon staff was distrustful of the Agnew staff, but because Nixon's campaign staff had long since been put together, including key people for the vice-presidential campaign, and things would be smoother with this arrangement. John Sears, the young New York lawyer who had been a Nixon aide all year, was named the liaison man for the Agnew campaign. He had been working with Agnew since before the convention. Nixon told White that it was important to have "this excellent talent" at work for the vice-presidential tour, and he detailed the other arrangements that were being made in Agnew's behalf—he was to have a private chartered plane, secretaries, mimeograph machines, the works. And top-level staff. "But he told us we would be on our own, except for scheduling, which had to be coordinated with his plans out of New York, and he told us if we didn't want the staff help he was offering we could turn it down," said White. Contrary to the charges later made in the press, White said, there was no assignment to compete with George Wallace or to try to win Southern states. John Sears said that at the time of the Mission Bay meetings, there was some thought of having Agnew attack Wallace, but the idea was put aside as the polls began to show that the coming election was not going to be close enough for the Wallace vote to be significant.

Then came the Democratic Convention in Chicago, and Democratic strength plummeted even further in the wake of the televised rioting around the headquarters hotel. Though in Chicago, unlike Miami, no one was killed, the riots still had a greater impact than those in Miami on the nation and on political fortunes. Strategy at that point became just to preserve the lead, as far as Agnew's role was concerned. With a staff that included White, Sears, Goodearle, and Annapolis aides Charles Bresler, Art Sohmer, Herbert Thompson (and Mrs. Thompson as Mrs. Agnew's press aide), and several newcomers, the Agnew campaign started in September to make as many headlines as the presidential candidates were making, an unusual and unwanted occurrence.

It began when he had breakfast with a group of Washington reporters in the second week in the month. Agnew had already made several speeches with a law-and-order theme. He had blamed the violence at Chicago during the Democratic convention on Communists. He had said that many of the campus riots of the previous spring had also been caused by Communists. Nixon had not made such charges. Reporters asked Agnew if these speeches meant he was assigned to take the "hard line" in the coming campaign, as Nixon had in his vice-presidential campaigns. Agnew's reply was, "It's all relative, if one is soft on communism and law and order, maybe the other man looks hard line. When I see this peace-at-any-cost line, Mr. Humphrey looks a lot like Neville Chamberlain and that makes Mr. Nixon look like Winston Churchill." Soft on communism? Or, as it was also reported, "squishy soft" on communism? That viewpoint sounded familiar to some reporters and editorialists. Agnew was pressed on the subject at another press conference later the same day. There were references to the late Senator Joseph McCarthy, who had made similar attacks on Democrats. Agnew shrugged off these reactions, saying it was inconvenient for candidates to have to worry about every connotation of every combination of the words.

The next day, with Agnew's remarks headlined in all the morning papers, House Republican Leader Gerald Ford and Senate Republican Leader Everett Dirksen held a press conference following a meeting of top party leaders on the Hill to say that they had seen no evidence that Humphrey was soft on communism. Both men also said that they did not like to see Republicans use the phrase "law and order"; they preferred "law and order with justice." This too was a knock at Agnew, who had been speaking of "law and order" and had said publicly that he didn't think there was anything wrong with the phrase. But Republican Senator Edward Brooke of Massachusetts, a Negro, had already complained that "law and order" implied repression. And Ford and Dirksen knew that the kind of posture Agnew was taking in the early days of the campaign could be bad politics. With a big lead, why dredge up the ghost of Joe McCarthy? Representative Ford put his criticism in a revealing way. The party had many good issues, he said, and therefore, "I don't think this one—soft on communism—should be pushed at this time."

The following day, while in Rochester to give a speech, Agnew apologized for his remarks. He said he had been in private conversation with Dirksen, but not with Nixon, concerning his charges. "If I had known my remarks were going to cast me as the Joe McCarthy of 1968 I would have turned five somersaults to avoid them. If I left an impression that the Vice-president was not a loyal American, I want to rectify that. He is a man of great integrity and I have great respect for him. My record is not one of inquisitorial procedures. I have never been a particular admirer of former Senator Joseph McCarthy. I didn't approve of the witch hunts that took place at that time and I still don't approve of them. I've never been one to go the low road in politics and I want to get off the low road."

The next day he was in Chicago. Since his remarks on the Chicago rioting were what has started off the roundelay, he was naturally asked about it once again. He said it wasn't up to him to place blame.

Off that hook, he got on another. In response to a question about civil rights on Irv Kupcinet's popular television show, he said that he was for advancing the rights of Negroes, but not if doing so meant breaking laws. He was against the Selma march and all such attempts to obtain desegregation in the South through direct action. (Later he would say he even disapproved of the peaceful and landmark Montgomery bus boycott, which he said was illegal.)

When pressed for his views on civil disobedience, he replied that under no circumstances could he condone it. Would he not drink out of a White Only water fountain to dramatize the situation if he were black? No, he would make the point in some other way. Until now, Agnew had probably been making only liberals mad. But as he was beginning to do with regularity, he went too far, and invited criticism and perhaps ridicule even from his supporters. He was asked about the traditions of men like Jesus, Gandhi, Martin Luther King, Jr., and Thoreau. "The people you have mentioned did not operate in a free society," he said grandly.

There were other gaffes in September (at the end of which the Republican lead in the polls began to dwindle). It was in Chicago that he made a casual and perhaps even affectionate but coarse reference to Polish-Americans. He said, "When I am moving in a crowd I don't look and say, 'Well, there's a Negro, there's an Italian, and there's a Greek, and there's a Polack.' " This remark drew instant criticism from sensitive Democrats. Sensitive in more ways than one. Even mock-pious attacks on Agnew on this point, however, could make him look bad. When a man gets a reputation as a stumbler, every little slip or hesitation looks like a pratfall. And Agnew wasn't helping to break out of this vicious circle. Nixon had charged collusion between Wallace and Humphrey supporters. Agnew was asked about this matter, but the question did not indicate who had made the charge of collusion. Agnew thought it had come from Humphrey and was directed at Nixon supporters. Here was a chance to retaliate. The charge, he said, "is not sufficiently dignified to required a comment. The word 'collusion' has nasty connotations. It is as bad as soft on communism."

Even his timing was bad. Early in the campaign there had been a problem concerning speechwriters. His favorite from Annapolis, Mrs. Rosenwald, was unable to travel because of illness in her family. The first two writers who came along on the tour were not producing the sort of thing Agnew and his top advisers wanted. Sears and White asked for help from the Nixon headquarters, and Stephen Hess, who had been a White House aide in the Eisenhower administration, was sent to Washington to talk to White about the job. He agreed to take it, but first had to finish up some work at Harvard, where he was a fellow at the Institute of Politics. By the time he joined the tour, Agnew had already made

most of his gaffes. Columnists Rowland Evans, Jr., and Robert Novak said he had been sent to prevent such embarrassments in the
future. The fact that Herbert Klein, Nixon's top publicist, issued a
press release on the Hess appointment added to the impression
that this was a Nixon maneuver. On top of that, the *Sun* had an
editorial praising Hess, a Johns Hopkins graduate, as if to suggest
that it was about time someone with his capability joined the Agnew staff. Agnew resented these reactions, and though he was civil
to Hess, he did not deal with him directly very often, and he followed the speeches Hess wrote even less often. Agnew preferred
instead to say the same things over and over again. On occasion,
what he said and what Hess wrote and released to the press were
contradictory.

Then, after Hess had joined the tour, Agnew was embroiled in
a further headline-making fiasco—the now too-well-known incident in which Agnew referred to a reporter as "the fat Jap" in what
he meant to be a jocular fashion. The statement reached the public
as Agnew arrived in Hawaii, with its many citizens of Japanese de-
scent, and he was predictably denounced by a Democratic senator
from the state.

The Democrats believed they were onto something in Agnew,
and began to concentrate their fire on him. There was evidence
that the public was not viewing the Agnew campaign with admira-
tion. In early September a Harris poll showed Senator Muskie preferred over Governor Agnew by only 33 to 30 percent. In mid-October the margin was 41 to 24 percent. One Democratic television
spot commercial featured a poster saying "Agnew for Vice-President," with a sound track of hysterical laughter. When protests
forced the Democrats to drop that commercial after only a few
days, they substituted one that showed an oscilloscope recording of
the beats of a heart, which could also be heard. The message was
to the effect that Hubert Humphrey's choice as running mate was
qualified to be a heartbeat away from the presidency, but Richard
Nixon's sure wasn't. The Democrats were also using newspaper advertisements to attack Agnew, and through him Nixon. One full-
page ad, complete with Agnew's picture, began, "President Agnew
said . . ." and then reproduced some of his worst gaffes. "President
Agnew?" it concluded. Another said, " 'Mr. Agnew says if you've
seen one slum you've seen them all. I say if you've seen one slum

you've seen too many.' [signed] Hubert Humphrey." It was unusual for a vice-presidential candidate to be so singled out. The attacks began to get to Agnew.

"He was always asking, 'Is Dick happy?' and explaining to us
what he meant by the controversial statements," a Nixon staff man
said. Mrs. Agnew described her husband as "very discouraged"
during the campaign. It seemed to her that Agnew would get worn
down as the day went on, but would make a determined effort to
start anew each morning to overcome his critics. George White
saw his friend in a similar light, and wondered, too, if he as campaign manager was doing something wrong. He asked John Mitchell several times if the criticism was hurting the ticket. Nixon had
been through a somewhat similar experience when he ran for vice-
president in 1952 and 1956, and apparently he took a philosophical
view. He kept relaying word to Agnew that it was just the press,
not to worry. Mitchell told White finally that far from being dismayed at the attacks on Agnew, they thought them advantageous
in a sense. "Did you ever stop to think if they weren't giving you
hell, they'd be giving it to us?" he told him on one visit to New
York.

Attacking Wallace

At the midpoint of the campaign, when the anti-Agnew criticism was at its height, Nixon speechwriter Patrick Buchanan
joined the Agnew tour for a brief Southern swing. He said later he
was there only to improve the speeches. Hess's scholarly speeches
didn't fit Agnew's style. They had been undelivered, but Agnew
stuck to Buchanan's texts. When criticism of Agnew began to shift
away from his miscues and toward the substance of what he was
saying, the object of the criticism most often was the sort of speech
he delivered on this tour. But Agnew did not invite attack just to
do his duty to Nixon. He believed in what he was reading. He had
said the same sort of things in the past. Basically, his new tough
speeches asked people who might be attracted to Wallace to vote
for Nixon instead. A vote for Wallace, he said, would help Humphrey. He provided reasons for voting for Nixon by taking just as
tough a line on certain matters as Wallace was taking. In Jackson-
ville, Florida, he charged that Federal aid was being given to mili-

tants in ghettos to buy their silence. Then he said that promising
the poor uplift which in fact could not be delivered resulted in
"the revolt, the civil disobedience and the irresponsible dissent
sweeping the country." It was possible to read into this kind of
statement a linking together of *all* poverty aid, all civil-rights programs, and all criminal activity. Many people so understood it and
charged Agnew with using coded appeals to racist sentiments. He
hotly denied the accusation, but this sort of speech became a staple, which he wouldn't or couldn't discard. It was the Agnew
Southern Strategy speech.

It is easy to see why both parties felt, about the first of October,
that Wallace was a threat: his standings in the polls were still high,
18 percent in the Harris poll, 20 percent in the Gallup. Agnew and
others had forecast a drop to 10 percent or less. Most of that support was in the South, but not all of it. The competition for Wallace
voters meant that the Southern Strategy could pay off in the North
as well. The statistics on Agnew's campaign tour are suggestive. He
made 108 separate visits. Of these, 25 were in the Southern or
Border states, 23 were in the Pacific states, 29 were in states in the
Great Lakes area. His strategy was to pay as much attention to the
South as to those regions with which, traditionally, Republicans have
been more associated.

According to Theodore White, Buchanan went back to Nixon
headquarters to report that Agnew should be kept on ice for the
rest of the campaign. Agnew's schedule had by now become one in
which he was kept away from the voters even more than Nixon
himself was kept at a distance. Agnew's staff called this approach
the "new politics," and said that they much preferred having him
speak on television instead of before a live rally crowd. Meanwhile, he was delivering the kind of speech recommended by
Buchanan almost every day. What follows is a description of one
Agnew week on the trail during the last half of the campaign. It
was a typical week embodying the two Buchanan proposals, regarding his scheduling and his message. It has been chosen for use
here because the author was on that trip.

Monday, October 14/Agnew lunched with *Time-Life* editorial executives in New York. He made some brief remarks at a
Greek-American All-Nationality Reception, and spoke at a rally in
a blue-collar neighborhood in Woodbridge, New Jersey. Then he

attended a dinner at New York's Waldorf-Astoria Hotel honoring James L. Buckley, the Conservative party's candidate for the Senate.

In the speech in Woodbridge he said he shared his hearers' disgust for "phony intellectuals . . . who don't understand what we mean by patriotism and hard work." He also talked of "the principal problem arising from this dissent" and then brought in "organized crime" in a way that yoked the two rhetorically at the very least. He attacked Attorney General Ramsey Clark, as Nixon had been doing, urged a Federal offensive against the narcotics problem, said a vote for Wallace was a vote for Humphrey, and left the crowd wildly excited. Agnew delivered his lines with a determined smile and occasional inflections, but with no real emotion, like a high-school drama student, yet his audience responded emotionally.

At the Waldorf he told the black-tied diners that there had to be a hard line on unruly students. Instead of "phony intellectuals" he criticized "pseudo intellectuals." He was as well received there as at Woodbridge. The references to "pseudo" and "phony" intellectuals were straight out of George Wallace's lexicon. Also in the Wallace manner was the mingling of attacks on students, dissent, crime. Agnew's appearance at the Buckley dinner was officially greeted with opposition by the campaign organization of Republican Senator Jacob Javits, whom Buckley was running against. Privately, Javits aides said John Mitchell had worked the visit out, and Javits had agreed to it.

Tuesday, October 15/Agnew flew to Indianapolis early Tuesday. At noon he spoke to five hundred of the city's business and professional elite, at a luncheon at the Indianapolis Athletic Club given by publisher Eugene Pulliam. Agnew told the establishment members gathered there that he would say to the poor, "Yes, we will listen to your complaints. You may tell us your symptoms and we will make the diagnosis, and we the establishment, for which I make no apologies for being a part of, will implement the cure." He also attacked both the relatively new War on Poverty and the more traditional Federal approach to the poor, the welfare system. He put in a plug for new towns and standardized welfare payments, his two original contributions to the campaign.

After the meeting he taped a television interview. Then he flew to Concordia College, in Fort Wayne, where he attacked Wallace, crime, and dissent, again linking the latter two. Then he flew to Pittsburgh, where he spent the night.

Wednesday, October 16/In the morning he met with the traveling press. In holding this meeting, he was giving in to pressure. He had not had a press conference since mid-September, and reporters assigned to the tour were complaining that they couldn't do their job if they didn't get to see him regularly. The meeting lasted ninety minutes and produced nothing new or startling. The tension between him and the press was quite evident. When a network reporter who had been traveling with Senator Muskie said the pace in the two campaigns was quite different, implying that Agnew was, as some stories had begun to say, being hidden, the candidate displayed real anger. When a woman reporter made an unjustified leap of logic in interpreting Agnew's answer to another question, he refused to let her off gracefully and insisted on exposing her error. He defended his decision not to campaign in slums on the ground that he had been in many slums as governor and county executive. "I don't feel there is an particular gain to be made by debating on a street corner. You certainly don't learn from poor people what to do about the condition of poverty. The poor are not equipped to solve their problems." For that matter, he continued, neither were the "pseudo intellectuals" and "pontificators." He would turn the problem over to engineers, architects, and others who deal with the "mechanical" aspect of the urban environment.

In the afternoon Agnew taped another television interview, and that night he drove thirty miles to Belle Vernon to speak to a suburban group. The pace was still leisurely. It was in Pittsburgh that a reporter claimed that when a door was opened by mistake he saw Agnew watching a soap opera on television at a time when he was officially reported to be in a staff meeting.

Thursday, October 17/The campaign plane, *Michelle Ann*, named after Agnew's only grandchild, took the short hop to Youngstown, Ohio. Agnew spoke at noon in the Paramount Theater to a crowd of about a thousand, again attacking George Wallace, who was thought to have a special appeal for the steelworkers of Youngstown. "I guess he's all right to some people. I wouldn't want my daughter to marry him," he said. Then he at-

tacked Wallace's running mate, Curtis LeMay. "We're on the verge
of potential nuclear disaster every minute, that can be unleashed
by a thoughtless finger on the red button. And if you have heard
the third-party candidate talk about the war in Vietnam, and if
you have heard his running mate talk very casually about the use
of nuclear capacity as a simple extension of conventional weapons,
you would be as frightened as I." Agnew's tone and facial expres-
sions conveyed the idea that he was no more frightened about this
than he was of the prospect of rain in Youngstown tomorrow, but
his audience was responsive and cheered and clapped. He went on
to give the speech in which welfare recipients, dissenters, crimi-
nals, and students all tumbled over one another.

That evening Agnew was the star at a rally in Detroit's huge
riverfront Cobo Hall. George Romney was there, along with enter-
tainers Kaye Stevens and Corbett Monica. The crowd numbered
about four thousand. Agnew continued his attack on students. He
had mentioned the Students for a Democratic Society several times
lately. The week before this tour began, he was heckled at Towson
State College, and in one of the few times he ever showed emotion
on the campaign trail, he replied to his hecklers, "You're sick,
you're sick." Unable to quiet them, he demanded to know if they
were members of SDS, and the question brought a roar of admission, false for most, from the audience. Without referring to that
episode, Agnew told the Cobo Hall crowd that there was an SDS
chapter at his hometown's college and that two professors had
founded it. "Now I say it's time we began to discourage the employment of this kind of person in our colleges and universities."
He got a roar of approval for that thought, and went on to describe SDS as "an organization led by people who preach the overthrow of the country." He would not name the professors. He said
the information came from police and FBI files.*

Friday, October 18/Agnew taped two television shows in Detroit in the morning, then flew home to Annapolis, with a stop in
Washington. It had been a very relaxed campaign week, in which
he appeared at eight public events and on four television shows. In

---

* The professors promptly identified themselves: Phillip Marcus and David
Chen, both of the physical-sciences department. Agnew wired the chairman of
the board of trustees and the college on October 18 asking an investigation.
Marcus was later fired, but not for "political" reasons according to the college.

Detroit Agnew had again proved that a man determined to make headlines can't be deterred. During one of the television interviews, he was asked about news stories to the effect that he wouldn't campaign in slums. He replied that he had not said he wouldn't, that he had been in slums before, and "to some extent I would have to say this: If you've seen one city slum you've seen them all." In a number of newspapers and on a number of news broadcasts the quote was later given without the qualification or the context, making Agnew appear to be coarse and unconcerned, and he was understandably vexed. Actually the statement should have been criticized as false, rather than as unfeeling or malicious. The Twelfth Street area of Detroit does not look like Los Angeles' Watts, for an obvious example. Even where slums *look* alike, there can be important demographic differences. Social decay is more than skin deep. Engineers and architects can't cure it. If Agnew is ignorant about slums and the poor, he is not unfeeling. He expressed compassion often during the 1968 campaign, but such statements seldom made news. In the speech to the Indianapolis establishment he had said that a poor black man living in a miserable ghetto should not be expected to compete for a job with a man in a comfortable suburban setting, that the former needed to have his environment improved before he could be a productive, competitive member of society. This is a humane view, even if not backed up with any specific program or pledge to improve the environment, even if it represents the wrong way to approach the problem of joblessness in the first place, and wider publicity to Agnew's expression of such sentiments as this would have softened his image. Agnew was alternately puzzled and angry at the press for not reporting "half of what I say, always the same half," as he put it to a friend. Yet in this case and others, the "nice" Agnewisms were overshadowed or erased completely from broadcasts and newspaper reports by his other remarks or activities of the day. This one-sided coverage was partly the fault of the press, but most politicians understand news and know that if they want both halves of a philosophy to reach the people, they must not always yoke the two, with "the same half" always presented in a more dramatic manner.

From "squishy soft" to "one slum," Agnew was still making the wrong kinds of headlines. Richard Nixon began to omit mention of his running mate. Nixon had made much of his belief in the citizen who worked hard, paid taxes, but did not loudly protest policies —"the forgotten man," part of "the silent majority." Joseph Daughen of the Philadelphia *Bulletin* noted how seldom Agnew was mentioned by campaigner Nixon and dubbed *him* the forgotten man.

Is Agnew Crooked, Too?

Then came one last final blow to Agnew. His philosophy had been attacked, his ability had been demeaned, his qualifications scorned—now his integrity was questioned. Along with everything else, he was accused of having used his position in government to improve his friends' and his own financial status. *The New York Times* made the charge in an editorial, not once but three times in the final two weeks of the campaign. As it turned out, from Agnew's point of view the episode was probably the best thing that happened to him during the campaign. Richard Nixon stopped ignoring him. He came to his defense, berating the *Times* for "the lowest kind of gutter politics," and declaring that it was hitting "below the belt." Other, unexpected supporters sprang up, among them the Washington *Post* and the Baltimore *Sun*. Nixon-Agnew campaign aides sensed that the public might be on Agnew's side. George White publicly threatened a libel suit, thus keeping the issue in the public eye. Everett I. Willis, a partner in the New York firm of Dewey, Ballantine, Bushby, Palmer and Wood, met with *Times* lawyers to discuss the editorial during the campaign. So did White; and after the election White maintained that had the Republican ticket lost, he would have sued. It would have been a hard suit to win, since Federal courts have given newspapers wide latitude in commenting on public figures. Win or lose in court, White and Agnew thought the controversy helped rather than hurt, and they kept it alive when others, including the *Times*, were ready to drop it.

Agnew had issued a financial statement on October 14. It showed a net worth of $111,084.44. Slightly over $36,000 was in cash; $27,000 was in stocks, including four hundred shares, worth $11,000, in the Chesapeake National Bank, whose letterhead listed "Spiro T. Agnew, Governor of Maryland" as a member of the board; $10,000 was in American Telephone and Telegraph debentures; and there was an equity of $11,000 in a $49,000 home in the Virgin Islands. He had sold his Towson home when he was elected governor, and bought the Virgin Islands place. The difference between the 1966 financial statement issued during the gubernatorial campaign and this 1968 statement was a gain in two years of $25,-000. His salary had been only $25,000 a year for each of those years, but he had had to make no outlay for housing, and he received a $20,000-a-year living allowance and a political-expense fund. Part of the increase in his net worth was accounted for by the sale of his Towson home for some $5,000 more than he had valued it; hence, the remainder of the increase amounted to only $10,000 a year.

On October 22, the *Times* carried a long news article about Agnew's financial background. The article recounted the controversies and charges of previous years, already familiar to Marylanders. These included his relationship with J. Walter Jones in the Chesapeake National Bank and in the Revell Highway property venture, the Steinbock charges of pressure on the Slade Avenue rezoning, the accusations concerning the Executive Assembly fund, and so forth. The article also stated that state funds totaling $200,000 were on deposit in the Chesapeake National Bank.

Four days later the *Times* editorialized as follows:

Richard M. Nixon, who prides himself on his investigative abilities, appears not to have done much checking into the background and associations of Spiro T. Agnew before choosing him as his running mate.

It now develops that as a Zoning Board member, as Chief Executive of Baltimore County and as Governor of Maryland, Mr. Agnew has been the political ally and financial partner of wealthy land speculators. These businessmen have made sizable fortunes out of developing land in suburban Baltimore over the past 15 years, in part because of favorable zoning and government decisions, and Mr. Agnew's financial net worth has also risen sharply.

In 1965 Mr. Agnew joined with these businessmen in purchasing a tract of land on the probable approach route of a new parallel span of the Chesapeake Bay Bridge. As Governor he approved this route. In response to public criticism Governor Agnew later sold his share of the land. With several of these same businessmen Governor Agnew is still a partner in a Virgin Islands land venture and in a bank . . . since Governor Agnew is responsible for the enforcement of the state banking laws and the state has public funds on deposit with this bank, it would seem highly improper for the governor to continue as a director and stock-holder. The same relationship existed from 1964–1966, when Mr. Agnew as County Executive, voted to deposit county funds in the bank. . . .

In his obtuse behavior as a public official in Maryland as well as in his egregious .comments in this campaign, Mr. Agnew has demonstrated that he is not fit to stand one step away from the presidency.

Agnew's own public reaction was to call the editorial "the major blooper of the year." He said further, "Specifically the *Times* charged, or inferred, that because of the favorable treatment given friends of mine, my financial worth had 'risen sharply.' This is a completely false statement. No improper treatment was given friends of mine while I was in office. Moreover if you eliminate some $35,000 to $40,000 that I inherited or was given by my parents, my net worth is considerably less than that of the other presidential or vice-presidential candidates . . . $74,000."

What came from his parents, according to the 1966 statement, was the family home on Murdock Road, worth $15,000, the $11,000 in Chesapeake National Bank stock, which Agnew was quoted as saying his father had left him, and some $11,000 in cash he said his mother had left him. But Agnew's father died before the Chesapeake National Bank was chartered, and the *Times* used this fact to suggest in its editorial that Agnew was not telling the truth about his finances. Agnew denied having ever said his father left any such stock; rather, he said, he bought the bank stock with the proceeds of the sale of other stock his father left him. His father left no will; his mother left only the Murdock Road house. Agnew's half brother, Roy Pollard, said in 1971 that he was not aware of any estate, that he received nothing after the death of his mother. "My brother's a lawyer. He handled it," he said. However, there are ways in which a parent can leave things of value to children—or to a child—without filing a detailed will.

The Washington *Post* said, "It is unfortunate that these charges against Governor Agnew have been raised so late in the campaign. The facts concerning them have been known for many months. Strictly on the basis of what has been spread on the public record, they do not raise serious questions about Mr. Agnew's honesty or integrity." The *Sun* rebuked the *Times* for "extravagantly overstat-[ing] its case." Faint praise, but, like a brief shower in the desert, unexpected and welcome. The Washington *Star* went further in commenting on the *Times* charges. It said, "Spiro T. Agnew has been a good governor of Maryland, the best in many years. He is obviously not the country's slickest politician. But any attempt to picture him as a bigot or as the sort of man who would deal from the bottom of the deck is both deplorable and devoid of any basis in fact." The *Star* also reminded the *Times* that on October 12, 1966, it knew "or had ample opportunity to know the details of the matters concerning which it so bitterly complains on the eve of an election in November, 1968." On October 12, 1966, the *Times*, which circulates in suburban Washington, had endorsed Agnew for governor of Maryland.

The *Star* had a good point. To be sure, Agnew's net worth had increased an unexplained $10,000 a year while he was governor, but he had had no real need to spend his own money during this period. In his four years as county executive, when he had no free home and his expenses were not underwritten, his worth, exclusive of what he claimed came from his parents, increased to $49,000. This rate of increase, too, comes to about $10,000 a year, assuming that the Martindale and Hubbell estimate of his 1962 net worth as between $10,000 and $20,000 was correct. That estimate is plausible, in view of the limited rewards of his law practice before 1962. After all, he had been a junior employee of a declining firm, then a part-time lawyer in Baltimore while working for the Court of Appeals committee, then a part-time labor lawyer in Towson, from 1957 to 1961, while serving on the zoning-appeals board, and then had been occupied with running for office. He could hardly have saved much money. So his fortunes were improving at the same pace before the *Times* endorsement of 1966 as in the period between the endorsement and the editorial attacking his fitness.

Though it did not figure in the campaign, a much more critical rumor involving Agnew's public activities and personal fortunes was widely circulating in Maryland in this period. It involved his handling in May, 1968, of a bill that would have required some Medicaid drugs to be of the generic rather than the brand-name type. These are much cheaper. The legislator who pushed for the bill estimated savings to the elderly poor and to the state of between $750,000 and $1,000,000. A special governor's committee recommended such a drug policy. Opponents of the bill were the state medical society and the drug manufacturers. The story was broadcast by some supporters of the bill in the legislature that a group of drug companies paid $250,000 to Agnew and certain legislators to get the bill killed. It was passed. Agnew vetoed it, and the legislature did not try to override his veto the following January. But no dramatic increase in Agnew's net worth showed up in his 1968 statement. Drew Pearson, the *Wall Street Journal,* the Baltimore *Evening Sun,* the New York *Post,* and some top Democratic party investigators followed up the charge and found no proof of it. Some Democrats in the state legislature still talk privately as if they believe there was a payoff. Jerry Kelly, the *Evening Sun's* top investigator, a skeptical and professional reporter, cites this talk when he says that suspicions about ethics swirled around Agnew's head more than in the case of any previous governor in modern times. It seems safe to say that if there had been a shred of evidence, someone would have found it. No one did, yet the rumors just grew stronger.

One reason put forth to explain this narrow-eyed view of Agnew is that he was so much involved with real-estate men. In Maryland, land used to be a symbol of the rich and the rectitudinous—in politics at least. But in the 1950's and 1960's speculation in land was so intimately involved with the activity of public officials, that a certain taint came to be associated with land deals, even when a conflict of interest could not be demonstrated. The most shocking deal Agnew was involved in came to light after the 1968 campaign. A month before he became vice-president, he signed deeds giving a developer in the resort of Ocean City 190 acres of wetlands on a bay there for a hundred dollars an acre. The developer paid the state ten cents a ton for fill dredged from the bottom of the bay. The resulting land was sold in lots, as many as twelve to the acre, for from four to eight thousand dollars each. Agnew, the state treasurer, and the state comptroller, sitting as the state Board of Public Works, provided this instant multimillion-dollar fortune for a developer despite warnings from state officials that the ecological damage to the bay would be immediate and irreversible. The board would not even wait for a full environmental study before consummating the affair. This was an unseemly action in a state noted for its oyster, crab, and clam industries, for the wetlands are vital breeding grounds for marine life. Also, the sale took recreation potential away from the public and gave it to private individuals. Even Agnew's staunch supporter Rogers C. B. Morton said the state had been shortchanged. Representative James Haley of Florida and the House Interior and Insular Affairs Committee charged that Agnew "overlooked the interests of the state." Maryland Senator Joseph Tydings called the deal "incredible."

The Associated Press investigated the whole transaction after Agnew became vice-president and concluded that there was no evidence that Agnew profited "financially or otherwise." Jerry Kelly says he believes Agnew just responded to the pleas of Ocean City and Worcester County officials that they needed a larger tax base. The attention focused on this affair is an example of how suspicious and vociferous Agnew's critics were. The governors before and after him also allowed developers to destroy wetlands for profit, but were not subjected to as much criticism. While governor, Agnew was involved in one other eyebrow-raising episode concerning land, laws, and profits. It will be discussed in the next chapter.

Agnew's answer to the charge that Chesapeake National Bank had received state funds while he was governor and county funds while he was county executive was that the state treasurer was responsible for depositing the former and the county finance director was responsible for depositing the latter. Both were Democrats. Agnew did participate in the county decision; but the state treasurer called a press conference to announce that as governor, Agnew was blameless: the $200,000 in state funds had been deposited in 1964, befqre Agnew came to Annapolis. Agnew also pointed out that since the Chesapeake was a national bank, not a state bank, the implication that state banking laws were crucial in its operations was incorrect. He also made the charge, which the *Times* grudgingly admitted, that the editorial distorted the time sequence of his purchase and resale of the Bay Bridge property. Furthermore, Agnew said, it wasn't the governor who decided on the bridge route, but other officials.

White, Agnew, and Nixon kept talking about the *Times* smear, hoping for political advantage. Campaign aides almost unanimously agreed that Agnew was coming out of the fight looking like a whipping boy rather than a crook. One aide said that he doubted that any electoral changes actually resulted from the episode, but that it almost put Maryland in the Republican column. Nixon-Agnew lost Governor Agnew's state by just over 20,000 votes out of more than 1,000,000 cast.

The campaign drew to its close for Agnew in too-typical fashion. He was slighted by his running mate, became involved in controversy on the trail and at home, and avoided the public and the press as much as possible. His last day of campaigning was Monday, November 4. He made just two appearances, in Charleston, West Virginia, and Richmond, Virginia. In Richmond a local Republican scheduled a press conference. Agnew's aides were furious and would agree only to one question at planeside. The question was, Who did he think would win the election? The Republicans' sixteen-point margin in the Gallup poll had dwindled to nothing. It was a toss-up. Agnew refused to predict. Then, at a rally in Richmond, a student in the crowd demanded to know why Agnew had not accepted more questions throughout the campaign. As the audience cheered Agnew, the student was hustled out by two men.

Agnew flew back to Maryland Monday evening, while the two presidential candidates concluded the campaign with nationally broadcast telethons. Humphrey had Muskie with him. Nixon had Bud Wilkinson, a former Oklahoma football coach. This was an obvious humiliation to Agnew. He was the forgotten man again, after the brief excitement of the libel charges. He was warmly received when his plane landed at Baltimore's Friendship Airport. A crowd of students jeered him at Annapolis, however, and continued picketing and yelling after he entered the mansion. Police arrested twenty-seven of the approximately one hundred demonstrators.

Agnew voted in a firehouse early Tuesday; then he and Dr. Emmet Queen drove to Baltimore County for a round of golf. There was a reception in the mansion that night for some 150 staff members, their families, and friends. The Governor mingled with the guests for most of the evening. There was also a party for Republicans at the Annapolis Statler-Hilton, and Agnew went there at about 3:30 A.M. to speak briefly, expressing the belief that they had won and the hope that Maryland might go Republican. He had called Nixon at his New York headquarters much earlier in the evening, and a few minutes before going to the Statler-Hilton, had received the return call, in which Nixon said he felt they had won.

They won barely, with a margin over Humphrey-Muskie of a half million out of 63 million votes cast for the major-party candidates; Wallace got just under 10 million. There have been several reports of dissatisfaction with Agnew's performance within the Nixon campaign staff. John Sears, the Nixon man assigned to the Agnew campaign, probably summed up the whole thing best, though, when he was asked if Agnew—or the choice of Agnew— would have been blamed if the Republican ticket had lost in 1968. He replied, "We didn't lose." An intense study of the campaign was therefore not necessary. Had there been one, it is possible that Agnew—or the choice of Agnew—would have won praise. Louis Harris, the pollster, spoke to the National Press Club in Washington two days after the election. He said his polling showed "a late drop [in Wallace' strength] in the New South and the Border states. . . . The beneficiary was Richard Nixon there, for Humphrey was hardly a Southern alternative. The calculated gamble Nixon had made on Spiro Agnew and Strom Thurmond finally paid off when he won 75 electoral votes in that region, and, in many ways, the Electoral College battle was settled right in the states of Florida, South Carolina, North Carolina, Virginia, Tennessee, Kentucky, and Oklahoma, where Nixon left the Humphrey cupboard bare."

Chapter Thirteen

The Veep

Routine Duties

THE CONSTITUTION of the United States assigns the vice-president two responsibilities: to preside over the Senate and vote there in case of ties, and to succeed a dead, disabled, or removed president. Several statutes and executive orders assign the vice-president further duties, such as service on certain administrative councils, but the real duty of any vice-president is to do what his president tells him to do. Richard Nixon had some very definite ideas about vice-presidents. He was the first president since Martin Van Buren to have served a full term as vice-president, the first since John Adams to have served two terms in that office. While still vice-president, Nixon told a biographer that according to his "interpretation" of the Constitution, "The first function of a Vice President—his first responsibility—is to support the President and the administration." Agnew felt absolutely loyal to Nixon, and agreed with his view of the office. For the most part he was a Nixonian vice-president, though on a few occasions his outspokenness revealed him to be opposed to the president on important matters.

Agnew came to Washington resigned to the fact that the reputation he had acquired during the campaign would be with him a while. He told an interviewer that nothing he could say would change what people thought of him, only what he did.

Agnew faced formidable problems on Capitol Hill. He was the first vice-president since World War II who had not previously been a senator. He had never served in any legislative body. The Senate is an awesome society, with complicated rules and customs. Agnew is a quick study, and those things that could be learned by rote he quickly learned. For instance, since he had to administer, the oath of office to new senators, he memorized it—something veterans Lyndon Johnson and Hubert Humphrey never did, or saw the need to do. Agnew had lunch with small groups of senators, but neither rote learning nor casual conversations could prepare a man for the Senate's intricacies. In his first year, he began making enemies.

For one thing, he tried to pressure Republican senators, notably the reluctant Len Jordan of Idaho, to support the bill for a tax surcharge, which was important to the Administration. There had been reports of much White House arm twisting in the House of Representatives. Senators, particularly those of the same party as the president, pride themselves on their independence from the executive branch. And though the vice-president is the presiding officer of the Senate, he is definitely considered a representative of the executive branch, so when Agnew began urging Republicans to line up behind the President, his activity was resented. Hubert Humphrey had lobbied. Lyndon Johnson had lobbied. "Every vice-president since I've been here has lobbied," said a Senate official who has been there since 1947. He sympathized with Agnew, but conceded that in some indefinable way, the new vice-president had crossed the line separating proper and improper lobbying.

Agnew's transgression may have been primarily symbolic. Senator Jordan is a touchy and independent man, even by Senate standards. Just before the vote, the Vice-president left the chair, strolled over to him, and while reiterating his own and the President's hope that Jordan would support the bill, placed his hand on the Senator's arm, as he would have done if he were actually going to twist it. Jordan was outraged. He later told a luncheon meeting of the Republican Policy Committee that he would automatically vote against any bill the Vice-president pressed him to support. Other senators at the meeting expressed displeasure at the Vice-president's unsenatorial conduct, but Senator Gordon Allott, the Policy Committee chairman, defended Agnew by saying that the Vice-president himself realized that he had needlessly upset some senators, and had learned a lesson. Allott had a written apology to prove it. Later, during the 1970 campaign, Agnew made more Senate Republicans angry, with his attacks on Senator Charles Goodell, who was seeking reelection in New York. Though they all knew, or should have known, that Agnew was carrying out orders of the President in this case, they felt his remarks were a little personal. More about that later. Democratic senators, particularly liberal ones, were cool to the new vice-president from the start, as a result of his role in the 1968 campaign. The chill became glacial before long. Agnew's outspokenness got him into trouble. One Senate custom that vice-presidents are expected to follow concerns the way in which members speak about each other, in the chamber and out; the worst enemies oil their criticisms so that no hint of the enmity is heard. If one senator believes another is deliberately not telling the truth, he may say, "My esteemed colleague has been misinformed if he believes that the statement he just made is true. I am sure the honorable gentleman will see upon closer examination that the facts in the case are as follows. . . ." But once when Agnew thought Senator J. William Fulbright of Arkansas had made a misstatement of fact, he said, "He lies in his teeth." Also, as we shall see in more detail later, in the 1970 campaign his repeated and very pointed attacks on a half dozen or so liberal Democratic senators and candidates for the Senate were more personal than custom allows. For example, when Representative John Tunney made routine but apparently erroneous accusations about spending cutbacks that would affect California's economy, Agnew charged, "He lied twice."

Agnew was also making enemies by his attacks on the Senate doves, who were trying to change American policy in Vietnam. Most of what he said about them was not much more personal or critical than what some of them were saying about him (Senator Fulbright called him "smart aleck" on one occasion, "upstart" on another), but, once more, his way of speaking was unsenatorial, in the senators' view. He attacked the Hatfield-McGovern proposal to cut off funds for the war as "a blueprint for the first defeat in the history of the United States," and said that while he was not questioning the sponsors' patriotism, he wondered if they "really give a damn." The total effect of the speech was "inflammatory," said Hatfield. Also, Agnew's criticizing of some senators while he was on trips abroad was regarded as very much a breach of etiquette. The net effect of all this was that after daily attendance for several months, Agnew seldom spent any time in the Senate or in his Senate Office Building suite. When a close vote was expected, and his tie-breaker might be crucial, he presided, but otherwise he was busy elsewhere.

For the first two months of the Nixon-Agnew administration,

the Vice-president was assigned an office in the White House. The President said this unusual arrangement had been adopted in order to familiarize the Vice-president with the job of president, but most outsiders interpreted it to mean that the President wanted to keep a close watch on Agnew, and prevent his making any more mistakes of the sort that had characterized his campaign. In any case, the arrangement did not last long. In the spring Agnew moved into an office in the Executive Office Building, next door on Pennsylvania Avenue, which vice-presidents traditionally use, and which almost all of Agnew's staff had occupied from the beginning. He also had an office on Capitol Hill, with a staff headed by veteran senatorial staff functionary Walter Mote.

Most of the people in the Pennsylvania Avenue office had been brought over from Maryland. C. Stanley Blair was chief of staff. Herbert Thompson was head of press relations. Arthur Sohmer was administrative assistant to the Vice-president. Frank DeCosta, Jr., who had succeeded the unhappy Dr. Ware in Annapolis as civil-rights adviser, was legislative assistant. Mrs. Rosenwald was a speechwriter. Jerome Wolff was a science adviser. Significantly, when Agnew sought a man with Washington experience to join his team, he selected C. D. Ward, who had been counsel for the National Association of Counties. The DeCosta appointment also tells a lot about Agnew. DeCosta is a Negro; he told Agnew he wanted a job that his legal background qualified him for, not a civil-rights type of job, and Agnew, in the fashion of the 1950's-liberal, was pleased to accommodate him. DeCosta was thirty-three when he came to Washington, a handsome man who used the words "Negro" and "black" interchangeably and unselfconsciously. He had grown up in comfortable, middle-class college-campus surroundings in the South ("I can't say I know what it is like to live in a black slum," he says), became a successful lawyer in Baltimore, then an assistant state attorney general, before joining Agnew. He lived in one of Baltimore's finest—and barely integrated—neighborhoods. Starting as legislative assistant to the Vice-president, he progressed to deputy chief of staff and counselor. Both men shared a belief in the old civil-rights goal of removing barriers to equal opportunity. Period. Whatever they felt about assisting the black poor was unrelated to what they felt about civil rights.

Under the law, Vice-president Agnew was a member of the National Security Council. President Nixon created a domestic equivalent, the Urban Affairs Council (later renamed the Domestic Council, and somewhat changed); Agnew was appointed vice-chairman of that, and usually presided at the meetings. The President also named him head of the new Office of Intergovernmental Relations, which was meant to make it easier for governors, mayors, and other local officials to get assistance from Washington. Some governors later complained that the office did not work as they had anticipated, but some mayors protested that the staff was much more responsive to governors than to them. Mayor Ivan Allen, Jr., of Atlanta and Vice-president Agnew engaged in a near shouting match at one meeting in the White House attended by a number of local officials, with Allen contending that it was difficult for a mayor to have to go through his governor to get Federal aid, particularly when, as in his case, the governor was Lester Maddox. Former Governor Agnew said the mayors would just have to do the best they could.

Another new assignment for the Vice-president was chairmanship of the Committee on School Desegregation, established to assist Southern schools deal with the problems of desegregation. At the end of the 1960's, fifteen years after the Supreme Court decision forbidding separate but equal schools, the South had finally run out of delays, and a great deal of school desegregation was taking place in the region. Agnew was apparently only a front man, the committee being run by Robert Mardian of the Justice Department, and George Schultz, the Secretary of Labor, who took over the new and powerful Office of Management and Budget. As defined by the President, Agnew's role with respect to school desegregation was more political than operational. He was popular in the South after the 1968 campaign, and became even more popular in 1969 and 1970 as he made speeches defending the South against its critics. One example of the political Agnew at work came when he spoke to a meeting of the Southern Governors Conference, at Williamsburg, Virginia. He had prepared a speech making the point that the Administration was not retreating on schools, but was being just as firm in Chicago as in the South. He changed that at the last minute, because, according to one report, he heard that Governor Lester Maddox of Georgia was planning a walkout to protest Nixon's efforts to require compliance with the law.

Agnew ad-libbed, "I'm against busing those children to other neighborhoods simply to achieve an integrated status of a larger geographical entity." Maddox didn't walk out, but then the governors turned around and approved a resolution that favored "restraint and good judgment" when busing was required. Thus the Administration had been made to appear more conservative than the Southern governors.

Agnew was not just speaking his own mind on this. The President made it clearer and clearer in the following months that he was very much against "busing just to achieve a racial mix," and even opposed his own Department of Health, Education, and Welfare on this matter, overruling departmental plans for Austin, Texas, schools and publicly rebuking the officials who had drafted and approved the plans. Race relations was always ticklish for the Administration, drawn one way by its traditions as the party of Lincoln, and another by its belief that not only the South but the suburbs would penalize a party that tried to do very much in this field. One of the biggest fights within the Nixon administration family was over the question of desegregating the suburbs by requiring that they include low-rent housing projects among their plans as a condition for receiving Federal grants for other programs. Secretary of Housing and Urban Development George Romney favored such an approach. Attorney General John Mitchell opposed it. Mitchell won, but Romney did get the President to support suits to prevent suburbs from deliberately zoning out low-rent projects. Agnew agreed with the presidential policy, but curiously, in view of his background, he was not a principal in the debate over the policy.

Indeed, President Nixon believed in vice-presidents being more political than policy-oriented. Vice-president Agnew accepted and fulfilled that job with gusto. He worked hard on all his committee assignments, too, but had relatively little impact on policy, whether domestic or foreign. In both of these areas, he and those who thought like him lost out in the arguments over important programs and initiatives.

New Towns, Welfare

The two Agnew ideas in which Richard Nixon had first expressed interest back in early 1968 dealt with aiding the cities, by creating new towns and by federalizing welfare. Agnew's point was that the influx of the rural poor was destroying the cities. Moving some of the poor out to new towns and encouraging others to remain in the rural South by making welfare payments uniform through federalization might tend to reduce the poverty population of the big cities, he believed. There is some question about his underlying theory. It is doubtful that by the late 1960's there was much migration directly from the rural South to the urban North. The more likely migration route was from the rural South, to the urban South, and then to the urban North. It is also questionable that welfare checks were as much a lure to migrants as were job opportunities. In Maryland, the welfare recipients were largely old residents, the average family having been there five years before applying for relief. Nevertheless, Agnew's ideas, being directed at the disproportionate poverty population in big cities, which was the core of the problem, would have helped some.

Agnew should have been an expert on new towns, since one of the few real ones was being developed in his state. That was Columbia, located between Baltimore and Washington. The developer, Baltimore mortgage banker James Rouse, had contributed to Agnew's gubernatorial campaign. When Agnew became governor, state assistance to Columbia in the form of new highways and so forth was among the requests he granted. One form of aid Agnew granted new-town developers stirred up another of those not-infrequent storms of accusations of impropriety against him. In 1968 the General Assembly passed a law aimed at closing a loophole in the state's farm-assessment law. Farmland was assessed and taxed at a lower rate than other land. Speculators bought farmland, developed it, and sold it, all the while paying taxes as if the land were being used for agricultural purposes. Some developers bought the land and held it for long periods while its value grew, but still paid the low farm-assessment tax. The new law said that farmland sold for seven times more than its assessed price would lose its farm classification and its low assessment. Thus it would be more highly taxed. The original 1968 bill exempted land being used for new towns, but the General Assembly deleted the exemption. Agnew vetoed the bill. Delegate Blair Lee met with Agnew for twenty minutes to try to talk him out of the veto, emerged "livid with anger," in the words of a witness, and charged Agnew with selling out the state to pay off big campaign contributors, several of whom were buying up farmland for development. Agnew later defended his veto by saying, "The greatest problem facing all of us today is that of the urban areas. . . . The only feasible answer seems to be an increased emphasis on the planning and orderly development of newly populated areas. . . . The capital to plan, develop, and maintain such population centers must be from private not public sources." The following January the General Assembly upheld the veto.

But Agnew's interest in new towns was abstract. He attended a ground breaking at Columbia before the town was officially opened, before there were any residents, then never returned to watch it grow. After he became vice-president several Cabinet members, led by George Romney, went to Columbia representing the Urban Affairs Council to take a detailed tour, but Agnew did not accompany them.

Shortly after he took office as vice-president, Agnew did convene two new-towns conferences of state, local, and Federal officials to discuss new-towns legislation. The meetings gave the idea much-needed visibility, and eventually Congress passed new-towns legislation, but it did not provide support for the kind of development that now interested Agnew—the so-called "free-standing" new towns, built miles away from any other city. The legislation emphasized, instead, satellite new towns, close to or in the suburbs of metropolitan areas, and "new towns in town," making use of reclaimed or previously unused land in an old city. Congressional Democrats and members of the Administration both took credit for the bill. An Urban Affairs Council subcommittee had recommended legislation much like that introduced by Democrats in the House, but Agnew's role in formulating this legislation was minimal, in part because of the organizational situation—the vice-president is not a member of any of the subcommittees, where the real work is done on proposals—but in part because so much of his time was spent on political chores for the President.

Agnew was more involved in the intra-administration fight over the President's most dramatic domestic proposal, his scheme for the reform of the welfare system, to be known as family assistance. Critics found the existing program hopeless, saddling state governments with ever-increasing costs, leading to the breakup of families in states where employed males were not eligible for aid no matter how little they earned, and seemingly paralyzing millions of the poor in a welfare culture where attempts at productive life were discouraged. The Nixon proposal was revolutionary in that it called for the establishment of a minimum welfare payment, to be guaranteed by the Federal Government, and for payments to the working poor to bring their income up to another minimum.

Agnew had originally favored federalizing welfare and establishing national standards for the level of welfare payments. Not long after he came into the Federal Government he discarded the idea of standards, believing that it would be too difficult to work out a formula to allow higher payments in high-cost areas than in low-cost areas, while making the same payments everywhere would be unfair to recipients in big cities of the North (since the compromise figure would be too low there) and to the working people in such places as rural communities (since the compromise figure would be higher than could be earned in some jobs in such areas). More fundamentally, he had begun to believe that the so-called cycle of welfare, in which a way of life based on receiving welfare is passed from generation to generation, had to be broken. To him this meant taking children out of the "environment" of a family on welfare and placing them with working-class families. He thought changes in the adoption laws and foster-parent programs would best serve that end. He became an expert in this field, and—even his critics within the Administration conceded— quite eloquent on the subject. As far as the guaranteed income and assistance to the working poor were concerned, he was never willing to go beyond endorsement of a pilot program, which he did recommend at one Urban Affairs Council meeting.

The Vice-president sided with the conservative Arthur Burns in the argument over the nature and scope of welfare reform. Burns was a White House counselor in 1969, when the argument was being conducted. He later became chairman of the Federal Reserve Board. His principal goal was to keep the program's cost down. Another White House official, the Democrat Daniel P. Moynihan, who was the President's urban-affairs adviser, was the leading advocate of the more liberal and expensive approach. When it began to look as if no compromise was going to be forthcoming, after several Cabinet, Cabinet committee, and Urban Affairs Council meetings, Agnew undertook to arrange a compromise between the Burns and the Moynihan views. He apparently acted on his own initiative, without being aware that the President had ordered Secretary Schultz to draft a proposal that would meet as many of the conservatives' objections as possible while still carrying out the major Nixon goals. Schultz did so, and by the summer of 1969, it had been made clear to all members of the administration that Schultz's plan was the one the President wanted.

In August, the President met with the Vice-president, most members of the Cabinet, and those staff members who had been working on welfare reform at Camp David, the Maryland mountain retreat. When the President had presented the program, Finch and Schultz were the only Cabinet members to endorse it. The President emphasized that his mind was made up, so the opponents did not make any lengthy or substantive comments—except for Vice-president Agnew. He delivered a long attack on the principle that the nation ought to guarantee anybody anything. He expressed his other misgivings in a manner that—since the President had made it clear that he was not to be swayed—some found embarrassing, even though they thought the Vice-president's argument was forceful and heartfelt. Finally the President declared, with a meaningful look at his Vice-president, that it was time for arguments to end and for all to "get on the team." But Agnew got in a last word. He had to leave the meeting to go to the Senate, where a close vote was expected on the anti-ballistic-missile system; he might have to cast a deciding vote. As he reached the door, he said to the President, "If there is a tie, may I telephone you before I vote and ask you whether you've changed your mind about this welfare program?"

Outside, in the eyes of the public, the Vice-president was a loyal member of the team, giving his support to the President's plans for welfare reform, and in particular, the President's proposal for revenue sharing—transferring Federal funds to state and local governments with no strings attached. Agnew was the leading campaigner for that program. In the first six months of 1971, for instance, he made eighteen separate speeches around the country on behalf of revenue sharing. The President's proposal earmarked 5 billion dollars for sharing. According to executive-department staff members who worked on the proposal, the choice of that figure was due in large part to Agnew. Governor Rockefeller of New York had wanted 10 billion dollars, and he probably spoke for his fellow governors. Both Attorney General Mitchell and George Schultz, director of the Office of Management and Budget, among others, argued inside the White House initially that no more than 2 billion dollars could be spared. Agnew fought for the compromise figure; among his persuasive arguments was the point that 2 billion dollars was too small an amount to gain any political benefit.

The Nixon version was being held up in Congress in the late summer of 1971. Representative Wilbur Mills and Senator Edmund Muskie were offering counterproposals. Mill's opposition was especially important, since he was chairman of the Ways and Means Committee. He wanted more money to go to the cities, but not unconditionally. Muskie also wanted more money to go to big cities, but was in favor of a no-strings approach. Both these men were Democrats and both had national ambitions in 1971, and they were looking to the cities, traditionally Democratic, in part perhaps because of those ambitions, though their argument that the cities needed the money more than state or county governments was undeniable. The Nixon proposal did not overlook the political fact that Republicans were stronger in statehouses and suburban courthouses. The controversy was like the one between the Cooper-Hughes and Hughes-Agnew-Lee tax-reform proposals for Maryland. In each case Agnew favored the program which was more beneficial to suburbia than to the cities. In Washington in 1971 the political impact of suburban growth was not yet as great as it had been in Annapolis in 1967. Also, the political rivalry between the parties was such that the Mills or the Muskie proposal would be supported by many Democrats who might otherwise have favored the Nixon plan. Furthermore, urban interests were better represented by lobbyists in Washington than suburban interests, an urban alliance having been formed during the years of the Johnson administration. However, in this respect it appeared that the suburbs might soon catch up. Suburban county officials began in earnest talking about a more effective Washington lobby at a National Association of Counties convention in 1971. Whatever formal lobby develops in the future, the sheer weight of suburban growth assures it of effectiveness.

Chapter Fourteen

A Household Word

Protesting the Protesting

IN SEPTEMBER, 1969, C. Stanley Blair and other top-level members of Agnew's staff met to consider a presidential command for a more active, visible, and political Agnew. The most politically charged issue of the day was the war in Vietnam. Plans were being made by the Vietnam Moratorium Committee to hold big end-the-war rallies in Washington and in major cities across the nation the following month. The announcement by many prominent Democrats who had supported President Johnson on the war issue, or who had been silent, that they would speak, or otherwise support the committee's Vietnam Moratorium Day, gave the growing and increasingly activist peace movement a political dimension. Apparently at this September meeting, and at subsequent meetings, the staff consensus was that Agnew should attack the war protesters and the very liberal young in general, and isolate them from the "mainstream" of American citizens.

It is hard to discover exactly how much coordination there was between the White House staff and the Agnew staff in the next four weeks. There appeared to be a very close working arrangement. Moratorium Day was to be on October 15. On the fourteenth, Agnew came out of a meeting with the President to lead the Administration counterattack. He told reporters that North Vietnam had sent an open letter to the American people in support of the Moratorium. "This message from a Communist regime is a shocking intrusion into the affairs of the American people by an enemy power," a grim-faced Agnew said. He said the Administration supported the right of Americans to demonstrate (even though President Nixon had said he would pay no attention to the demonstration), but the North Vietnam message proved—or would be interpreted as proving—that many well-meaning persons were being used to support that country's aims. He asked the organizers of the Moratorium Day to disavow the message.

Some Moratorium leaders, and some other opponents of the Administration and its policies, believed Nixon was using Agnew and the North Vietnam message to chill the protest, to take as much political heat from it as possible, even to discourage attendance. That may have been true. It was also true, however, that Agnew was honestly outraged by the intruding message—and by the protest, itself, message or no. He had spoken against antiwar politics and demonstrations as early as 1967, arguing not only that President Johnson deserved support but that if there were unity on the war issue, more attention could be paid to other issues which, Agnew said, were more important.

The Moratorium itself was a success from the organizers' point of view. There were large crowds in many big cities—40,000 in Washington, 100,000 in Boston—and news-making events also took place in many small and medium-sized towns. The protesters were a good cross section in age and social class. The events were for the most part extremely orderly. The Moratorium indicated that the peace movement was a political force to be reckoned with. So on the following Sunday, October 19, when Vice-president Agnew went to New Orleans to deliver a speech attacking the activities of the fifteenth and the point of view they signified, he probably was being both political and philosophical. He delivered a speech heard round the world.

Most of the long speech was a reasoned marshaling of the arguments supporting President Nixon's policies in Vietnam and in other areas of military and nonmilitary activity. It was boiler plate, prepared by the White House staff, good but routine. The preliminary remarks made the news.

Sometimes [he began] it appears that we are reaching a time when our senses and our minds will no longer respond to moderate stimulation. We seem to be approaching an age of the gross. Persuasion through speeches and books is too often discarded for disruptive demonstrations aimed at bludgeoning the unconvinced into action.

The young—and by this I don't mean by any stretch of the imagination all the young, but I am talking about those who claim to speak for the young—at the zenith of physical power and sensitivity, overwhelm themselves with drugs and artificial stimulants. Subtlety is lost, and fine distinctions based on acute reasoning are carelessly ignored in a head-

long jump to a predetermined conclusion. Life is visceral rather than intellectual, and the most visceral practitioners of life are those who characterize themselves as intellectuals.

Truth is "revealed" rather than logically proved, and the principal
infatuations of today revolve around the social sciences, those subjects
which can accommodate any opinion and about which the most reckless
conjecture cannot be discredited.

Education is being redefined at the demand of the uneducated to suit
the ideas of the uneducated. The student now goes to college to pro-
claim rather than to learn. The lessons of the past are ignored and oblit-
erated in a contemporary antagonism known as the generation gap. A
spirit of national masochism prevails, encouraged by an effete corps of
impudent snobs who characterize themselves as intellectuals.

It is in this setting of dangerous oversimplification that the war in
Vietnam achieves its greatest distortion.

The recent Vietnam Moratorium is a reflection of the confusion that
exists in America today. Thousands of well motivated young people, con-
ditioned since childhood to respond to great emotional appeals, saw fit to
demonstrate for peace. Most did not stop to consider that the leaders of
the Moratorium had billed it as a massive public outpouring of sentiment
against the foreign policy of the President of the United States. Most did
not care to be reminded that the leaders of the Moratorium refused to
disassociate themselves from the objective enunciated by the enemy in
Hanoi.

If the Moratorium had any use whatever, it served as an emotional
purgative for those who feel the need to cleanse themselves of their lack
of ability to offer a constructive solution to the problem.

Unfortunately, we have not seen the end. The hard-core dissidents
and professional anarchists within the so-called "peace movement" will
continue to exacerbate the situation. November 15 is already planned—
wilder, more violent, and equally barren of constructive result.

Those words made headlines, and so did the reaction to them.
Senator Mike Mansfield, the Senate Democratic Leader, announced that the speech embarrassed him. Senator George McGovern, the leading Democratic critic of the war, said, "If Mr. Agnew's
speech is a measure of this administration's moral and mental sensitivity, God help America." Senators J. William Fulbright and
Edmund S. Muskie also attacked Agnew. Even the Senate Republican Leader, Hugh Scott of Pennsylvania, denounced Agnew's
"name-calling," though without mentioning Agnew's name.

The New York Times may have spoken for most of Agnew's adversaries when it said:

Vice President Agnew demonstrated a truly monumental insensitivity to
the most profound concern of millions of Americans—and particularly the

nation's youth—when he described last week's Vietnam Moratorium as the creation of "an effete corps of impudent snobs who characterize themselves as intellectuals." . . . The ominous strains in Mr. Agnew's words are that they equate support of the war with manliness, while describing as effete those who call for a redoubling of the nation's dedication to peace. It is the mark of insecure nations and politicians to mistake unquestioning support of military ventures as the test of patriotism. This is exactly the approach to the American destiny which the most articulate and politically alert sector of the nation's young intellectuals have questioned and rejected. Mr. Agnew's incredible obtuseness can only add to the frustration of millions of Americans—young and old alike—who believe that rational dissent must be given a fair hearing. His insensitivity to this principle of American democracy will give comfort to those who preach the gospel of disruption and violence.

On two separate occasions in the following week presidential press secretary Ron Ziegler declared that the President had not seen the Agnew text in advance. He said pointedly that the White House had seen in advance the speech Secretary of State William Rogers delivered on October 20, one saying that the Moratorium protesters displayed a "dignified" concern for peace in Vietnam— "and we listen to these voices with respect." It almost seemed that at his briefings Ziegler spent more time that week answering questions about Agnew than answering questions about Nixon. There were more questions about Agnew's speech than about the war itself. Many questioners were trying to find out how much the President had to do with the delivery of the speech, directly or indirectly, and what his reaction to it had been.

Neither the President nor his staff had anything to do with the news-making first part of the Vice-president's remarks. Mrs. Rosenwald had written an introduction for the boiler plate, but as he had been doing increasingly in the past few months, Agnew had torn up her speech and written his own, coming down to his Executive Office Building suite on Saturday, October 18, to draft it in longhand, then calling a typist. The President's influence on the composition of the speech had been indirect, arising first, out of his summer suggestion that Agnew become more political, and second, out of his expression to Agnew of his own enmity to the Moratorium, at their meeting on the fourteenth, according to one version of the conversations there.

Certainly the decision to use the Vice-president in this way was paying off from Agnew's point of view. "Agnew" was a "household word," said Senator Mansfield. It sure was. In immediate response to his speech he received five thousand letters, with better than two to one in support of him. By October 27, the White House staff had come to the conclusion that Agnew's New Orleans speech had been on balance helpful, despite the liberal and Democratic response that had dominated the newspapers and television. At a staff conference that day, James Keogh, the President's editor and writer, reported that on a trip to his home in Omaha, he had found that Agnew was very popular. White House counselor Harry Dent, Senator Thurmond's old assistant, said he had noticed the same thing on a visit to Sacramento. Presidential aides who had previously denied that Nixon had approved the New Orleans speech, began telling reporters in Washington that the Vice-president had been given freedom and blessings to continue. On October 30, President Nixon finally commented. He was addressing a nationalities group at a White House reception. Agnew was also there. The President said, "I am very proud to have the Vice-president with his Greek background in our administration, and he has done a great job for this administration."

The next day the Vice-president made another speech, in Harrisburg, Pennsylvania. Again he attacked dissent and protest and political leaders who did not object to protests. One journalist called the speech a perfect statement of middle American impatience. It was also a perfect statement of Agnew's impatience, and of his philosophy with respect to protest. It was his *summa* on the democratic process, so to speak. This speech was prepared by Mrs. Rosenwald. Because so many of her recent efforts had been discarded, she was careful to put this one together almost exclusively from statements previously made by Agnew, in speeches, in memoranda, or in conversation. Then Agnew edited the speech to intensify the "flavor," as she later put it. For instance, he was said to be the author of these headline-making (and editorial-making) thoughts:

"It is time to question the credentials of [the protesters'] leaders. And, if in questioning, we disturb a few people, I say it is time they were disturbed. If, in challenging, we polarize the American people, I say it is time for a positive polarization."

And:

"America cannot afford to write off a whole generation for the decadent thinking of a few. America cannot afford to divide over their demagoguery, or to be deceived by their duplicity, or to let their license destroy liberty. We can, however, afford to separate them from our society—with no more regret than we should feel over discarding rotten apples from a barrel."

Agnew had topped what many had thought was an untoppable effort—the New Orleans speech—but he was just beginning. He was to deliver two more speeches that first fall of his vice-presidency that would start a debate and a conflict that have not yet ended.

The Media Blasts: Television

Both Herbert Thompson and Mrs. Rosenwald wrote speeches for Agnew during his early months in Washington. So did some members of the White House staff, on occasion. That is a routine arrangement. In 1971, Lyndon Johnson aide John Roche described in his newspaper column how he had written all of Vice-president Hubert Humphrey's speeches on Vietnam. But until after the Harrisburg speech, no major or important address had been written for the Vice-president by White House writers. Three days after Agnew spoke in Harrisburg, President Nixon went on television, on all three networks, to appeal to "the great silent majority" to support his Vietnam policies. His own tone was softer and more understanding of his opponents than the Vice-president's had been, but he was emphatic about sticking with the policies he had been following. Afterward, as is customary, network journalists commented on the broadcast. Much of what they said was critical of the President, his policies, and his speech. Patrick Buchanan was in charge of a news-monitoring operation for the President; he was also his "conservative" speechwriter. (Raymond Price had become the "liberal" writer. There were several other presidential speechwriters, working under Keogh.) Buchanan wrote a long and blistering attack on the performance of the networks following the November 3 speech. This was to be delivered by Agnew. The supercharged quality of the speech caused Mrs. Rosenwald concern. She thought it a little too hot in spots, and suggested some changes, as did Herbert Thompson. Only a few important changes were made, however. The result was almost a white paper on network journalism, if not, as the networks interpreted it, blackmail.

Agnew delivered the speech at a meeting of the Midwest Regional Republican Committee in Des Moines, Iowa, on November 13. The second Vietnam demonstration had just started in Washington, a three-day affair that was to bring 250,000 antiwar protesters, mostly young, to the capital (and 100,000 to San Francisco in a West Coast version). Advance notice of the nature of the Vice-president's speech caused the three television networks to cancel their usual Thursday prime-time fare and broadcast it instead, providing the greatest political publicity windfall ever enjoyed by a vice-president—an audience estimated by one network official at fifty million. Agnew attacked the networks and their top newsmen specifically for their comment on the President's speech and generally for their role in preparing the news day by day. "When the President completed his address—an address that he spent weeks in preparing—his words and policies were subject to instant analysis and querulous criticism," Agnew said. He charged that the majority of the commentators were hostile to the President.* He said that while "every American has a right to disagree with the President of the United States . . . the President of the United States has a right to communicate directly with the people who elected him, and the people of this country have a right to make up their minds and form their own opinions about a Presidential address without having the President's words and thoughts characterized through the prejudices of hostile critics before they can be digested. . . . The purpose of my remarks tonight is to focus your attention on this little group of men who not only enjoy a right of instant rebuttal to every Presidential address, but more importantly, wield a free hand in selecting, presenting and interpreting the great issues of our Nation."

Agnew identified this "little group" as the "anchormen" and top news executives of the three networks. He said their coverage and commentary "make or break . . . a moratorium or a war." In his view, their power over public opinion was the most concentrated

---

* The commentators had been professional journalists, with the exception of Averell Harriman. Agnew was most bitter about Harriman's remarks. He compared him to the Ancient Mariner, "under some heavy compulsion to justify his failures to anyone who will listen," and said he had failed when he was the United States negotiator with North Vietnam.

in history. "What do Americans know of these men?" he asked. His answer was that Americans know that they all live in Washington or New York, "read the same newspapers and draw their political views from the same sources. Worse, they talk constantly to one another, thereby providing artificial reinforcement to their shared viewpoints." They are not objective and they do not share the views of most Americans, he continued, and wasn't it time to question this concentration of power enjoyed by "a monopoly sanctioned and licensed by the government. . . . [?] Perhaps it is time that the networks were made more responsive to the views of the nation and more responsible to the people they serve."

Such talk is threatening to broadcast journalists, who are well aware of the government's licensing power over the television and radio stations which the networks own. Agnew then went on: "I am not asking for government censorship or any other kind of censorship." Whatever calming effect this remark might have had, was quickly overcome by what followed: "Advocates for the networks have claimed a First Amendment right to the same unlimited freedoms held by the great newspapers of America. The situations are not identical." The undeniable net import of the speech so far was that the networks had better watch it or they would lose the licenses for the stations they owned, and they had better not try to pull any of that First Amendment stuff, either. Agnew went on to quote some liberals in opposition to the power of the networks—among them Walter Lippmann, at length. Then he returned to criticizing the nature of network news. Particularly galling to him was the emphasis on controversy and conflict.

The speech was bold, and the howls of the network officials and journalists were prompt. So were criticisms of the speech by the newspapers, which had not been attacked. Yet. That the speech had had at least some little intimidating effect on the networks seems indicated by the fact that they did carry it, unscheduled. According to one newspaper television critic several months later, another immediate effect was a reduction in the coverage of the Vietnam demonstration in Washington that weekend; less time was devoted to it, this critic calculated, than to a patriotic rally in Washington the following summer. There has been much talk and disagreement in the broadcast industry about the ultimate net effect of the speech. It is impossible to say with certainty that this or that network news decision after November, 1969, was made because of fear of losing a license. The Columbia Broadcasting System's presentation of its now-famous program "The Selling of the Pentagon" long after the Agnew speech suggests that it was going on as before. The National Broadcasting Company and the American Broadcasting Company also aired criticisms of Administration activities with regularity after the speech.

The immediate reaction of the networks was to condemn Agnew, the President, and the speech as meant to be intimidating. The immediate reaction of the public was surprisingly pro-Agnew. NBC reported 1,900 telephone calls supporting Agnew and 1,600 opposing him. The White House reported 450 for Agnew's argument and 50 against it. An Associated Press survey of calls to twenty-one stations around the country turned up a two-to-one Agnew majority. The Republican National Committee commissioned a poll and found Agnew supported by 64 percent, with 24 percent opposed and the rest undecided. CBS said the letters it received were heavily pro-Agnew. And an ABC poll showed that 52 percent agreed with the proposition that the networks were biased, while only 33 percent did not agree—but a majority supported the right of the network to comment on a presidential talk. Finally, CBS devoted a full hour to the subject on the November 25 broadcast of the program "Sixty Minutes," interviewing all the anchormen, sending Walter Cronkite back to his hometown of St. Joseph, Missouri "to find out what people there think of him and all of us," as one of the hosts, Harry Reasoner, put it. (Mike Wallace was the other host. Reasoner later became anchorman on ABC's news show. Broadcast gossip had it that the moderately conservative Reasoner had replaced the liberal Frank Reynolds there because the White House had constantly complained about Reynolds.) What people thought of them, judging by the remarks televised at a luncheon the St. Joseph Chamber of Commerce put on for Cronkite, was that the networks were wrong. On specifics Cronkite could make points. For instance, the "instant analysis" criticized by Agnew was for Nixon's November 3 speech based on prior access to the text and a briefing of the newsmen by Henry Kissinger. But the general suspicion felt toward the networks came through clearly despite such arguments.

The middle section of this CBS program consisted of a discussion of the Agnew speech by the commentators. David Brinkley said that all administrations complained about news coverage. "All that's new is that this time—this time—it came in the form of a threat," he said. Howard K. Smith of ABC agreed that "there is a problem" of being negative. "I think we should welcome criticism. We need it. But I think we can insist it stop well short of intimidation." Eric Sevareid of CBS accused Agnew of using "patriotism as a club to try to silence his critics."

The theme that there was open, naked intimidation in the Agnew message was one the network men came back to again and again on that program and elsewhere. The third segment of the CBS show included appearances by President Nixon's director of communications, Herbert Klein, and President Johnson's first press secretary, Bill Moyers. Klein indicated that the speech had not been a presidential effort. He was asked whose decision it was "for the Vice-president to go ahead with this whole enterprise?"

"The decision was that of the Vice-president. He is his own man, he's an elected official, and it was his decision."

Klein was invited to appear on the program after Patrick Buchanan, who wrote the speech, and Clark Mollenhoff, also of the White House staff, had turned Wallace and Reasoner down. Mollenhoff was quoted later by the newspapers he formerly worked for, the Des Moines *Register* and *Tribune,* as saying the White House had prepared the speech. Klein did not say specifically that this hadn't happened; he only implied it. Moyers said such vice-presidential independence would have been very unusual in the previous administration, and added—very much to the point—that often President Johnson had Vice-president Humphrey express "the administration philosophy on issues that the President himself did not wish to speak to."

One ironic thing about the Vice-president's attack on the networks is that while he certainly agreed with the statements he was reading, he was, as he put it "a printed media man." His interest in newspapers and magazines was much more intense than his interest in broadcasting. And he had more grudges against specific journals than he had against any television journalists. In his Des Moines speech he made several statements which seemed to praise newspapers for separating news and opinion in a way he said the networks did not. His closing words were to that effect. Then a week later he took out after the printed media.

The Media Blasts: Newspapers

Long before the advent of what the Vice-president's staff came to refer to as the media blasts, Spiro Agnew had had his troubles with newspapers. Public officials do, sooner or later. It is not at all uncommon for officeholders to expect the press to limit itself to relaying to the public only that part of public business that the officials believe is "news." County executives and presidents are no exceptions. Agnew is unusual only in that, more than most, he has always retaliated when angry. When he was county executive he cut off official advertising in the Catonsville *Herald-Argus* and the Reisterstown *Community News,* because the owner wrote critically of his administration. "It's not a personal vendetta," Agnew said at the time. "It's because he consistently goes beyond the bounds of correct reporting. He never carries our side of the story. He never will print our replies to charges he has aired." When he was governor, Agnew at one point decided that reporters for the afternoon papers, the Baltimore *Evening Sun,* the Baltimore *News-American,* and the Washington *Star,* were "against" him, and stopped the practice of making important announcements alternately in the mornings and in the afternoon, giving all the news to the morning reporters instead.

The vice-presidential campaign left him with personal grudges against three newspapers in particular—the Baltimore *Sun,* the Washington *Post,* and *The New York Times.* He was angry at the *Sun* for two reasons. One, as he explained it later, concerned the conduct of the paper's staff just after he was nominated for the vice-presidency. Since he was unknown to most of the nation, reporters from everywhere descended on the *Sun's* convention headquarters for information about him. The *Sun's* reporters and editors, Agnew believed, described him in unflattering terms. The second reason Agnew disliked the *Sun* was that he felt his hometown newspaper should have been more proud of his honor. Instead, when the paper endorsed Richard Nixon for president, it also said, "Mr. Nixon's choice of Governor Agnew as the Vice-pres-

idential nominee has been a major flaw in his campaign." Agnew
was offended at the *Times* because of its editorials questioning his
ability and his integrity. He was angry at the *Post* because of the
Caligula's-horse editorial and other criticisms, and because he believed its news coverage of him was unfair. Members of Agnew's
staff like to point out that the "fat Jap" remark was made in a relaxed moment in the rear of a plane, in circumstances when what a
candidate says is completely off the record, and that the *Post* not
only used the remark, but took it out of the long story the reporter
filed and printed it as a separate front-page story several days afterward, after Agnew had arrived in Hawaii. Richard Harwood,
then the national news editor of the *Post*, now its full-time in-house
journalism critic, was responsible for that decision. He later called
it "a cheap shot" at Agnew. Agnew's retaliation was to exclude
Post reporters from his campaign plane, a decision quickly overridden by Herbert Klein. After he became vice-president, Agnew
barred representatives of the *Post* and the *Sun* from his plane on
his first two long international journeys.

But personal grudges, vendettas or not, constituted only one of
the elements in his attitude toward the press. In 1968, he was also
beginning to think differently of the press as a whole. He came to
see it as an entity, an estate, with its own philosophy and an interest in government different from that of other estates. This view
was a popular one in the Nixon administration. The first bit of advice John Mitchell gave George White in San Diego, just after the
convention, was, "the press is going left and the country is going
right." Daniel P. Moynihan, the presidential adviser and urban expert, charged in a long article in *Commentary* that the press had
become an Ivy Leaguish elite group, at least in Washington and
New York. And though this assertion cannot yet be substantiated
statistically, there is evidence that the best and most influential
newspapers are drawing increasingly on the prestigious schools for
young talent. This development may just reflect the fact that the
salaries offered by newspapers are increasingly competitive with
those of other businesses, rather than indicating any philosophical
or political trend. There is, however, also a growing feeling within
journalism that it has an adversary responsibility in a free society.
The Nixon-Agnew idea that the press must serve the government
in some way has been most eloquently and succinctly rejected by

Tom Wicker, Washington-based associate editor of *The New York Times*. He said in April, 1971, "We are even being told at exalted levels that the American press has something of a Marxist function —that it is our duty to serve the interests of the state—let's make it clear, and I believe we never have fully done so, that the press of America is not an adjunct of politics or an appendage of the government, but an estate of its own, with its own responsibilities and its own commitments." A short time before, Agnew had told Massachusetts editors he favored an "adversary, probing, suspicious" relationships between government and the press, but he wanted it to work both ways, so that he would probe the press as much as the press probed government. He had made this point also in his second media speech, in November, 1969.

The antinewspaper speech followed the Des Moines appearance by exactly a week. It was delivered in Montgomery, Alabama, and was once again a Nixon team effort, not initiated by the Agnew staff. Indeed, Mrs. Rosenwald and others on the Agnew staff thought the speech was a poor one, unfair and strained. She refused to work on it. Agnew, however, liked the speech and after some changes he delivered it, fully committed and even surer of himself than he had been the week before. The part of the speech that received the most attention was his warning against the "trend toward the monopolization of the great public information vehicles and the concentration of more and more power over public opinion in fewer and fewer hands." That this was a trend and that it represented a threat, almost no one could doubt. In Montgomery, for example, the only two daily newspapers were owned by the same corporation. There was only one television station. But Agnew did not mention that situation. Instead he attacked the Washington *Post* Company, which owned the paper, a television station and a radio station in Washington, and *Newsweek* magazine, "all grinding out the same editorial line—and this is not a subject you have seen debated on the editorial pages of the Washington *Post* or *The New York Times*." Then he attacked the *Times* for its "irresponsible" news judgments, which he blamed in part on the absence of competition from other papers. He gave as an example a story that had made the front page of other papers—the endorsement by 359 members of Congress of a Nixon policy in Vietnam—but had not even appeared in the *Times*.

As it turned out, the *Times* had carried the story, in a later edition than the one Agnew (or Buchanan) had seen. Also, the *Times* had recently published an editorial opposing monopolies in journalism. Agnew was also off base in using the *Times* as an example of a paper without competition, since the other morning newspaper in New York is the *Daily News*, which has the largest circulation in America (and is a solid supporter of Agnew and Nixon, and their policies and points of view). As for the *Post* Company situation, while the *Post* is the only morning paper in the capital, there are two afternoon papers owned by other corporations, making Washington one of only three cities in the country with newspapers representing three separate owners; furthermore, there are several radio stations and four VHF television stations in Washington. Therefore, many people interpreted the speech not as a comment on journalistic monopoly, but as an attack on the *Post* and the *Times*, thorns in the Administration's side. Senator Alan Cranston, a California Democrat, called the speech part of the Administration's "reign of verbal terror against the news media." Senator Jacob Javits said, "If in fact it is the enormous power and prestige of the President that stands behind the Vice-president's recent speeches—speeches that tend to intimidate those who invoke the traditions and rights guaranteed by the Bill of Rights—then we are in for a grave crisis."

There was little doubt that the President was behind the Vice-president. On December 8, the President was asked at a press conference, "What, if anything, in those speeches is there with which you disagree?"

His answer was, ". . . the Vice-president does not clear his speeches with me, just as I did not clear my speeches with President Eisenhower. However I believe that the Vice-president rendered a public service in talking in a very dignified and courageous way about a problem that many Americans are concerned about, that is, the coverage by the news media and particularly television news media of public figures." Despite the tricky opening, this answer did serve to keep the Agnew remarks in focus: "coverage . . . of public figures," *not* concentration of power, was what was bothering the Administration.

Meanwhile, Agnew's press aide, Herbert Thompson, said the Vice-president planned no more such speeches for a while. "He has said his piece and focused attention on the media. He takes great satisfaction in having promoted discussion among the media and the public and he sees nothing to be gained by continuing to take part in the dialogue." It was not until the following spring, after the American-Vietnamese invasion of Cambodia had set off rioting on campuses and the killing of students at Kent State and Jackson State by law officials, events that led to severe editorial criticism of the President's actions and the Vice-president's rhetoric, that Mr. Agnew returned to the dialogue. Speaking at a Republican party dinner in Houston, Agnew quoted at length from many newspapers and magazines (again the grist came from Buchanan, who maintained a press-monitoring operation, but Agnew initiated the idea this time) that condemned Nixon and Agnew. Presented all together, selected for their impact, the criticisms did have an almost hysterical tone. All of this led up to Agnew's point—that he would continue to speak out just as angrily as he had in the past.

Ladies and gentlemen, you have heard a lot of wild, hot rhetoric tonight—none of it mine. This goes on daily in the editorial pages of some very large, very reputable newspapers in this country—not all of them in the East by a long shot. And it pours out of the television set and the radio in a daily torrent, assailing our ears so incessantly we no longer register shock at the irresponsibility and thoughtlessness behind the statements.

"But you are the Vice President," they say to me. "You should choose your language more carefully."

Nonsense. I have sworn I will uphold the Constitution against all enemies, foreign and domestic. Those who would tear our country apart or try to bring down its government are enemies, whether here or abroad, whether destroying libraries and classrooms on a college campus, or firing at American troops from a rice paddy in Southeast Asia.

I have an obligation to all of the people of the United States to call things as I see them, and I have an obligation to the President to support his actions in the best manner that I can. I choose my own words, and I set the tone of my speeches. As he said at his recent press conference, I am responsible for what I say. And I intend to be heard above the din even if it means raising my voice. . . .

It does bother me, however, that the press—as a group—regards the First Amendment as its own private preserve. Every time I criticize what I consider to be excesses or faults in the news business, I am accused of repression, and the leaders of the various media professional groups wave the First Amendment as they denounce me. That happens to be *my* amendment too. It guarantees *my* free speech as much as it does their freedom of the press. So I hope that will be remembered the next time a "muzzle Agnew" campaign is launched. There is room for all of us—and for our divergent views—under the First Amendment.

The gulf between the Vice-president and the press had become so great it could never be spanned. They were at war. If Agnew's remarks in Houston do not prove that, perhaps these words from William B. Arthur, editor of *Look* magazine, do. He delivered a lengthy speech to a professional journalism fraternity on the subject of "Agnewism." His conclusion was, ". . . be unafraid. Fight them on all fronts. Fight them and make sure they know that the only silence they will obtain is over our dead bodies. And when we answer our enemies, let's don't always be so polite. Let's remind them from time to time that if they don't like a free press in a free country, then they can find what they do like in a place such as the U.S.S.R., or perhaps a Nazi Germany would suit them better. Or, maybe a place called hell."

Chapter Fifteen

Students and Radiclibs

Big Man on Campus

WHEN A MAGAZINE EDITOR could tell the Vice-president of the United States to go to hell, and when editorial cartoonists could, as the Washington *Post*'s Herblock did, draw a cartoon in which the ammunition used for shooting down students was labeled with Agnewian phrases, it was obvious that for the Fourth Estate, Agnew had become a real enemy. This was the situation in the spring of 1970. But another segment of American society was even more antipathetic to the Vice-president. This segment was the university community, particularly its student members. Agnew's anti-protest speeches of the previous fall had been aimed at students, faculty members, and college administrators. After the Kent State shootings, which were followed by the slaying of students at Mississippi's Jackson State College and by the shutting down of hundreds of colleges across the country that bitter spring, Agnew reacted to criticism of his attacks by escalating his rhetoric. He seemed to be going beyond what his aim had originally been in 1969—the isolation of the rebellious students from the others. He seemed to be trying to isolate the entire university community from the rest of the country, using it as object of attack because that approach was popular with working-class Democrats and independents as well as with the conservative core of the Republican party. Certainly this was the interpretation many liberal and moderate members of the university community put on the Agnew attacks.

Whether Agnew's speeches were isolating the "bad" students from the good, or the entire university from the other elements of society, one thing was clear: he was isolating the Administration from the universities. In October, 1970, the University Index Collegian Opinion Poll asked 1,124 students, "How would you rate your opinion of the Vice-president?" The results were: "very favorable,"

7.95 percent; "somewhat favorable," 19.8 percent; "very unfavorable," 34.9 percent; "somewhat unfavorable," 29.0 percent. Only one Democratic student in seven said Agnew represented his views, and only four Republican students in ten did.

In April, 1970, Agnew's attacks on the academic community began to focus more on the universities themselves than on protesting students. Two weeks before the invasion of Cambodia, he criticized the plans of the University of Michigan to make the student body there 10 percent black by 1973. "The new socialism," he called it. Michigan President Robben Fleming replied to this and other Agnew remarks by saying, "It is sad to see the Vice-president . . . launch superficial attacks on universities for their failure to curb turbulence and for eroding standards by admitting black students. Every study of campus turbulence shows that it is directly related to national policies which are largely beyond the control of universities, but which are unpopular with the youth of the country."

The fact that every study also showed that student dissent, and especially student violence, was unpopular with the majority of the voters, explains in part what Agnew and the Administration were up to, and why, for instance, the anti-university speech just quoted was made at a party fund-raising dinner in Iowa, and his even earlier criticism of such educational policies as student determination of curricula and faculty was made in a Lincoln Day speech to the Illinois party faithful. That is not to say that there was no justification for Agnew's criticism of academic policies, or that he did not believe what he was saying. The new ideas bubbling up on campuses had some sincere opponents even among educators. Agnew was and always had been a firm believer in authority. The thought that students should participate as equals with professors or deans in deciding policy was abhorrent to him. He was a stern father himself, and had refused to allow his youngest daughter to participate in an antiwar protest. He said publicly and privately that he believed many youths were attracted to such dictators as Fidel Castro, Mao Tse-tung, and Ho Chi Minh because they needed authoritarian adults to help them and were not finding them in their families or on their campuses.

He was continually expressing these views in speeches and articles. That spring, after he had angered Michigan's President Fleming, he singled out Yale's president, Kingman Brewster, Jr., and the Cornell administration, again at a party fund-raising event, this time in Florida. Brewster had declared that he doubted that Black Panthers or other black revolutionaries could get a fair trial in the United States. Agnew in his speech paraphrased that statement, saying, "I do not feel that the students at Yale can get a fair impression of their country under the tutelage of Kingman Brewster." He called on Yale alumni to have Brewster fired. As for Cornell, it had been in the news when black revolutionaries took over a building. Newspaper photographs showing them holding rifles, with cartridge belts slung over their shoulders, had shocked even those who were sympathetic with black and university problems. Cornell had become something of a symbol for those who held little hope that the universities could deal with the urgency of young black intellectuals. Agnew told the Florida Republicans that the Cornell administration was so permissive that it had done nothing when students there "beat a dormitory president into unconsciousness." Cornell President Dale Corson wired him the next day that no such thing had happened. The event Agnew referred to had taken place at the University of Connecticut. Agnew responded that even so, Cornell had allowed violence to go unpunished, and he stood by his general point. If you've seen one university president, you've seen them all.

Two days later, Agnew met with Republican governors in Lexington, Kentucky, and carried on the debate. Again the setting made it appear this was a conflict between politicians and academicians, as indeed, Agnew pointed out, in many cases it had to be. After first concluding his argument with Cornell by criticizing its administration for granting amnesty to the gun-toting blacks, he went on to say that it should not even be up to college administrators to decide whether to punish student offenders whose lawbreaking harmed other students or interfered with their rights. "There is a general feeling in the country [on campuses] that you are sort of a fink if you complain . . . that it is anti-intellectual and anti-freedom to call in police." He said he favored government action, such as the cutting off Federal aid, to penalize colleges that were "overpermissive." President Nixon had made similar observations just the day before. But his remarks, and Agnew's too, were promptly knocked off the front pages by the Cambodia invasion, which the President announced on the evening Agnew spoke to the governors.

The announcement touched off rioting on many campuses. On May 1 a perturbed President Nixon went to the Pentagon for a briefing on the progress of the invasion, then a day old. In an impromptu discussion with some employees there, he referred to "those bums, you know, blowing up the campuses. . . . Here they are burning up the books, storming around about this issue. You name it. Get rid of the war [and] there will be another one." That was the one presidential statement that Herblock used, along with several vice-presidential remarks, in labeling the bullets in his cartoon. Nixon later said at a press conference that he was only talking about the violent, destructive students, not about dissenters and protesters in general.

National Guardsmen at Kent State shot and killed four students on May 4. Following that incident, many colleges closed, and many others were kept open by Guardsmen or other law-enforcement agencies. The situation was unprecedented in American education. On May 7, Harvard's President Nathan Pusey and seven other university presidents met with Nixon at the White House to discuss the crisis. The meeting lasted an hour and a half. The presidents told Nixon how particularly unpopular Agnew was on campuses, and how his remarks were increasing the tensions rather than isolating the violence-prone students. The President replied that he did not want to contribute to their problems, which he understood, and promised that they would see prompt evidence of a change in tone in Agnew's speeches, and his own. Agnew made his next speech the following Friday, in Boise, Idaho, on the eve of another hastily called war protest in Washington. He told the audience he was not going to deliver part of the prepared speech. The first part of the already printed text was an attack on "choleric young intellectuals and bitter elders" who were criticizing the President for the Cambodia decision. "If my abandonment of the first two pages of my speech in some small way will help to cool the violent situation in the United States, I'm going to do it," he said. The following day he spoke at the Confederate monument at Georgia's Stone Mountain substituting for the President, who had been scheduled to appear. Nixon had told the college presidents to watch this speech particularly and White House staff members had

●

spent the week alerting reporters to the tone of the coming speech. It was both a gesture of respect to the South, calling for an end to discrimination against it in national affairs, and a plea for lowered voices, or at least for the need to stay together. "We are reminded here today that we have paid too great a price for being one nation to let ourselves come apart at the seams," Agnew said.

Though college officials had been the principal critics of Agnew's pre-Kent State rhetoric, two of the most outspoken attacks on Agnew that spring came from within the Nixon administration. Secretary of the Interior Walter Hickel wrote a letter to the President after the Kent State tragedy asking for changes in the Administration's stance. The letter was leaked to the press. One of the most quoted and requoted parts was, "I believe the Vice President has initially answered a deep seated mood of America in his public statements. However, a continued attack on the young—not on their attitudes so much as their motives—can serve little purpose other than to further cement those attitudes to a solidity impossible to penetrate with reason." About the same time, Secretary of Health, Education, and Welfare Robert Finch met with a group of students on a grassy mall near his department's headquarters. He was asked what led to the shootings at Kent State. "A whole series of causative things including some of the Agnew rhetoric," he replied, according to the Associated Press, whose reporter was standing almost at Finch's shoulder during the meeting. The students persisted: "Did the Agnew rhetoric contribute to the deaths?" Finch is said to have answered, "It contributed to heating up the climate in which the Kent State students were killed." As soon as the story moved on the Associated Press wires, Finch issued a denial. "Neither by direct statement nor by allusion have I ever indicated that any statement by the Vice-president contributed to the tragedy at Kent State." The quick spasm of intra-administration public fighting was over after that, at least at the Cabinet level. Eight youthful members of the White House staff fanned out to visit colleges, and reported to the President in early June that students were almost universally disheartened by the Cambodia invasion and especially disliked the Agnew speeches, which they regarded as generalized attacks on all students.

Not long after that, President Nixon named a special Presidential Commission on Campus Unrest, headed by former

Pennsylvania Governor William Scranton, to "identify the principal causes of campus violence, particularly in the specific occurrences this spring." Vice-president Agnew could not keep out of the spotlight on this issue. One of the members of the Scranton Commission, a twenty-two-year-old Negro student at Harvard, Joseph Rhodes, Jr., told an interviewer, "One of the things I want to figure out is who gave what orders to send police on campus and were they thinking about campus bums when they pulled the trigger. If the President's and the Vice-president's statements are killing people, I want to know that." He also accused California Governor Ronald Reagan of being "bent on killing people for his own political gain." These were hardly judicious statements. Agnew, naturally, responded. Rhodes "should resign . . . [he] showed a transparent bias that will make him counterproductive to the work of the Commission." The White House decided that forcing Rhodes off the Commission would be even more counterproductive, and the matter was not pursued by either side.

In his effort to smooth relations with the academic world, the President had taken other stops besides muzzling Agnew (of course, both men denied that any muzzling had occurred) and appointing a presidential commission of inquiry. He brought Vanderbilt University Chancellor Alexander Heard into the White House to serve as special adviser on campus problems, and he continued to meet with university officials. In late June, Nixon met with another group of college presidents to hear their complaints. Heard and Robert Finch, who was newly transferred from Health, Education, and Welfare to the White House as presidential counselor, also attended. Finch's liberal reputation on both civil rights and student dissent made his appearance at the meeting symbolic. Meanwhile, a group of eleven University of Minnesota professors met with Agnew himself to discuss the situation. They told him of their problems and of fears which they were about to present to the President in a letter. They talked for two hours and came away convinced of two things: Agnew was sincerely troubled, and interested in their problems, and he was unconvinced that he needed to make any changes in his style. Their point was that far from separating the bad apples from the rest, Agnew's utterances had the effect of separating the good apples from society. In the letter they left for the President, they said, "We find among our bright, hard-working, ambitious, well-read students a widespread distrust of their government, a growing despair about the political process, a mixture of fear and resentment toward America's leadership. These are not lazy, violent, irresponsible rebels—they are competent and conscientious young people, quietly pursuing their studies to be physicians, businessmen, lawyers, engineers, psychologists, biologists, teachers and so forth."

Agnew had not come face to face with representatives of the college community before. Now he and his staff felt he should get together with a group of students. They were aware that they were losing the battle to put across his views. But almost every conceivable forum seemed dangerous to them. A suitable opportunity finally arose, a television confrontation on the syndicated David Frost show. The Vice-president and five students would just sit and talk. The show was taped in New York in September and immediately shown around the country. That both Agnew and his critics seemed pleased afterward, and convinced that their side had "won," is a testimony to the honesty of unrehearsed television, or perhaps to the solidified prejudices of all concerned. The highlights of the program were these exchanges: Richard Silverman of the University of Washington, a Ph.D. candidate in the field of urban violence, said to the Vice-president, "You have done more to build and create an atmosphere and milieu of violence than anyone else I know." Agnew replied calmly that there had been violence on campuses long before anyone ever heard of him. "To use me as a convenient *bête noir* for violence caused by the disgusting permissive attitude of the people in charge of educational institutions is one of the most ridiculous charges I have ever heard." Eva Jefferson of Northwestern University accused Agnew of trying to make parents afraid of their children. Agnew's response was to chide her for having testified to the Scranton Commission that bombing buildings was the only way students thought they could get attention. She said she wasn't *advocating* violence, but she accepted it. Agnew said that was wrong, too. Frost asked Agnew if the Nixon administration wasn't more lenient with the construction workers who had recently beaten up some students in New York than it was with students who resorted to violence. Agnew said he saw a distinction, "a fundamental difference": the campus disorders were not spontaneous and the hard-hat rioting had been. It had also been "a wave of defense of a country, not a wave to destroy a country." Agnew and the students were talking to each other on wavelengths even more separated than those Agnew and the Baltimore black leaders had been on when they so utterly failed to communicate several years before.

Later that month, the Scranton Commission issued its report. It was a condemnation of both the violent students and the national administration. It appealed to the President "to bring us together before more lives are lost, more property damaged and more universities disrupted. . . . A nation driven to use the weapons of war upon its youth is a nation on the verge of chaos." Its appeal for a "cease fire" was meant to apply to rhetoric, too. The report made it clear that the investigators found fault with the present President, and placed their hope in him alone. Chairman Scranton made the same point at a news conference. Speaking of the increasingly strident tone of the rhetoric on both sides, he remarked, "Since last spring up to this very minute, there has not been the kind of leadership to bring about the kind of reconciliation we're talking about." In the report itself there was this placing of responsibility: "Only the President has the platform and prestige to urge all Americans at once to step back from the battle line into which they are forming."

The President was off to Europe as the report was issued. He would have nothing to say about it until much later. But Vice-president Agnew, speaking in North Dakota, had something to say. The fact that he read his blistering statement from a prepared text suggested that the Administration was speaking, not just the Vice-president. He was scathing, labeling the whole report "scapegoating of the most irresponsible sort." He called the suggestion for a cease fire "neutrality between the fireman and the arsonist." And he said, concerning what he assumed to be criticism of his own rhetoric, "The suggestion that vigorous public condemnation of antisocial behavior is somehow, *ex post facto*, a cause of that conduct is more of the same remorseless nonsense we have been hearing for years." The Scranton report also blamed much of the unrest on campuses on the continuation of poverty and racism in America. Agnew, after defending the President at length, declared this to be "totally false and utterly unacceptable." He summed the whole report up in the kind of alliterative phrase that was becoming char-

acteristic of the Agnew style that fall; it was, he said, "more pab-
lum for permissiveness." Presidential-counselor Finch promptly
said he disagreed with the Vice-president, and wondered aloud if
Agnew had even read the report.

Who was speaking for the President? Nixon finally got around
to commenting on the report in December, in a letter to Scranton.
It began, "Dear Bill," and ended, "with personal regards, Sincerely," but in between it rejected the notion that "only the President" could cool off the nation's campuses: "Moral authority in a
great and diverse nation such as ours does not reside in the Presidency alone. There are thousands upon thousands of individuals
—clergy, teachers, public officials, scholars, writers—to whom seg-
ments of the nation look for moral, intellectual and political leadership."

As for speaking out too strongly, the President said that there
were some leaders who had spoken or acted "with forthrightness
and courage," and he approved of this activity as necessary and
desirable in a free society. "High in that category I would place
the Vice President of the United States. History will look favorably
I believe upon these men and women. It may well look severely
upon these others—on and off campus—who for whatever reason
refused or failed to speak out forthrightly against the inequities
visited upon the academic community."

Those Awful Radical Liberals

Vice-president Agnew's attack on the Scranton Commission report was made in North Dakota, where he was campaigning for
Republican Representative Thomas Kleppe. Kleppe was giving up
his safe seat in the House to challenge Democratic Senator Quen-
tin Burdick. President Nixon had persuaded Kleppe and several
other Republican representatives to make such challenges. The
Senate had been a thorn in the President's side in 1969 and 1970. It
had rejected two of his nominees to the Supreme Court and had
challenged him on many domestic and national-defense issues. He
had won the fight for expanding the anti-ballistic-missile system by
only one vote, for example. The Senate offered an unusually good
opportunity, in the view of some Republican strategists, including
the President, because the famous class of 1958 was coming up for

reelection. In 1958 there had been a recession, and the Democrats had registered a net gain of fifteen seats. Several Democrats had won in states, such as Maine, that traditionally elected Republicans. In the normal course of political events the Democratic bonanza would have been counteracted in the next election for those seats. But that election, in 1964, was anything but normal. That was the year of Lyndon Johnson's victory over Barry Goldwater, and the Democratic presidential landslide was as beneficial to Democratic senatorial candidates as the Eisenhower recession had been. The counteraction was delayed six more years—to 1970.

In 1969 the Republican National Committee worked out a list of sixteen target states in which it believed there was the best opportunity to replace a Democratic senator with a Republican. These were Connecticut, Florida, Indiana, Maryland, Michigan, Minnesota, Missouri, New Jersey, New Mexico, Nevada, North Dakota, Ohio, Tennessee, Texas, Utah, and Wyoming. These states— along with California and Illinois, where Republican incumbents were in trouble, and New York, where a Republican was to be dumped—were to get special attention in the 1970 campaign. Republican leaders believed they could expect a net gain of seven Senate seats, which would give their party a majority in the Senate. The party set up an unprecedented off-year election budget, something over 13 million dollars, with much of that sum earmarked for the "target state" senatorial races. Probably even more than that was spent; record keeping in this area is not good. Much of the money was raised by Vice-president Agnew, who was the party's champion fund raiser. One estimate is that Republicans paid 5.5 million dollars in 1970 to hear him speak.

However, raising funds was only part of Agnew's 1970 role. The President was to campaign in twenty-three states in the last stages of the campaign, but in the earlier stages the Vice-president was to be the Administration's spokesman and the leading attacker of the Democratic candidates for the Senate. He had already become the party's best-known critic of liberalism and its supposed softness on crime, violence, pornography, drugs, and those other matters that had come to be lumped together as "the social issue." That issue had been defined by Democratic authors Richard Scammon and Ben Wattenberg in a new book, *The Real Majority*, which was being read by all the political operators in the White House that summer. The Scammon-Wattenberg book said the crucial voter was the middle-aged, middle- or working-class white Democrat who would vote for the candidate of either party who offered the most assurance on the social issue.°

Nixon gave Agnew plenty of support. In August he commanded the whole Cabinet, except the Secretaries of Defense and State, who traditionally stay out of political campaigns, and the Postmaster General, who was involved in taking the Post Office out of politics, to work for the election of Republican senators. Also that summer he gave the Vice-president his choice of White House staff members to use in the coming campaign. Agnew selected Bryce Harlow, the White House counselor who had been a friend of Nixon's since the Eisenhower years, as chief of the campaign; he also chose Nixon's speechwriters Patrick Buchanan and William Safire, and urban specialist and researcher Martin Anderson. Carl de Bloom, editor of the Columbus *Dispatch,* took leave to join the staff as press aide, as did Victor Gold, a public-relations man who had worked for Barry Goldwater in 1964 (and would become Agnew's full-time press aide after the campaign). On September 9, Nixon sent Agnew off on a two-month tour, with a ninety-minute pep talk to him and other top Republicans. In this meeting at the White House he stressed the need for winning the votes of Democrats and independents with the social-issue appeal. The President emphasized that if Agnew kept the Democrats on the defensive on that issue, they couldn't use the growing inflation and unemployment against the Republicans.

The next day, first in Springfield, Illinois, then in Casper, Wyoming, the Vice-president showed how he meant to go about it. In Illinois the incumbent senator was a Republican, Ralph Smith, who had been appointed when Everett Dirksen died. The Democratic challenger, Adlai Stevenson III, was favored. Agnew attacked Stevenson for having criticized police activity during the Democratic convention in Chicago in 1968. Then the Vice-president set forth what the issue was, in his view. "The issue is whether a free people operating under a free and representative system of government will govern the United States, or whether they will cede that power to some of the people, the irresponsible

---

° A 1970 Gallup poll rated crime a more important issue in the congressional campaigns than inflation, war, pollution, or anything else.

people, the lawbreakers on the streets and campuses and their fol-
lowers, their sycophants, and the people who subscribe to their activities behind the scenes, the radical liberals." The last phrase was
to be his motif in this campaign. He shortened it, in another reference in Springfield, to "radiclibs," and he used the two tags over
and over in the coming weeks. Several senators qualified for the
title, he declared, and asserted, further, that "radiclibs" had taken
control of the Democratic party. He named no individuals at this
stop, nor in Casper later in the day, where he said, on behalf of
Representative John Wold, who was challenging Senator Gale
McGee, that many liberal Democrats, "sheep in wolves' clothing,"
were now rushing to the right and talking tough on the social
issue, "but I intend to blow the whistle on them." He included
most of the Democratic senators he was to campaign against in
what he called "the Come-Lately Club," charging that they "came
late to the law and order campaign." On this tour he also attacked
rock music and the drug culture, asserting that many radio stations
played popular songs that were disguised advertisements for LSD
and other such drugs.

Except for one late embrace of the economic issue, the main
themes of the Agnew campaign were sounded in the first day's
speaking, including the use of silly language: "pusillanimous pussy-
footing," he said in Springfield, of the Democrats' behavior. Before
the week was over he would also have given quotation collectors
these: "nattering nabobs of negativism," "hopeless, hysterical hypo-
chondriacs of history," and "paralyzing permissive philosophy per-
vades every policy they espouse."

Agnew often resorted to fancy language. He had long been a
fan of the *Reader's Digest* feature "It Pays to Increase Your Word
Power," according to one biographer. Historian Arthur Schlesinger,
Jr., had belittled his use of big words in an article in *The New
York Times* prior to the 1970 campaign, noting that in consecutive
speeches Agnew had used the words "struthious" and "tomentose,"
and speculating that he was up to S and T in reading through a
dictionary. He labeled the Vice-president an autodidact, which led
a letter writer to observe that Schlesinger wasn't very far along in
his dictionary. Early in the 1970 campaign the alliteration began to
draw more attention to itself than the content of the speeches was
getting, and Agnew and his borrowed speechwriters dropped it.

From Wyoming, the Vice-president went to California, and there he defined a radical liberal. He said there were seven or eight of them in the Senate, but he wouldn't name them yet because he wanted to keep up the interest. "A radical liberal," he explained at a press conference, "is a person, normally of the legislative type, and people in government who seem to find a great necessity for applauding our enemies, castigating our friends, running down the processes of our government, attempting to overthrow tradition regardless of whether it has been proven to be effective in the past. They are the people who seem to see solutions in the most unusual portions of the periphery of American opinion, but who never look to a reasonable, representative system for answers to their questions, and who always find theatrical attention-getting devices which they say will solve the problems, but which we say only provide good copy."

The next week, after flying back east, he named the first radiclib, Senator Philip Hart of Michigan. Hart was singled out after a confrontation at the Saginaw, Michigan, airport between the Vice-president and the very sort of youths he objected to. Some three thousand adults were at the airport to meet the vice-presidential party. About two hundred youths tried to interrupt his speech by chanting, "One-two-three-four, we don't want your fucking war!" Manna from heaven! "Ladies and gentlemen," Agnew said, "that is exactly what we are running against in this country today." Then he attacked Hart. Later in the day in Grand Rapids, Agnew defined the voter he and the President were trying to persuade to give them the sort of Senate they needed, using a phrase from 1968, "the forgotten American" ". . . this forgotten American has strong family ties and keeps faith with his religion. He is fed up with the tired rationales and the general permissiveness that have brought rioting in the streets and on the campuses. He is fed up with watching college buildings destroyed in the name of academic freedom, especially when the destruction drives up the tuition he must scrape to pay. He does not enjoy being called a bigot for wanting his children to go to a public school in their own neighborhood. For too long this American has been forgotten—but on this election day the forgotten American won't forget."

Many public figures and journalists criticized Agnew for anti-campus rhetoric. He defended it as being not anticampus or anti-student, but antiviolence and antilawlessness, and usually the distinction was clear. Often the press coverage of his speeches did make his remarks seem more all-encompassing than they were. But sometimes his delivery blurred the distinction. For instance, what was a reporter or an audience to make of his saying of Senator Vance Hartke of Indiana, "I believe he represents some people in Berkeley, California. I believe he represents some people in Madison, Wisconsin, some people at Columbia University in New York, but I don't believe he represents the people of Indiana"? Whether Agnew intended it or not, such a speech set the college community apart *as a community*. When Agnew attacked Senator Albert Gore of Tennessee for having "radical friends in Manhattan and Georgetown," whatever his intent, he was certainly not bringing together the people of different regions. Gore was also attacked as the "Southern regional chairman of the Eastern liberal establishment." Similarly, Senator Frank Moss of Utah was "Western regional chairman of the Eastern liberal establishment." However effective this sort of stump language was politically, it was not unifying or healing.

Radiclibs . . . obscene disrupters . . . the elite of Washington and New York . . . in an Agnew campaign speech all these blended together in such a way that the sins of one target became the sins of all. The effect was like that of his 1968 campaign speeches after Buchanan had joined him on the tour. Crime certainly was a problem and an issue, in 1970, but there was some question as to whether Agnew and the President were really trying to rally people behind solutions to the problem—or were simply trying to exploit it. That is a serious question to raise about public officials, but it was often raised. Less serious but more to the point was the charge that though Nixon and Agnew did offer certain ideas for reducing crime—stricter judges, more police, more money for anti-crime apparatus, preventive detention, no-knock warrants—these solutions were simplistic, one-sided, and in some cases against the American tradition. A true debate on the crime issue was never really joined in 1970, however, in part because the Agnew onslaught caused many Democrats to do just what Agnew accused them of—"pinning on sheriff's badges," and agreeing with the Republicans on law and order.

The Southern Strategy had been first of all a strategy for electing a president, but in 1970 Nixon and Agnew did see an opportunity to elect Republican governors and senators in Florida and Tennessee, a governor in South Carolina, and a senator in Texas. Agnew visited all four states during the campaign, as well as Alabama, Georgia, and North Carolina. He made a frankly Southern pitch in North Carolina. The Nixon administration "likes it down South," he said, and was following a strategy of treating the South "as an equal." He pledged placement of a Southerner on the Supreme Court and protection from imports for the textile industry, and came out again for neighborhood schools—in other words, against busing.

Hartke, Gore, and Moss all joined Hart on Agnew's radiclib list. Before the campaign was over, so did Senators Birch Bayh of Indiana, J. William Fulbright of Arkansas, Charles Goodell of New York, Edward Kennedy of Massachusetts, George McGovern of South Dakota, Edmund Muskie of Maine, and Joseph Tydings of Maryland. Bayh, Fulbright and McGovern were not candidates for reelection.

All but Goodell were Democrats. He was a New York Republican who was being read out of the party, with Agnew doing the reading. Goodell had been a moderately conservative member of the House of Representatives from western New York. In 1968 Governor Rockefeller appointed him to fill out the term of the assassinated Senator Robert Kennedy. Goodell felt he had to change his stance on many issues to represent his new liberal constituency. He voted against President Nixon on many issues, including confirmation of the controversial Supreme Court nominees, Clement Haynsworth and G. Harrold Carswell, and expansion of the antiballistic-missile system. On September 30, in Minot, North Dakota, Agnew told an interviewer that by voting and speaking as he had, Goodell had left the Republican party, and he, Agnew, would not support him. He said Goodell had joined "those awful radical liberals."

Goodell was running against a liberal Democrat, Richard Ottinger, and a Conservative-party candidate, James Buckley. Agnew did not endorse Buckley. But just his public announcement that he would not support Goodell was enough to cause an uproar. Party was party, after all. Senator Barry Goldwater said that if he lived in New York he wouldn't vote for Goodell, but National Chairman

Rogers Morton, in New York on the day of Agnew's statement, quickly and enthusiastically endorsed Goodell. So did many of his Republican colleagues in the Senate, not all of them liberals. Senators Charles Mathias, Charles Percy, Mark Hatfield, and Edward Brooke all promptly criticized Agnew. Senate Minority Leader Hugh Scott, noting that the President was in Europe, said, "While the President is away, there are those who like to play President," suggesting that Agnew was acting without presidential approval. Governor Rockefeller said he expected to get the matter straightened out, implying that the President would override Agnew.

Agnew went blithely on. He knew where the President stood. In the first week in October he flew to New York to say that he could not support Goodell or Ottinger. He declined to say he couldn't support Buckley. Some leading conservative New York Republicans chose that occasion to make it clear that they were supporting Buckley. Nixon's old friend and White House aide Murray Chotiner expressed amazement at the debate going on in the party and in the press over whether Agnew was speaking for himself. He said vice-presidents didn't speak out without presidential approval. Agnew himself put it this way, while in Florida: "As Vice-president of the Nixon administration, I'm not on a frolic. And while everything I say has not received express clearance from the President, I have a sense of purpose and definition in what I'm trying to accomplish."

Some liberal Republicans still disputed this. Eighteen Senate Republicans endorsed Goodell; seven campaigned for him in New York. Senator Clifford Case of New Jersey said the President was aware of their concern about the party being divided by a jettisoning of Goodell, and Robert Finch said the White House had a "hands-off policy." The President returned from Europe and demonstrated that this meant hands off Goodell. His plane was met at a suburban New York airport by Buckley supporters, and Nixon told them, "I appreciate the fact that he's for me." Only a few days before, Agnew had called Goodell "the Christine Jorgensen of the Republican Party," a remark Senator William Saxbe of Ohio denounced as being in bad taste.° During the rest of October, Agnew's "divisiveness" was less an issue in Republican ranks than his "taste," but this was in large part because the President, by refus-

° The phrase was a speechwriter's discard.

ing to speak out, made it clear that Agnew was only doing his duty with respect to Goodell.

The existence of a debate about whether or not Agnew was acting on his own in this and other matters in the fall of 1970 is puzzling, in the light of recent Republican history. In 1954 the Republican vice-president—Richard Nixon—had campaigned in a style as personal and slashing as Agnew's. White House aide Sherman Adams later wrote of that campaign, "Eisenhower had set a plain example for Nixon in keeping away from extremes himself . . . but this did not mean, as some Republicans seemed to think, that Eisenhower wanted his spokesmen to be kind to Democrats in their campaign oratory. He told Nixon and others, including myself, that he was well aware that somebody had to do the hard-hitting infighting, and he had no objections to it as long as no one expected him to do it. Far from being displeased with Nixon's performance in the 1954 campaign, Eisenhower wrote him a warm letter of praise for it." Eisenhower himself, by the way, could campaign in a "hard-hitting" manner, and interestingly, in view of the "radical liberal" epithet of 1970, in the 1958 campaign he had declaimed against "senator[s] of the radical persuasion."

Senator Tydings was surprised at being included on the radiclib list. Although a liberal, he had been an Administration stalwart in working for tough anticrime bills. (He had been prosecutor before coming to the Senate.) Also, he had withheld endorsement from Agnew's Democratic opponent in 1966, to Agnew's great benefit. But Agnew came to Baltimore to attack him, and that may have been the straw that broke Tydings' back, for he was to lose the election. He had angered some liberals by his tough anticrime stand. He had outraged conservatives by fighting for strict gun-control laws. *Life* magazine accused him of impropriety and conflicts of interest. The Democratic governor of the state was cool to him because he had opposed the machine six years before. Parts of Maryland's large Catholic community were offended by Tydings' urging birth control. And George Mahoney had run against him in the primary with a somewhat better-natured slogan than in 1966 —"Yes, Again." Agnew alluded to some of that in denouncing Tydings in a speech in Baltimore. He endorsed Representative J. Glenn Beall, Jr., whose father Tydings had unseated in 1964, but he cast adrift his former aide C. Stanley Blair, who was running for governor. For though he endorsed Blair, he said pointedly that "no outsider can win or lose an election," and that his loss "would not be a rejection of Ted Agnew by the voters of Maryland." Blair was heading for a landslide defeat, and Agnew knew it.

Who Won?

Despite his disclaimer of influence in Blair's race, Agnew must have known by that late date—the next-to-last week in the campaign—that he himself was a noncandidate who might make a difference, one way or the other, in elections not only in Maryland but in states where he was truly an outsider. California Republicans were reported to have indicated to the White House that an Agnew campaign speech was not desirable there, where incumbent Senator George Murphy was losing to Representative John Tunney. Missouri, New Jersey, and Ohio Republicans asked that no Agnew visit be scheduled. Even in Tennessee, the Republican candidate for the senate was leery of Agnew. Up until his Baltimore visit, on October 20, the Vice-president had campaigned heavily in the original target states. Of the twenty-eight appearances he had made in September and October, eighteen had been in target states. After the twentieth, he made twelve appearances, only two of which were in target states. Democratic National Chairman Lawrence O'Brien claimed that Agnew had become an issue for the Democrats, their best except for the condition of the economy. He said, "People used to cheer Agnew on, now they ask, 'Who's he picking on now?' "

Despite O'Brien, however, and despite the fact that in some states Republicans thought Agnew would harm a senatorial candidate's efforts, Agnew's campaigning had not hurt him generally with the public, if a Gallup poll published in late October was to be believed. It concluded, "With Republicans, particularly those of a conservative stripe, [Agnew] has achieved a level of popularity reached only by Republican Presidents of recent years. With Democrats, excepting those in the South, he is the most unpopular man holding high office in the past decade. With independent voters . . . he gets a mixed reception. More like him than dislike him."

The trend of his "favorable/unfavorable" ratings in the poll showed a steady rise of *both* responses since 1968.°

In his final speeches Agnew devoted as much time to the economy issue as he did to law and order. The President had taken over the latter issue. On October 29 a rock was thrown at the President's car at a rally in San Jose, California. On the thirtieth, Nixon delivered a very tough and emotional law-and-order speech in Phoenix. On November 1, the President and the Vice-president conferred, and Agnew then attacked the Democrats for the "tactic of the big lie" concerning the economy. The President's Phoenix speech was rebroadcast nationally on election eve, making it more or less official that law and order was the issue the party wanted to be judged on. Agnew flew home to vote at Rodgers Forge School in Towson. He predicted that the Republicans would pick up from four to six seats in the Senate, including the Maryland seat. He was right about Maryland and wrong about the Senate total.

Glenn Beall ousted Tydings by running strongly in Baltimore County, the rural western mountain counties, and the Eastern Shore counties. Nationally, Republicans gained Senate seats in Maryland, Connecticut, Ohio, and Tennessee. They lost seats to Democrats in Illinois and California, and to the Conservative Buckley in New York. In Virginia the incumbent senator, conservative Democrat Harry Byrd, Jr., won as a third-party candidate. In Texas the Democrats won, but liberal Democratic Senator Ralph Yarborough had lost in the primary to conservative Lloyd Bentsen. Buckley had run as a Nixon supporter and promised to vote with the Republicans in the Senate. Noting all this, Agnew and Nixon expressed pleasure at the outcome, claiming a net gain of four "ideologically," and "a working majority." But the Republican who won in Connecticut was a liberal, Lowell Weicker, Jr., and Senator-elect Bentsen quickly announced that he considered himself a member of "the loyal opposition," so in fact the net gain was two, ideologically and nominally.

Since the announced Republican goal had been seven Senate

° But Agnew thought the net result of the campaigning was harmful to him, personally, he told reporters later. During the campaign he lamented to Bryce Harlow that he was becoming known as a bloodthirsty politician. Harlow assured him that he was doing a necessary job, much like the one Nixon had done when he was vice-president. The implication was, It hasn't hurt Nixon, look where he is today.

seats and control of that body, and since there had also been a net loss to the Republicans of twelve seats in the House of Representatives and eleven governorships, most journalists, most Democrats, and some Republicans claimed that the President, the Vice-president, and their party had lost in the election.

Some Republican governors were particularly concerned about the results. Their number had been cut by over a third, from thirty-two to twenty-one. At a meeting of the Republican Governors Conference in Sun Valley, Idaho, six weeks after the election, the bitterest governors expressed their feelings to Vice-president Agnew, after he delivered a speech defending the outcome of the campaign. He said that he, and the President, had done the only thing they could do—"attack"; election campaigns were *supposed* to divide the country. The governors, he asserted, were misled about his campaign by the press, and too many Republicans were too deferential to the press ("eager to pat the backside of Sander Vanocur to get on the boob tube," is the way he put it, according to one governor). The only point Agnew conceded to the governors was that liaison between the statehouses and the White House had been poor. Oregon Governor Tom McCall called the Vice-president's remarks, "A rotten, bigoted, little speech." Six other governors also criticized the speech, to Agnew or to the press. According to press reports filed from Sun Valley, only California Governor Ronald Reagan defended Agnew. The Vice-president later said that only five of the twenty-one governors he met with were critical of him or of his campaign efforts, and he brushed off their comments as inconsequential.

In terms of what they set out to do, the President and Vice-president certainly "lost" the 1970 election. Instead of seven Senate seats they won only two. Of the radiclibs up for reelection, Hart, Hartke, Kennedy, Muskie, and Moss won, while Goodell, Gore, and Tydings lost. But by historical standards, the Republicans could legitimately claim a victory. In most off-year elections, the party in control of the White House loses seats in the House and Senate. Since the end of World War II, the President's party has lost more House seats than the Republicans lost in 1970 in every off-year election but one, and has failed to do as well in Senate races as the Republicans did in 1970 in every election but one. This record was the basis for Nixon's victory claims in November,

1970. Significantly, the two exceptions both occurred in 1962, following John Kennedy's very narrow victory over Nixon in 1960. The closer the presidential vote, the less likely it is to have a coattail effect, and thus there are fewer coattail riders to be ousted from office in the off-year voting. Actually, in the Senate, Republicans had gained seats in both the Presidential year of 1968 (five) and the off year of 1970 (two) for the first time since 1940–1942. Since the 1970 gains were made despite rising inflation, increasing unemployment, and the failure of President Nixon to end the war two years after he had pledged to, it could be argued not only that the Republicans had won the election, but that they had won it precisely by diverting attention from all other principal issues to the social issue. Historically, the existence of war, unemployment, and inflation have been harmful to a President's party.

If the President really read the election results as a victory, and the *New Republic*'s astute White House reporter John Osborne has written that he did, then the 1972 campaign could be a repeat of 1970. *New York Times* reporter James Naughton, who has probably spent more time with Agnew than any other reporter in the past two years, interpreted the 1970 attack on liberal Republicans as "a White House attempt to construct a new majority [in 1972] by welding together Republican journeymen and hard-hat Democrats." Naughton believed that the fact that presidential contenders Muskie, Kennedy, and McGovern were named as radiclibs, and that other leading Democrats who might be the presidential candidate in 1972, like Hubert Humphrey and Ramsey Clark, were attacked as radical or almost radical, proved that 1970 was a trial run for 1972, assuming that no significant changes in national and international affairs occurred in the meantime. In any event, what did 1970 say about 1972 as far as Spiro Agnew was concerned? The 1970 campaign was still under way when the first Dump Agnew story appeared, and a great many followed in the months after the campaign was over, as shall be discussed later.

Chapter Sixteen

Diplomat Agnew

Selling Nixon's Doctrine

ONE REASON FOR the eclipse of governors by senators at the national level of politics in recent years has been that national security and foreign affairs are such overriding concerns. Governors get little time to develop reputations in those areas. Governor Agnew was no exception, but once he had been exposed to professional briefings in those matters, he began to think of himself as at least a semiexpert. This attitude started to develop during the 1968 campaign; at one point in that period he complained that he was never asked about foreign matters, never given an opportunity to show off his newly found "expertise," as he put it. When he got to be vice-president, his education really began. President Nixon believed only the president could make foreign policy, and slighted even his secretary of state, in the view of many, but he encouraged Agnew to learn all he could about such matters. The method chosen had two main elements. First, Agnew was thoroughly and regularly briefed. He received the morning and afternoon summaries from the State Department's operations center, and the daily Central Intelligence Agency's presidential briefing report. He was given a staff assistant for foreign policy, Kent Crane, formerly of the State Department, and a brainy young general, Michael Dunn, to advise him on national defense. But his prime education in this regard came not from Crane or Dunn or the daily briefing papers, but from the President's own assistant for national security, Henry Kissinger. Kissinger sent him reading material intermittently, often called by telephone to keep him up-to-date on matters of interest, and met with him privately once a week, like Mark Hopkins with a student on a log, to teach him the intricacies of his new fascination. Agnew called Kissinger his "main prop."

The second element in the education of Spiro Agnew consisted of the international missions assigned to him by the President. He went on four of these in his first three years in office. They were low-level missions, as befits a vice-president; they had political implications, at home and abroad, as they apparently were intended to have; and they stirred up controversy, as everything the Vice-president did seemed to do.

On the initial trip, Agnew and his party first went to Manila, for the second inauguration of President Ferdinand Marcos. Several Asian leaders also attended, and Agnew was dispatched to tell them more about the new American policy which President Nixon had proclaimed that summer. This was the "Nixon Doctrine," which, simply put, was a commitment to avoid any more Vietnam wars and even any more Korean wars. The President said the United States would help nations help themselves, protect them against aggression from nuclear powers, and at the same time stand by its treaty commitments. The President was stressing the first two parts, telling a war-weary America that the nation would maintain a low profile in Asia. This doctrine, the policy of withdrawing troops from Vietnam, the pressure of Senate war critics to cut back foreign military aid (the Senate was even then holding up arms for South Korea and Nationalist China), and other manifestations of American war-weariness were making the nation's Asian allies nervous. Agnew's mission was to reassure these allies that the President was just as committed to standing by them in accordance with existing treaties as he was to the other parts of the Nixon Doctrine.

From the Marcos inaugural in Manila (where Agnew's car was the object of firecrackers thrown by antiwar demonstrators), the Vice-president made an unscheduled trip to South Vietnam, where he met with that country's President Nguyen Van Thieu and Vice-president Nguyen Cao Ky and some American soldiers at a fire base. "We really appreciate what you fellows are doing out here," he said. "Don't let anybody tell you the people back home aren't with you, because they are, one hundred percent." He rapped "certain publications" in the United States for contending the American people no longer supported the war. Commenting on controversial American political matters was a slight departure from diplomatic propriety even in this setting, and foreshadowed a much more flagrant breach of etiquette on a later world tour.

Agnew then flew to Taipei to assure Chiang Kai-shek that his island country had nothing to fear from some tentative steps by the United States toward friendlier relations with Communist China. He told top-level officials that the Nixon Doctrine did *not* mean that United States was no longer interested in being a Pacific power. As for those dealings with China—the relaxation of travel restrictions, and the like—Agnew discussed them for newsmen traveling with him, after they left Formosa: "China is a country of 800 million people. They cannot be ignored . . . those steps that have been taken with Communist China are just baby crawling motions. . . . I think diplomacy, modern diplomacy, requires that initiatives are taken with any country. We don't want always to exist at arm's length with a hostile attitude toward the rest of the world."

This viewpoint was not new; Richard Nixon had expressed it in public and private since before he was elected president. However, reporters traveling with Agnew, particularly those who had observed him most closely in his first year in office, were impressed with the ease and confidence he displayed in discussing such matters, with reporters and with foreign dignitaries.

The trip's itinerary was similar to one followed by Richard Nixon in 1953, when he was vice-president. Agnew went to Singapore, Thailand, Nepal, Afghanistan, Malaysia, Australia, and New Zealand. At almost every stop he managed to make some statement assuring the nation he was then visiting that the Nixon Doctrine was not a threat. In Singapore, for instance, he said the United States might extend aid to Singapore, and to Malaysia, New Zealand, and Australia, to fill the vacuum Great Britain was leaving as it withdrew its defense forces. Later, in Australia, he made a much stronger speech, written by State Department and National Security Council staff members. He said it was America's "destiny" to master the problems of the day so that there would be a generation of peace. With the staunchly anti-Communist Australian Prime Minister John G. Gorton at his side, Agnew said, "For our part America will never shrink from this destiny, this challenge, this opportunity." Gorton said, "You have never been more welcome than you are here in the capital city of Australia." Senator Fulbright complained that Agnew was making promises he couldn't keep, and other Democrats were critical of the Vice-president's diplomacy, but the Administration was reportedly very satisfied with the way he was handling himself. Secretary of State Rogers and a crowd of some five hundred welcomed him back home when his plane returned to Washington.

The return was in January the trip having begun on the day after Christmas. In August, 1970, on the eve of his hectic campaign tour, Agnew again flew to Asia. His mission was much the same as previously. Just before he left, he met with the President, Kissinger, and Rogers at the Western White House in San Clemente. He said afterward that his mission was "to reaffirm the essentials of the Nixon Doctrine, which of course involves our dedication to retaining the American presence in Asia and living up to our treaty obligations there." Again, the emphasis was on the part of the doctrine that the old, anti-Communist American allies like best. The August tour was to take Agnew to those allies who were most nervous, who had been most closely tied to American policies in Asia in the past—South Korea, Nationalist China, Thailand, and South Vietnam. He also made a surprise stop in Cambodia, where a new pro-American government was struggling against the threat of the Communists and North Vietnamese. All the nations on the itinerary were states that had some reason to be concerned about American policy, present or anticipated. The United States was withdrawing some of the elements of its two divisions in South Korea. The Senate had voted to cut off special United States assistance to South Vietnamese and Thai troops in Cambodia. Cambodia itself had been told quite clearly that it could expect no aid in the form of American forces.

A few hours out over the Pacific, not long after the meeting with the President and his two top foreign-policy aides, Agnew began offering assurances to the Asian allies. He told newsmen on the plane—and his statement was promptly reported to the world —"We are going to do everything we can to help the Lon Nol government [because] the whole matter of Cambodia is related to the security of our troops in Vietnam." He said that without non-Communist control of the six hundred-mile border between South Vietnam and Cambodia, Vietnamization would fail. Vietnamization, the turning over of the entire war effort to South Vietnam, was the key Nixon goal, and if what the Vice-president said was reassuring to Lon Nol, it was not reassuring to the American public. So when Agnew flew to Cambodia later in the trip he said that what he really believed was that if Cambodia fell to the Communists, Viet-namization would take longer, but would still succeed. He promised Lon Nol money and arms, and explained that his visit there was a signal to the Communists that such American aid would be forthcoming.

It was later revealed by White House staff members that the true Agnew mission to Asia was to affirm Nixon's resolve to de-emphasize the American presence in the Far East. In his public statements before he left, and in some of those he made along the way, Agnew stressed our concern with honoring commitments and standing by old friends, but in private conversations with top foreign government officials he was adding the message that the President was determined that the nation would do all that the Nixon Doctrine implied—maintaining a low profile, with no more Americans fighting on Asian soil. Even in his public statements on this subject, Agnew was allowed to go further than other Administration spokesmen. After his tour's first stop, in Korea, where he told a small welcoming crowd that "Americans keep their promises and . . . regard their commitments as binding," and where he fended off Chung Hee Park's pleas that the United States not withdraw troops until after the Korean army was modernized, Agnew announced that not only were two divisions coming home, but within five years *all* United States troops might be out of South Korea. He was firm again in private talks in Formosa, and in Vietnam he chose to emphasize in his public statements that American troop withdrawals there would not be slowed. In Thailand he told the press that absolutely no commitments were made to that government. His conversations were described as "very guarded." Again, he was being firm. In Bangkok, Agnew made a diplomatic stumble similar to the one he had committed on the first trip, speaking once more of American domestic problems. Some observers believed he was not stumbling, but was deliberately using the exposure at home which his foreign tours gave him to make political hay. This time he expressed his disagreement with the dovish senators and said he would return to America to campaign for the election of senators who would give the President more support on foreign policy.*

This statement caused some Democratic anger back home, but it was nothing to the controversy the Vice-president was to ignite with remarks on his next foreign tour.

A Palace Tour

The third trip began in late June, 1971. The first stop was South Korea, where President Park was to be reinaugurated, and here the tone of the month ahead was set. The Vice-president spent six days in Seoul, playing golf when it didn't rain, and cards and Ping-Pong in his hotel when it did. He had some conversations with Korean leaders, but he had insisted en route across the Pacific that "I'm not going there on a negotiating or substantive mission." His press secretary, Victor Gold, said the trip to Korea had "no other purpose" but a ceremonial one. The day Agnew flew south from Seoul toward Singapore, Secretary of Defense Melvin Laird left Washington for talks with Japanese and South Korean leaders, as if to emphasize that the Vice-president's trip was exactly what he and Gold had indicated it was. The other stops on the thirty-two-day tour, with the Agnew explanation for each, were as follows: Singapore ("logistical reasons . . . informal" visit with Prime Minister Lee Kuan Yew); Kuwait ("they had been asking for . . . a high-level American visitor"); Saudi Arabia, Ethiopia, and the Democratic Republic of the Congo (to reciprocate visits of their national leaders to the United States; also, Agnew had received personal invitations from King Faisal of Saudi Arabia and Emperor Haile Selassie of Ethiopia; Kenya ("I don't believe there have been any American visitors in Nairobi in some time"); Spain (conversations between Agnew and Prince Juan Carlos at the previous space shot); Portugal ("geographic proximity"); and Morocco ("convenient"). The overall mission? "I see this trip as a chance to carry a message of friendship, and an explanation of the Nixon for-

---

* The most undiplomatic remark the Vice-president made was an obvious slip; it was aimed not at domestic adversaries but at an international ally. He was asked on this trip if Chiang Kai-shek wanted more United States jets for his air force. Agnew replied, "I guess he would like to have anything he can get. I've never seen him refuse anything."

eign policy to quite a few nations in Africa as well as Europe,"
Agnew told the reporters traveling with him.

In Singapore, he played golf with Prime Minister Lee. He also
criticized the American press. Shortly before, *The New York Times*
and several other newspapers had published the Pentagon Papers,
a compilation of studies and official documents based upon largely
top-secret papers relating to the decisions that led to the war in
Vietnam. Agnew was asked about the fact that Lee had just closed
three Singapore papers and jailed some employees. The Vice-president said he flatly objected to curtailing a free press, but then he attacked the American press and accused it of being prepared to describe any Communist offensive in South Vietnam as a victory
"because so many of our people in the national media are too ready
to assist the North Vietnamese by their overemphasis on what's taking place. I don't think they mean to assist them but we've gone
through this terrible introspective, almost masochistic twinge of
conscience in our country regarding the Vietnam war where we
look with favor on anything good that happens to the enemy." In
Kuwait, Agnew stayed at the royal palace, and met with Sheik
Sabah al-Salem al-Sabah, but practically no one else. In Saudi Arabia, he had his first and last contact with any people other than
officials—six hundred Americans who worked for the American
government and for American businesses there, at a party at the
embassy on the banks of the Red Sea. American and local reporters were beginning to refer to the vice-presidential tour as a "palace tour," and in American publications there were unflattering
comparisons of the Agnew style with the more outgoing, meet-the-
locals style Humphrey, Johnson, and even Nixon had displayed on
world tours. In Ethiopia, the Vice-president was still aloof, and he
told the reporters with him that his talks with Arab leaders had
been "very constructive," and had suggested new ways to reach an
Arab-Israeli settlement in the Middle East. He also said that every
leader he had talked to was appalled at the Pentagon Papers and
the cutbacks in military and space spending in the United States.

The leaders he was visiting were among the most authoritarian
in the non-Communist world, and an announcement by President
Nixon while Agnew was in Asia made some people believe Agnew
had been purposely sent to assure such conservatives of American
faith in them during a revolutionary shift in the United States pos-

ture in international affairs. The new situation was brought about by President Nixon's announcement on July 15, 1971, that he was going to visit Communist leaders in China, ending twenty-two years without any direct communication between the United States and Communist China. The preparations for the trip were made by Henry Kissinger on a secret flight to Peking (from Pakistan, where he was thought to be in seclusion because of an illness contracted while on a fact-finding visit), July 9–11. How much Agnew knew of the preparations is not certain. He was finishing his visits to Kenya and the Congo when the official announcement was made. Two days after the presidential bombshell, he met with reporters traveling with him in the back of the plane and parried questions about his foreknowledge. "I can't comment," he said. Weeks later he told another reporter, "I don't think it's reasonable to expect a person in my position to be uninformed of the direction of the President. Other than that I would have no comment." The reporter, Godfrey Sperling, Jr., of the *Christian Science Monitor*, wrote that "it has been learned that Mr. Agnew did know in advance of his recent world tour that someone was being sent to Peking, but it is not known if he was told the emissary was Dr. Kissinger, or that he knew the precise date."

What gave the affair a certain spice for Agnew critics particularly was that the issue of China was the one thing that had publicly revealed an Agnew-Nixon split, a strong difference of opinion. The Vice-president had not publicly voiced his disagreements with the President on welfare reform, even though he was opposed to the program finally agreed on. In the National Security Council he had argued against going too far too fast in ending the China–United States separation. When the Chinese invited an American table-tennis team to their country, and when they allowed several American reporters to accompany the team, the President and Secretary of State Rogers let it be known that they considered the episode to be the beginning of improved relations in many ways, and they regarded the publicity that accompanied the touring Americans as desirable. Agnew not only did not share the official enthusiasm about the trip, but was outraged at the coverage it was getting. As he put it later, "My judgment, as I indicated, was sure, we should begin to ease our relations with mainland China, but because they invite our table-tennis team to play their table-tennis team does not mean they have changed their attitude toward humanity. . . . My principal complaint, however, was that the visit of these few Americans was not reported as a meaningful encounter of sportsmen but was used as a vehicle to praise the Chinese system and way of life." Agnew's views on the subject became public in April, following an informal midnight meeting with several reporters at Williamsburg, Virginia, where a Republican Governors Conference was in progress. Agnew summoned the reporters for drinks and off-the-record talks about his poor press relations. He brought up the subject of China, and the next day his views were in all the papers. (He and press aide Victor Gold thought that their confidence had been violated. The Vice-president had also expressed his misgivings about China policy to some governors, who relayed the story to reporters.) White House press officials promptly denied for the record that there was any "difference of opinion" between the President and the Vice-president. Off the record, newsmen were told differently. As the Washington *Post* reported, ". . . the President reportedly made known to associates his surprise, concern and displeasure over criticisms of a policy he has worked on for months and takes great pride in." Secretary Rogers publicly praised even the press coverage the Vice-president objected to. What Nixon said to Agnew after the episode is not known, but at the next meeting of the Cabinet, a few days after the Williamsburg conference, as the President entered the room, he glared disapprovingly at the Vice-president.

The airborne press conference at which Agnew refused to comment on the China trip was held as the Vice-president flew from his last meeting with a black African leader toward a celebration in Spain. That leader was General Joseph Mobutu. The two met in his office high on Mount Stanley, with the General's caged leopard looking on. The President-General was leader of the only legal political party in the country, head of the army, a very tough man with student dissenters, by no means democratic. The man who thought Martin Luther King wasn't a good American was impressed. And now as the plane flew toward Spain, he said so! He began the press conference by announcing, "I have just, as you know, completed my visit to three African nations, and never in my life have I been more impressed than with the quality of leadership of Ethiopia, Kenya, and the Congo. I have seen leaders of those countries are dedicated, enlightened, dynamic, and extremely apt for the task that faces them. They have impressed me with their understanding of their internal problems, their moderateness, and their recognition of the difficulties that face their relationship with the remainder of the world and show every ability to solve these problems. This is in distinct contrast—the quality of this leadership—with many of those in the United States who have arrogated unto themselves the position of black leaders, those who spend their time in querulous complaint and constant recriminations against the state of society. The black leadership in the United States, not all of it but most of it, could learn much by observing the work that has been done in these countries by people like Haile Selassie, his Prime Minister, President Jomo Kenyatta, and his distinguished ministers, and of course President Mobutu and President of the National Assembly Bo-Boliko."

Agnew would not name the black leaders he had in mind, but made it clear that his use of "many" and "most" in referring to them was deliberate. He told questioners that the ones he had in mind "comprise a very substantial cross-section of what describes itself as the black leadership."

Reaction by blacks and by white liberals was instant and predictably outraged. Even the White House disassociated itself from the Agnew remarks. The most outspoken attack on Agnew came from Representative William Clay of Missouri, a Negro. During a round-robin type denunciation of the Vice-president on the floor of the House, Clay said, "In my opinion, Mr. Speaker, our Vice-president is seriously ill. He has all the symptoms of an intellectual misfit. His recent tirade against black leadership is just part of a game played by him—called mental masturbation. Apparently Mr. Agnew is an intellectual sadist who experiences intellectual orgasms by attacking, humiliating, and kicking the oppressed." He concluded by calling Agnew "this buffoon."

"I thank the gentleman from Missouri for his constructive criticism," said Representative Charles Diggs of Michigan, who was handling the debate.

In Spain, the Vice-president attended the National Day reception, honoring General Franco's overthrow of the old republic. The Vice-president was the first high-level American to attend the affair. Then he vacationed at the elegant Sotogrande, meeting his wife and two of their daughters. He made two more official visits, to Morocco and to Portugal, and then returned home. The press did not see.him after the press conference on the plane. Criticism of his tour had reached a crescendo. Inaccuracies in some reports, and the reporting of trivia, had so angered him that he did not even say good-bye to the newsmen who had traveled with him for thirty-two days, though the stories and comments he most objected to were not in the publications they represented.

Homage to Greece

Vice-president Agnew wanted to make another stop on that third tour—Greece. Although he had never been a part of the Baltimore Greek community he had been thinking of visiting his father's home, the village of Gargalianoi, ever since his father's death in 1963, according to some friends. But each summer something came up. After he became vice-president the opportunities for world travel were greatly increased, but Greece posed a special problem. A group of colonels led by George Papadopoulos had taken over the government in 1967, suspending democratic rule and many personal liberties. Greek-American relations became quite cool. Few government officials were allowed to visit there, since the colonels always used such visits to enhance their own reputation as the legitimate government. Agnew even had trouble getting White House permission for his secretary to go to Greece alone to do some genealogical research. In the summer of 1971, when he asked to visit Greece while in the Mediterranean area, he was promptly turned down. About the same time, the State Department was publicly expressing dissatisfaction with the Greek colonels and Papadopoulos, now premier, for not returning the country to democratic, constitutional rule. Also in 1971, the House of Representatives voted to suspend military aid to Greece, even though that country was a North Atlantic Treaty Organization ally. Against this background, with the House-passed ban pending in the Senate, it was announced that Vice-president Agnew was going to represent the United States at the celebration of the 2,500th anniversary of the establishment of the Persian Empire. The Shah of Iran was giving an elaborate party in October in a tent city in the Iranian desert. The announcement of the Vice-pres-

234   *Spiro Agnew's America*

ident's trip added that he would also visit the NATO allies Turkey and Greece while in the area.

The visits to Turkey and Iran were uneventful, except for some protest bombings in Turkey, and diplomats on the scenes gave Agnew high marks for the way he conducted himself. The visit to his father's homeland, however, as was probably inevitable, generated controversy. It was scheduled to be divided into two parts. The first part was official, involving talks with the Greek government about NATO problems. Following that, Agnew was to take on the status of a private tourist and visit the famous Greek ruins, the beautiful Ionian Islands, and Gargalianoi. He did follow this itinerary, but not ever really as a private citizen. The principal reason was that he arrived in Greece as a known supporter of the regime (he had defended it against critics in speeches as long ago as 1968), and once there, began making statements in praise of it. So Papadopoulos stuck by his side almost everywhere he went. The Vice-president's statements were of great benefit to the Papadopoulos regime, fortifying it against its internal critics. Those critics believed that only strong and constant American disapproval of the colonels could weaken their hold on the country. Agnew in part simply affirmed the Administration position that as a NATO ally, Greece was a vital friend even while in the control of a dictatorship. Thus he said that he knew the President would continue military aid to the country even if Congress passed its pending bill. (The bill allowed the President to do that under certain circumstances.) But in some of his statements Agnew went beyond that position, as when he said in one speech in Greece, "I recognize and appreciate the achievements that are going forward under the present Greek government." On another occasion he praised "the spirit of patriotism and unity" he found in the country.

Agnew twice met in private with Papadopoulos. He told reporters after those meetings that he was greatly impressed with the Premier, and believed that democracy would be restored in Greece, but he didn't say when. There was widespread speculation that Agnew was publicly praising Papadopoulos while privately telling him he had to bring back democracy. That is almost certainly not true. Agnew indicated to some friends that he did not believe such an approach would work, and that it was not his mission to try it, in any event. He probably told Papadopoulos of the favorable effect on Greek relations with America of a gradual but visible return to democracy, without pressing the point. "He came to honor Papadopolous, not to bury him," a foreign diplomat in Athens told a reporter for the Washington *Star*. The diplomat saw the Agnew visit as one prompted by Washington fears of an angry Greece perhaps pulling out of NATO or otherwise weakening America's strategic position in the eastern Mediterranean. Since Agnew was Greek and was known to like authoritarian leaders, he was perfect for the mission of assuring Papadopoulos that aid would continue. Agnew did not comment on this speculation, but his aides praised the *Star* story.

The highlight of the private part of the visit was the brief trip to Gargalianoi. Some Agnew cousins still lived there. All the inhabitants of the town, and thousands of people from the countryside, were present for the occasion. The Vice-president and Mrs. Agnew were accompanied by Premier Papadopoulos. Agnew unveiled a plaque commemorating his visit, laid a wreath on the Anagnostopoulos grave site, made a brief and obviously emotional speech about his father, then had lunch with government officials and local relatives. The Gargalianoi visit was unlike his earlier visits to foreign lands. Here Agnew showed genuine interest in the common people of the area, but there were still reminders of the palace-touring Agnew. The lunch was held in a resort hotel and occupied over half the vice-presidential party's five hours in Gargalianoi. He attended that lunch instead of a village feast planned in his honor.

Chapter Seventeen

1972 and Beyond

Suburban Strategy

"THE SUBURBS BEAT US," said Jake Arvey on election night, 1952. He was the Democratic boss in Illinois. His candidate, Adlai Stevenson, received the usual large Democratic majority in Chicago, 161,000 votes, but Dwight Eisenhower's margin in Chicago's suburbs was 277,000. There were similar patterns elsewhere, too. "In 1952, in fact, for the first time since the New Deal, the commuter country around New York, Chicago, Cleveland, Detroit and Milwaukee rolled up heavier majorities for the Republicans than those cities gave Democrats," Samuel Lubell has pointed out. The suburbs had generally been Republican, but nothing like they were in 1952 and 1956. According to a study by Frederick Wirt of the voting through the years in 260 suburban communities, Herbert Hoover received 51.3 percent of the vote in 1932, and Thomas Dewey received 52.4 percent in 1948, but Eisenhower received 56.4 in 1952 and a thundering 60 percent in 1956. The simple explanation for the Republican hue of suburbia was that this area contained more property-owning, tax-conscious, conservative voters than the city or the nonmetropolitan areas.

But in 1968, Republicans followed no conscious "suburban strategy." In accordance with conventional political science, it was assumed that where a voter lived was not a determinant of voting behavior. In the words of one campaign staff member, "Many suburbanites were still city Democrats who had moved." And indeed the voting pattern in Wirt's 260 suburban areas suggested that there might no longer be a Republican majority in the suburbs in the 1960's. Richard Nixon received only 47.3 percent of the votes in those communities in 1960, and Barry Goldwater in 1964 received only 33.8 percent.

Republican campaign planners had more than just election results to convince them that being a suburbanite did not automatically tend to make a voter a Republican. Almost every sociological investigation of the subject came to the same conclusion. For instance, "Compared with the importance of political climate, occupation and religion, suburban residence seems in itself to be politically irrelevant," Jerome G. Manis and Leo C. Stine concluded after studying a suburb of Kalamazoo, Michigan. Sociologist and planner Herbert J. Gans, who lived and worked in Levittown, New Jersey, agreed, basing his view on the way newcomers changed registration.

However, perhaps it is significant that Republicans made a small gain at the expense of Democrats in registration changes in Levittown, and that a few sociologists and political scientists were finding evidence of Republican gains in some suburbs. Fred I. Greenstein and Raymond E. Wolfinger studied the 1952 election results and decided that even when comparisons were controlled for education, income, occupation, religion, and ethnicity, Republican strength was greater in suburbia than in cities. They speculated that "environmental conversion is taking place." Irving Tallman and Ramona Morgner studied blue-collar families in Minneapolis and in a suburb of that city in the mid-1960's. Almost three out of four of the men in the urban sample were Democrats, but less than half of those in the suburban sample were.

Such studies may mean that place of residence in itself affects voting behavior, but even if these studies are wrong and the conventional wisdom is correct, it is still possible to argue that a suburban strategy would work at the national level. Those who believe place of residence has had no effect on voting behavior in presidential elections would probably agree with this statement, made by Joseph Zikmund: "The urban stockbroker and the suburban stockbroker are likely to differ politically only on intra-metropolitan issues, and the same holds true for the urban blue collar worker and his suburban counterpart." Traditionally, only candidates for local and state offices have been concerned with such issues. But increasingly in recent years intra-metropolitan issues are being debated by presidential candidates, as well as by congressional candidates. And increasingly at the national level the Republicans are regarded as the party that sides with suburban interests, while the Democrats are identified with urban interests.

Under Nixon's original revenue-sharing plan, for example, Maryland's rich Montgomery County would have received about two-thirds as much per capita as poor Baltimore city. Senator Muskie's revenue-sharing proposal would have awarded the city six times as much per capita as the county. The decision to enact one plan instead of the other, with its resulting impact on expenditures for county services and perhaps even on county tax rates, would directly affect the suburban stockbroker and the suburban blue-collar worker in the same way. *They* would agree on which candidate and party they favored on that issue, more than likely. The urban and the suburban stockbroker would disagree, as would the urban and the suburban blue-collar worker.

An even more important local or intra-metropolitan issue that presidential candidates are preempting is crime. Fear of crime is one of the most important facts of life in metropolitan areas. The presidential candidate who can offer the stockbroker and the blue-collar worker the most assurances on that issue is likely to get their votes. That is true in both city and suburbs, but it is more true in the suburbs. *Life* magazine asked Louis Harris to study attitudes toward crime in Baltimore in 1969. He found that in low-crime suburban neighborhoods the "strong fear of being a victim" was much greater than it was in high-crime urban neighborhoods. Furthermore, as a study for the National Commission on the Causes and Prevention of Violence said, "The perception of threat appears to be a great equalizer of class distinctions." So even if crime were the only "local" issue that a Republican presidential candidate preempted, many whose social status or philosophy might normally lead them to vote Democratic would be persuaded otherwise. And crime is not the only local issue so exploitable.

An issue that could become even more important in presidential politics is school busing. Where cities are predominantly black and their suburbs are white, this intra-metropolitan issue is a volatile one. A few courts have ruled that busing may be required in Northern metropolitan areas as well as Southern ones if it is needed to end segregated schools. President Nixon and Vice-president Agnew have come out most strongly against busing. Enforcement of court rulings or Federal statutes in this field would probably have to be by the Federal Government, so this "local" issue, too, is going to figure in presidential elections in 1972 and after. In

1970 a Gallup poll showed three-to-one opposition to busing in every region.

Then there is housing. The Open Housing Act of 1968 has not so far opened up the suburbs to the Negro. Unless there is more vigorous enforcement of the law and of other Federal initiatives, the black-white polarization of metropolitan areas is not going to be reversed. Most suburbs would oppose such vigorous enforcement.

Significantly, on every one of these issues the Nixon-Agnew position has been conservative and pro-suburb. To a degree, the 1968 election campaign by the Republicans involved a *de facto* suburban strategy. On intra-metropolitan issues, such as busing, the Republican presidential and vice-presidential candidates took positions that suburban voters favored. The result was warming to the Republican party. Nixon ran better in Baltimore County in 1968 than he had run in 1960. He got about half the vote both times, but the 1968 election involved a three-way race. With the Wallace vote distributed as the Michigan-Scammon-Wattenberg studies concluded it would have gone, Nixon would have received approximately 58 percent of the 1968 vote, an impressive gain over 1960. Part of that increase was due to the coattail effect—his running mate's being a home-county boy—but only part. St. Louis County, like Baltimore County, does not include any of its neighboring city —it is pure suburbia. In 1960 Nixon received 48 percent of that county's vote. In 1968, with his share of the Wallace vote, Nixon would have received 53 percent. Even in New York City's three suburban counties, which had become home for thousands of formerly very loyal city Democrats, Nixon held his own from 1960 to 1968, again with about 58 percent of the vote, scratching Wallace.

In the suburbs, just holding one's own meant winning, because suburban growth in the 1960's was so great. In 1960, the 58 percent share of the vote in New York's Westchester, Nassau, and Suffolk counties was approximately 10 percent of the New York state total vote; in 1968, it was 12 percent. Such growth, at the expense of the cities, was taking place everywhere. In 1960 St. Louis County cast 17 percent of the state's total vote, and St. Louis city cast 16 percent. In 1968 the county cast 21 percent of the total and the city, 12 percent. Baltimore County cast 18 percent of the Maryland total and Baltimore city cast 30 percent in 1960. In 1968 the city cast only 22 percent of the total and the county cast 17 percent, but the latter figure declined only because of the phenomenal growth of the other suburban counties. The Baltimore County vote total was 15 percent greater than it had been in 1960, while the city's was 10 percent smaller. Montgomery County's vote total in 1968 was 50 percent greater than it had been in 1960, and Prince Georges' was almost 70 percent greater!

All across the nation, suburban population has been booming, so much so that the 1970 census showed for the first time more people living in the suburbs of metropolitan areas than in the central cities or in the nonmetropolitan areas. As early as 1964 there were more *voters* in suburbia than in the central cities or the nonmetropolitan areas, though not many more: 25.9 million in suburbia, 25.5 million in nonmetropolitan areas, 25.2 million in the cities. By 1968 the suburbs were pulling away, with 28.1 million, compared to 27.5 million in nonmetropolitan areas and only 23.1 million in the central cities. The lead was expected to lengthen in 1972's presidential election. Most of the suburban growth in population and voters was white, so the proportion of whites in suburbia remained about what it was in 1960—95 percent. While most of the white growth came about through natural increase, a politically significant fact was that one-third of it resulted from emigration from the central cities. Nearly one-fifth the white population of the biggest cities moved to the suburbs during the decade. The central cities, meanwhile, became 21 percent black in 1970, up from 16 percent in 1960.

If these trends continue in the decade ahead, racial and economic polarization in the metropolitan areas is likely to become worse. And if there is still some uncertainty about the increase in polarization, there is none about this: the proportion of the total population of the nation that is suburban is going to increase still more. The generation born during the "baby boom" after World War II is in the period of high family formation, and will need housing. The suburbs will provide it. In 1970 the value of residential construction in Baltimore County was six times what it was in Baltimore city. Even taking into account the difference in average home costs, that is quite a gap. The average difference in costs is great, however, and this difference is another reason the suburbs are likely to remain just as white as ever, and the cities just as black. Negroes as a group are poorer than whites, and often cannot afford a suburban home. The median value of an owner-occupied Baltimore city house in 1970 was $10,000; in the county the figure was $17,700; in Montgomery County it was $32,700!

Such discrepancies, which are much greater than they were in 1960, are both a result and a cause of the continuing white-black polarization, and the increasing rich-poor polarization, in metropolitan America. In terms of constant dollars, the value of owner-occupied housing in Baltimore city was lower in 1970 than in 1960, a sure sign of declining economic health. Even Forest Park, still middle class, was showing signs in the new decade of further change. Here and there in the neighborhood were the seeds of slums—houses with bald yards, peeling paint, rotted screens. The decline in municipal services was made evident by the many filthy streets. Street crimes occurred with increasing frequency. The population of the census tract in which 3707 Sequoia is located was 95 percent black in 1970. The Baltimore area was even more polarized than the rest of the nation (ahead of the trend again). The city wasn't 21 percent black, but 47 percent, while for the county the figure was not 5 percent, but 3.5 percent. Towson's population growth from 1960 to 1970 was from 19,090 to 77,809. Negroes represented less than 1 percent of that increase.

A concomitant theme during the 1960's was the proportionately greater increase in the number of jobs in suburbs than in cities across the nation. In Baltimore County, there were some 50 percent more jobs in 1970 than in 1960, compared to less than 10 percent more in Baltimore city. (Many of the new jobs in the county had been taken from the city: between 1955 and 1965, 491 firms with 4,476 jobs moved from the city to the county.) Commutation from county to city apparently declined (no final figures are available as this is written), and even in 1960 slightly more Baltimore County working men and women were employed in the county than in the city. Thus the economic dependency of suburbia on the city is decreasing, and therefore the need for political compromise and cooperation on the issues which pit city resident against county resident is decreasing as well.

For all these reasons, a competition for suburban votes seems likely to emerge at the national level, and the Republican party seems more likely, by reasons of tradition and political sociology, to be successful in contriving a strategy for winning that competition than the Democrats. Politicians like Agnew will certainly be prominent in the future—men raised in one-class, one-race neighborhoods; politically trained in nearly one-class, one-race communities; elected to state offices, then national offices, by a suburban bloc that is not only one-class and one-race but appears to be developing an anti-urban attitude in political matters, its members being antiblack and antipoor whenever the needs of those groups conflict with their own. So the polarization and tension could continue. The times are not the result of Spiro Angew. Sprio Agnew is the result of the times, of the fity-plus years of urban-suburban development with which his lifetime coincides.

Dump Agnew

Will the nation's most successful suburban politician be around to help in the competition for the suburban vote in the election of 1972, or thereafter? Even before the 1970 campaign was over, David Broder wrote in the Washington *Post* that if the Republican senatorial candidate in Texas, Representative George Bush, gained election to the Senate, he would be a likely replacement for Agnew on the 1972 ticket. Broder had scooped the nation on Agnew once, and the Vice-president, his staff, and his friends couldn't help wondering if he was doing it again. But Agnew's comment on the story was that he felt very secure in his job; and as it turned out, Bush lost the race, which probably ruled him out, if indeed he had ever been ruled in.

But that Texas election didn't end the Dump Agnew stories, and the most persistent one in 1971 foresaw another Texan, John Connally, on the ticket with Nixon in 1972. Connally was a former governor of the state, a former secretary of the Navy, a former aide to Lyndon Johnson, a Democrat of great presence, executive ability, and ambition. He surprised the nation by coming to Washington in 1971 as secretary of the treasury and immediately dazzled the capital with his drive and salesmanship. Connally's appointment had not even been confirmed when predictions began to appear in print that he might supplant Agnew on the Republican ticket in 1972. Connally's name was the one most often mentioned when Dump Agnew articles appeared, but it was not the only one.

Governor Nelson Rockefeller was often mentioned. Rogers Morton, by now secretary of the interior, was suggested in one story, Secretary of Defense Melvin Laird in another. Newly elected Senator Robert A. Taft, Jr., of Ohio was touted in another article.* The liberal Republican Ripon Society said *some*body other than Agnew should be on the ticket, unless he changed his ways.

The reason for all this talk about replacing Agnew was that widespread opposition to him existed among students (a potentially important bloc now that the voting age had been lowered to eighteen by constitutional amendment), Negroes, liberal Republicans, and independents. While many voters in those groups might not support President Nixon under any circumstances, it was presumed that a certain percentage who might not otherwise vote would be spurred to action, and to voting Democratic, just by their dislike of Agnew. The intensity of liberal opposition to Agnew was suggested by some of the responses to him in the press. For example, when the Vice-president told a group of governors that liberals were "so blinded by total dedication to individual freedom that they cannot see the steady erosion of collective freedom," the journalist I. F. Stone exploded that this was "strange language from an American vice president in the capital of the so-called free world. This is not Jeffersonism. It is a compote of decayed Leninism and leftovers from the Fascist era." The Vice-president also said, "The leaders in the movement to plead America guilty . . . are to be found in all walks of life: the government, the university, the church, business and labor, the news media, the professions." William V. Shannon responded in *The New York Times:* "A leading politician has not made such a broad-brush indictment since the days of Joe McCarthy." After a number of guards and inmates were killed in a prison uprising in Attica, New York, the Vice-president complained about those who extended equal sympathy to all the dead. "To compare the loss of life by those who violate the society's law with a loss of life of those whose job it is to uphold it . . . [is] an insult to reason," he wrote in *The New York Times*. Norman Cousins responded with a coldly logical and furious editorial in the *Saturday*

* Senator Edward Brooke of Massachusetts, a Negro, was suggested by some Republicans as a vice-presidential candidate whose presence on the ticket would heal racial divisions. An Oliver Quayle poll taken in New York State in late 1971 showed a Nixon-Brooke ticket running better than a Nixon-Agnew ticket.

Review, comparing Agnew to Hitler for believing that some lives were worth more than others, and that government officials had the right to decide which were which.

There was a second side to this coin. Agnew was as popular with conservatives as he was unpopular with liberals. In 1971, President Nixon had a minirevolt on his hands, as conservatives grumbled about his initiatives to China, his economic policies, his family-assistance plan, a moderately liberal health plan, and other activities conservatives had long opposed—and had long assumed that Nixon opposed. In the summer of 1971, there were such straws in the wind as the opening of Draft Reagan drives in a number of states; critical editorials in the conservative weekly *Human Events,* including one that questioned whether Nixon should be reelected; a statement by a group of nationally prominent conservatives, among them William F. Buckley, that they were suspending their support of the President for the time being. In the South, as the courts and the Departments of Justice and of Health, Education, and Welfare pressed slowly but surely ahead on desegregation, Alabama Governor George Wallace's popularity appeared to rise while President Nixon's dropped.

With these conservatives, Vice-president Agnew was popular, for his outspokenness on China policy and for his symbolic reputation as one of the Administration's most trustworthy "men of the right." Several Southern state Republican officials told reporters in 1970 and 1971 that Agnew was more popular than the President in their region. According to one report, Mississippi Governor John Bell Williams said to Governor Wallace while both were guests on Air Force One (the President was in the South to open a new waterway): "I'll tell you one thing. If you run in my state next year and if Spiro Agnew is on the ticket and he comes in and campaigns against you, he'll clobber you." The American Conservative Union said in 1971, "The time has come to say what should not have to be said at all: The dumping of Vice President Spiro Agnew from the 1972 Republican ticket would be unacceptable to American conservatives." (The American Conservative Union had dismissed Agnew as a liberal when he was elected governor in 1966.) Senators Barry Goldwater, John Tower, Robert Dole, and James Buckley, all leading conservatives, endorsed an Agnew candidacy. Herbert Klein, the President's director of communications, predicted that Agnew would be on the ticket again, and so did Rogers Morton. Morton had nominated Agnew in 1968, and he told a Maryland audience in 1971 that he intended to nominate him again in 1972—and nominate him for the presidency in 1976. So the question for 1972 was: Would Agnew be a victim or a beneficiary of the liberal-conservative polarization which he had helped create?

The Vice-president himself often thought about his chances for the presidency, not only in 1976 but in 1972 as well. Whenever he heard speculation about the President's stepping down or being forced out as Lyndon Johnson had been, Agnew allowed his mind to weigh his chances against those of the other likely contenders. He told the author in August, 1971, "I'm not ready to concede that anybody else should get the mantle. There are three questions you would have to answer. First, do I have a chance of winning the nomination? My answer would be rather heavily in the affirmative. Second, could I win the election? I have to think I would have a good chance. Third, what does the presidency do to a man and to his family, and is it worth it?" He had not progressed to the third question because, he said, "I know the President is not going to withdraw. As for my opposing him, I'm not built that way. I'm in the vice-presidency because he selected me and for no other reason. I could never be disloyal like that."

One of the unlikeliest—but sweetest or bitterest, depending on your point of view—of the many 1972 "scenarios" public officials and journalists were swapping in Washington in 1971 had Nixon forced out by conservatives, Governor Ronald Reagan as the candidate of the right, and Vice-president Agnew opposing him as the candidate of the liberal and moderate Republicans! Stephen Hess said of Agnew in 1968 that if all the conflicting elements in the Republican party were fed into a computer, it would probably print out SPIRO AGNEW. Even after all that happened in 1968 and later it is conceivable that in a showdown between Reagan and Agnew, Agnew would be the choice of most of whatever liberal Republicans were left. Conservatives would also accept him, so he could be the great party unifier. In 1970 Senator Mark Hatfield, the liberal Oregon Republican, castigated Agnew for his campaign tactics, calling them out of the Republican tradition, but later, on reflection, he announced that Agnew was really a "good soldier" and had earned a place on the 1972 ticket. About the same time, a group of conservatives in Glendale, California, had some "Agnew 72" buttons made and sent them out with a letter that said, "Our purpose is to create a gentle reminder that if the leadership of the Republican party, including the President of the United States, should fail to stand up courageously for the principles enunciated by Mr. Agnew, he will become our choice for President in 1972."

Most scenarios and most activity relating to Agnew and 1972 dealt with the vice-presidential nomination. Some of Agnew's friends were urging him to coerce the President by allowing them to start an Agnew reelection committee. The presidential reelection organization in 1971 was pointedly named the "Nixon"—not the "Nixon-Agnew"—reelection committee. Whether Agnew would agree to pressuring the President through a reelection committee or in any other fashion is questionable as this is written. He told a number of people in 1971 that his concept of loyalty to Nixon was such that he would accept without questioning or complaint a presidential decision to "dump" him in 1972. But in the summer of 1971 Lee Edwards, a Washington publicist with close ties to the Republican right, announced organization of an "Americans for Agnew" group whose purpose was to insure that Agnew would be on the ticket in 1972, as the vice-presidential candidate. The right-wing Young Americans for Freedom went further. At their 1971 convention, they booed down the name of Richard Nixon and endorsed Agnew for president in 1972. Not all of Agnew's backers belonged to the right wing of the Republican party. At the 1971 Governors Conference, such moderates as Tom McCall of Oregon, Daniel Evans of Washington, Linwood Holton of Virginia, and Thomas Meskill of Connecticut praised Agnew and expressed the hope that he would be on the ticket in 1972. All of these individuals and groups realized that the decision was Richard Nixon's alone. (Though he could leave it up to the convention, technically.) "The polls will determine Agnew's fate," a Nixon adviser said in 1971. Polls were being taken even then, but the crucial ones would be those taken in 1972, as the convention drew near. Nixon would probably prefer to keep Agnew. Not to do so would make his original decision look bad. Also, as a former vice-president he empathized with him. In mid-1971 he urged party leaders to "do what you can to help the Vice-president. He's got a tough job and he's doing it well. He's been attacked and maligned unfairly."

One story often heard was that Agnew *wanted* to quit the job in order to make more money, but that his pride wouldn't allow him to quit because people might believe he had been dumped. He could make a lot of money by writing books and a syndicated newspaper column, conducting a television commentary show, lecturing, and perhaps lending his name and fame to a law firm. He could probably become a millionaire. My own belief is that this story is wrong on both counts. He himself described the sort of pride that would keep him from stepping down as "ego," and denied he felt that way; in 1966 he was urged to run again for county executive, and was told that not to do so was an admission of defeat. The appeal was to his pride, and he ignored it. That he would like to make a great deal of money is probably true, but as he is the first to point out, the vice-presidency provides him with everything money can buy, and then some.

The Trappings of Wealth

When the Agnews moved to Washington, Judy was quoted as saying she thought they would look for a place in the Maryland suburbs. She explained later that all she meant was that with daughter Kim still living at home and going to school, her first thought was of the school situation. Like so many suburban parents, she was in dread of urban schools. There is no official vice-presidential residence, but vice-presidents are expected to live in the capital. So the Agnews rented a four-bedroom apartment in the Sheraton-Park Hotel. Kim was enrolled in the nearby National Cathedral School.*

Their public social life changed dramatically, as he became a celebrity and a political leader. They entertained officially a great deal, at Blair House or the State Department reception quarters, and were occasional guests at the White House, often at the large affairs, less often "on the second floor," with the President and Mrs.

---

* The Agnews are Episcopalians, but like about two-thirds of their coreligionists, if the Gallup poll is to be believed, they are not regular churchgoers. But Agnew knows what he wants when he goes to church. "I think that one of the best things that could happen would be for religious leaders to begin listening a little more closely to their congregations instead of attempting to project a point of view they may have brought with them from the seminary," he told the Baltimore *Catholic Review*.

Nixon alone, or with just a few other guests. Their private social life also changed, although they continued to see old friends, meeting once a month with eleven couples they called "the crowd," usually at the home of one of the eight couples in the group who still lived in Baltimore County. There was very little of what Governor Agnew once described as his idea of a good evening at home, pizza and televison. The Agnews entertained at small and very informal dinners in their apartment whenever possible. Lyndon and Lady Bird Johnson were guests once. (The Johnsons had lived in the same apartment.) Governor and Mrs. Ronald Reagan were "real good friends," in the words of an intimate; they had been guests of the Agnews in Washington, and the Agnews had been their house guests in California. The two men had met when Agnew was still governor. California had become a favorite spot of the Agnews. According to one report, the Vice-president planned to buy Bob Hope's Palm Springs home. The Agnews had been house guests there, and Mrs. Hope stayed with the Agnews when she came to Washington for Tricia Nixon's wedding. The Hopes and the Agnews had met after he became vice-president. There is probably no better indication of Agnew's celebrity and new status in life in the eyes of the Middle America he is supposed to speak for than this: He was now able to surprise Judy on her birthday by bringing Bob Hope home for a drink, after which the three of them went out to dinner.

The Vice-president's status brought him other new friends. Astronauts Eugene Cernan and Tom Stafford were two of them. He played tennis with Dinah Shore and golf with Doug Sanders. Mrs. Agnew and Susan were house guests of Miss Shore's on one California visit. Sanders and his wife were house guests in Washington at least once. Mr. and Mrs. Arnold Palmer were dinner guests at least once. And Agnew played golf with other leading professionals. As a golfer, he was best known for having hit Doug Sanders with a drive, also for hitting some spectators on another occasion. But he was not that bad a player; his handicap was about 20 and he played as regularly as he could; at Burning Tree when in Washington. He didn't take up the game until he was county executive. At that time, one story goes, he was lifting weights; this activity aggravated an arthritic elbow and he was advised to switch to something less strenuous, so he tried golf instead. Another story was that he was urged to take up golf by J. Walter Jones, who said he would meet a lot of people who could be valuable to him at the Country Club of Baltimore.

The incidents involving Agnew's poor aim became a staple for jokes. He took up tennis in Washington. Once he was playing tennis before a crowd with Joseph Blatchford, director of the Peace Corps, as his partner, and hit him in the back of the head with a serve. Blatchford then donned a motorcyclist's helmet. All this was very funny, but some of his advisers felt that the picture of Agnew as a clown and a poor player was not in his best interest. Agnew's response to these objections was twofold. First of all, he pointed out, when you hit somebody with a golf ball, you can hardly *avoid* being laughed at; and second, the average golfer, he felt, probably identified with him because of such errors. However, a close friend said that Agnew was deeply humiliated by the incidents.

Like that average golfer (who is also a voter), Agnew was a long-time sports buff. Professional football was his favorite spectator sport. He was a loyal Baltimore Colts fan, a season-ticket holder, who had to watch the games from the press box after becoming vice-president, because the security arrangements could be more easily made that way. He had the whole team and their wives down to Annapolis for a party when he was governor, and after he became vice-president he was host at a buffet supper for the players and their wives.

The Agnew children were all close by in 1971. Kim lived with her parents in Washington. She turned sixteen years old in 1971. J. Rand Agnew, twenty-five, who had been married and divorced, and was a Vietnam veteran, was back at school in Towson in 1971. He and his daughter Michelle Ann were regular visitors to the apartment at the Sheraton-Park, as were his two sisters, Pamela Agnew Dehaven, twenty-eight, a social worker, who with her husband, a teacher, was also living in Baltimore County; and Susan, twenty-four, who was working in a state hospital on the Eastern Shore of Maryland. She had been engaged to a state-police sergeant in 1970, but called it off in 1971.

This was the life style of the Agnews in the vice-presidency, and it was embellished with the perquisites of his high office. At his disposal were planes, limousines, servants; there was much travel, many honors, all the "trappings of wealth." He used that phrase in explaining why he rejected the proposition, often heard, that he would like to leave political life in 1972 in order to become rich. He lived like a millionaire already. No private fortune could provide him any greater comforts and prestige than did the government of the United States. Nor could any private organization provide him with power as did his role in government—power to act, power to command, power to persuade or at least to reinforce the ideas of his constituency. "He won't admit it, but he likes power," said one of his intimate friends; however, only a few of the others would agree. Some of his old friends were spreading the story in 1971 that Agnew was bored with the job and anxious to quit. My own view, after spending a year investigating the man's history, was that he would give up the job at Nixon's request, but otherwise would not. I asked him in August, 1971, in the last of a series of interviews, if he liked being vice-president. He made a joke about not liking any work, then suddenly said with emphasis, "Yes. Yes, of course I like being vice-president."

Richard Nixon once was quoted as saying after he became a rich attorney that at last he had proved himself. That was a strange statement—a journalist observed—from a man who at that time had already been a representative, a senator, a vice-president, and a presidential nominee, but the making of money is the yardstick by which some ambitious men measure their lives. Nixon learned that he wasn't one of those men, and was soon confessing to friends that if he didn't get back into politics and government he would die. Agnew, despite all his talk about boredom at Annapolis and in Towson, his occasional complaints about the job of the vice-presidency, his aloofness, his "nonpolitical" bluntness, was very likely the same sort of man. He might leave government for "making some money," as he has been threatening to do ever since he first entered politics; he might leave elective office in 1972 for political reasons. But I suspect he would, like Nixon, soon be back.

Index